Shackleton Base

South Ice

keep mss
4/05

SOUTH POLE

T A R

ICE BAR

Ross Se

NEW Z

The Crossing of Antarctica

THE COMMONWEALTH TRANS-ANTARCTIC EXPEDITION
1955–1958

THE CROSSING OF

LITTLE, BROWN AND

ANTARCTICA

THE COMMONWEALTH TRANS-ANTARCTIC EXPEDITION 1955–1958

by SIR VIVIAN FUCHS and

SIR EDMUND HILLARY · *Illustrated*

COMPANY · BOSTON · TORONTO

Dedicated by gracious permission
to
HER MAJESTY THE QUEEN
Patron of the Expedition

Acknowledgments

In the short time at my disposal for writing this book, it has been difficult to find readily all the relative material, and I am indebted to all members of the expedition for their wholehearted assistance at all times. It is natural that much of the information I have incorporated was derived from the accounts of others, both in the field and at home.

Particular thanks are due to Kenneth Blaiklock, Roy Homard and Peter Jeffries for details of life at Shackleton during the first winter; to David Stratton and John Lewis, who provided, respectively, the stories of the sledge parties in the Shackleton Range and the account of the transpolar flight; to Richard Brooke and George Marsh for information concerning the Northern and Southern survey parties from Scott Base; to David Pratt, who compiled the technical appendixes; and to George Lowe, who provided the majority of the photographs.

Finally, I wish to acknowledge the help given by Mrs. Eleanor Honnywill of our London office, whose suggestions and corrections have been invaluable throughout the preparation of the book.

V. E. F.

The Commonwealth Trans-Antarctic Expedition 1955–1958

Expedition Leader: Dr. Vivian E. Fuchs

1955–1957   ADVANCE PARTY   (M.V. *Theron*)

K. V. Blaiklock, *Leader: Surveyor*
R. A. Lenton, *Deputy Leader: Carpenter and Radio Operator*
R. H. A. Stewart, *Meteorologist*
P. H. Jeffries, *Meteorologist*
J. J. La Grange, *Meteorologist* (South Africa)
Sergeant Major D. E. L. (Roy) Homard, REME, *Engineer*
Dr. R. Goldsmith, *Medical Officer*

1956–1958   TRANSPOLAR PARTY   (M.V. *Magga Dan*)

* Dr. V. E. Fuchs, *Leader: Geologist*
* D. G. Stratton, *Deputy Leader: Surveyor*
K. V. Blaiklock, *Surveyor*
* D. L. Pratt, *Engineer*
Sergeant Major D. E. L. (Roy) Homard, REME, *Engineer*
R. A. Lenton, *Carpenter, Radio Operator*
J. J. La Grange, *Meteorologist* (South Africa)
J. G. D. Pratt, *Geophysicist*
Dr. A. F. Rogers, *Medical Officer and Physiologist*
Dr. H. Lister, *Glaciologist*
Dr. P. J. Stephenson, *Geologist* (Australia)
* W. G. Lowe, *Photographer* (New Zealand)

Royal Air Force Contingent

* Squadron Leader J. H. Lewis, *Senior Pilot*
* Flight Lieutenant G. M. Haslop, *Second Pilot* (New Zealand)
* Flight Sergeant P. Weston, *Aircraft Mechanic*
Sergeant E. (Taffy) Williams, *Radio Operator*

* Accompanied the Advance Party in the *Theron*, returning in February 1956.

vii

THE TRANS-ANTARCTIC EXPEDITION

1956–1958 ROSS SEA PARTY (HMNZS *Endeavour*)

* Sir Edmund Hillary, *Leader*
* J. H. (Bob) Miller, *Deputy Leader: Surveyor*
Lieutenant Commander F. R. Brooke, RN, *Surveyor* (Great Britain)
R. A. Carlyon, *Surveyor*
Dr. R. W. Balham, *Meteorologist, Biologist*
B. M. Gunn, *Geologist*
G. Warren, *Geologist*
Dr. G. W. Marsh, *Medical Officer and in charge of Dogs*
(Great Britain)
M. H. Douglas, *Mechanic*
M. R. Ellis, *Engineer*
J. E. Gawn, *Radio Operator*
Chief Petty Officer P. D. Mulgrew, RNZN, *Radio Operator*
H. H. Ayres, *Mountaineer*
J. G. Bates, *Mechanic, Carpenter*
E. S. Bucknell, *Cook*

Royal New Zealand Air Force Contingent
* Squadron Leader J. R. Claydon, *Senior Pilot*
Flying Officer W. J. Cranfield, *Second Pilot*
Sergeant L. W. Tarr, *Aircraft Mechanic*

MEMBERS OF THE NEW ZEALAND INTERNATIONAL GEO-PHYSICAL YEAR PARTY WHO SHARED SCOTT BASE

Dr. T. Hatherton, *Leader: Geophysicist*
V. B. Gerard, *Geophysicist*
W. J. P. Macdonald, *Technician*
R. H. Orr, *Technician*
H. N. Sandford, *Radio Mechanic*

* Accompanied the Advance Party in the *Theron*, returning in February 1956.

Contents

The reader may justifiably feel that the color illustrations in this book are a somewhat romantic interpretation of the coloring in Antarctica. I would like to emphasize therefore that the colors seen may be both varied and vivid according to the season and the time of day. These pictures, taken by George Lowe and Jon Stephenson, give an excellent idea of the colors as they really are.

V. E. F.

List of Illustrations

COLOR

xi

LIST OF ILLUSTRATIONS

Between pages 236 and 237

Sno-cat Able before Mount Huggins

Mount Harmsworth, from the Skelton Glacier

Sno-cat Haywire on the Skelton Glacier

Looking across the open water of McMurdo Sound to the Western Mountains

Camp on the Portal, entrance to the Skelton Glacier

Emperor penguins watch the loading of HMNZS *Endeavour* at Scott Base

Sunset over the Western Mountains

BLACK AND WHITE

Between pages 44 and 45

Coastal cliffs at the approach to Halley Bay

M.V. *Theron* at the edge of the fast ice in Halley Bay

M.V. *Theron* unloading beside the ice edge at Shackleton

Supply dumps on the sea ice at the foot of the Filchner Ice Shelf

Frost smoke drifting away from the shore lead at Shackleton

Part of the great east-west chasm forty miles south of Shackleton

Incipient break-up of the floating ice shelf in the vicinity of Vahsel Bay

Seven of the Advance Party in their Sno-cat crate

The framework of the main base hut

Snow filling the half-built base hut to the roof joists after a blizzard

A view of the Tottan mountains east of Halley Bay

Fitting a wing to the Otter at Halley Bay

Icebergs breaking away from the crevassed edge of the Dawson-Lambton Glacier

The *Magga Dan* lying in the dock cut in the sea ice

Looking west over Shackleton

David Pratt and Hal Lister measuring snow density

Between pages 108 and 109

The installations at Scott Base on Ross Island

The sea ice of McMurdo Sound

The wintering party at Scott Base

Dog teams had their troubles with the crevasses

A crevasse rescue of sledge and dogs

Bob Miller and Jon

xii

LIST OF ILLUSTRATIONS

Icy conditions near Mount Suess
Surveyors at work
Near Mount Suess
"Dry" (ice-free) valley
The Mount Markham area
View over the Ross Ice Shelf
Ferguson tractor and the radio "caboose"
The depots, meeting place between ground and air transport
Mount Erebus
HMNZS *Endeavour*

Between pages 140 and 141
The aluminum framework of the hut at South Ice
The South Ice hut completed and drifted over
Stores in one of the snow tunnels at South Ice
Constructing underground winter quarters for the dogs at Shackleton
Sawing seal meat for the dogs during the winter
Feeding time in the underground dog tunnels at Shackleton
Windscoop at the eastern end of the base hut at Shackleton
Hannes La Grange attending to the wind-speed recorder
Aurora over Shackleton during the winter
Discussing the siting of South Ice
Sledge repairs in the carpenter's shop at Shackleton
Gordon Haslop taking his turn in the galley
Geoffrey Pratt at work while wearing the IMP
Roy Homard using the acetylene cutter
Typical view in the Theron Mountains
Surveying in the Shackleton Mountains

Between pages 268 and 269
Sno-cat Able at speed
Recovering Sno-cat Able from a crevasse
Vehicles halted among high sastrugi
A Weasel trapped by an invisible crevasse
Firing a seismic shot to sound the depth of the ice
Snow cairn built by the dog party
A typical Sno-cat load of five tons

LIST OF ILLUSTRATIONS

Maps

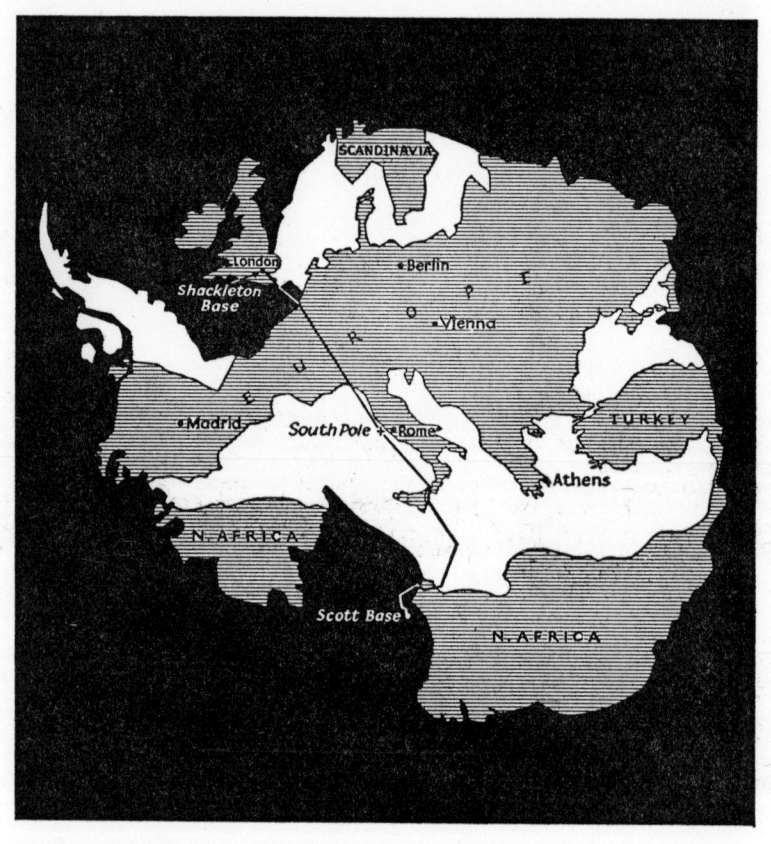

Map of Europe and North Africa superimposed on map of
Antarctica, showing comparative distances.

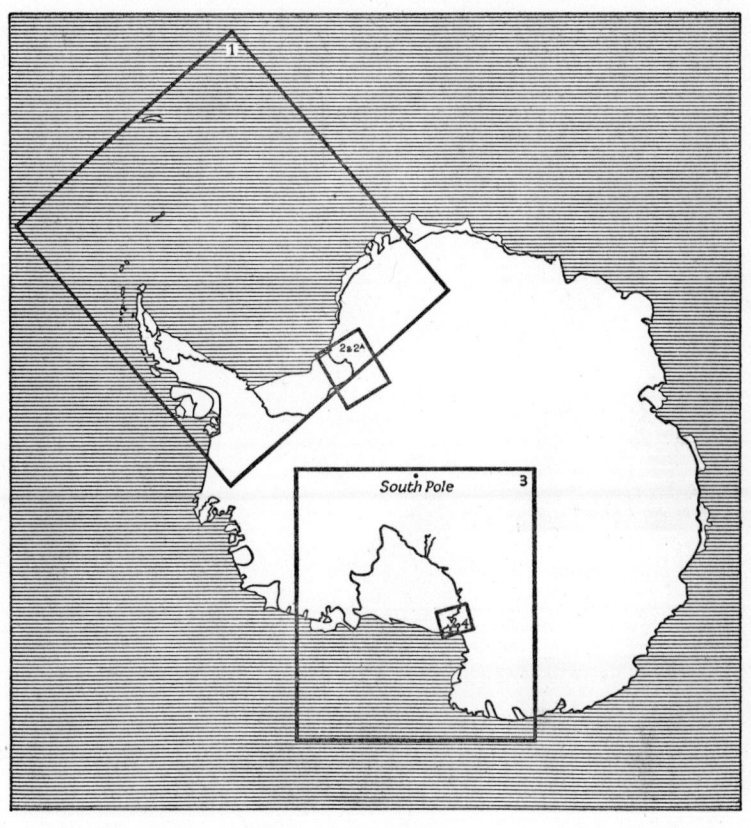

Key Map. The numbered insets refer to the detailed maps which appear in the text, and relate them to the Polar Continent as a whole.

The Crossing of Antarctica

THE COMMONWEALTH TRANS-ANTARCTIC EXPEDITION
1955–1958

I

The Beginning

IN EARLY DECEMBER 1949, Ray Adie and I had been confined to our sleeping bags for three days and still the wind tore its whirling burden of snow past the tent, blotting the mountains of Alexander Land from our view. From time to time one of us would go outside to feed the two dog teams or dig up their traces from the rapidly accumulating drift. It was important to do this so that the dogs could stand up, and also to prevent them from being asphyxiated by being buried too deep beneath the surface. Long since we had plotted our recent additions to the map and written our geological notes and journals. Now we waited for the blizzard to abate so that we could continue southward; but we were coming to the end of our food and would not be able to travel much further. Therefore we began to discuss how the geology of the area was related to the remainder of the Antarctic continent. Already we were working at the extreme range of an unsupported dog sledge party, for when we got back to our base at Stonington Island, our journey would have exceeded a thousand miles. This led us to think of means by which a journey could be made deep into the continent.

With time on my hands I began to list the various requirements and even the possible cost of such a plan. If one could go as far as the Pole, why not continue to the far side of the continent rather than return along the same route? In doing so an expedition would leave the Falkland Islands Dependencies and enter both Australian and New Zealand Antarctic territories before reaching the coast of the Ross Sea. Clearly it would be desirable to invite those countries to participate. South Africa too (Adie was a South African) might well be interested in a land which so closely affects the weather of all the continents in the Southern Hemisphere.

To launch such an expedition would require time and a great deal of money: probably, I thought, about a quarter of a million pounds. It could only be done by establishing bases on both sides of the continent, by using aircraft for reconnaissance and in support of dog teams and mechanical transport. The latter would be essential to carry the heavy loads the party would require in order to ensure any sort of proper scientific program. The heaviest commitment would undoubtedly be the seismic sounding of the ice depth, for which much electrical equipment, and the power to run it, must be provided, together with at least half a ton of explosive for the necessary "shots." It was a fascinating idea to play with and occupied the remainder of the time that the blizzard lasted, but we were already in the midst of an expedition which would take some time to complete.

Six weeks later we were back at our Stonington Island base, where the idea was mentioned; but no one took the matter very seriously and I discovered several years later that there was some betting against its ever taking shape.

On my way home early in 1950 I cabled Mr. (now Sir) James Wordie, Master of St. John's College, Cambridge, who had been Shackleton's Chief of Scientific Staff and who had taken me on an expedition to northeast Greenland in 1929. I told him of the idea then, and later discussed it with him in person. At that time it was clear that nothing could be done, but he did not forget, and in 1953 it was he who asked me if I was still interested in carrying the project through. He also attended certain official meetings where Sir Miles Clifford, then Governor of the Falkland Islands, was present, and as I was working for the Falkland Islands Dependencies it was Sir Miles who asked me to produce plans for a journey across the Antarctic.

The first tentative outline was for a party to travel from the head of the Weddell Sea to McMurdo Sound in the Ross Sea, a distance of nearly two thousand miles. They would use tracked vehicles with dogs and aircraft in support. At various stages vehicles would be abandoned, having served their purpose as traveling depots. On the Ross Sea side a party was to reconnoiter a route from the polar plateau down through the mountains to a base established in McMurdo Sound. They would also lay food and fuel depots along the

2

expedition's route, thereby reducing the load which would otherwise have to be carried across the continent.

Such a journey would permit the exploration of an entirely unknown area between the Weddell Sea and the Pole and make possible the mapping of the western side of the mountains surveyed by the Scott and Shackleton expeditions from the east. From the Weddell Sea base an inland station was to be established and manned during the winter for meteorological and glaciological purposes, and this would also be the main depot from which the crossing party would set off fully supplied. During the course of the journey seismic soundings and a gravity traverse would be made to discover the depth of the polar ice sheet and the form of the rock surface beneath.

The next step was to obtain the support of those whose knowledge and enthusiasm would always be available to further polar work, and the response from many who had little time to spare was generous and immediate. Early in 1955 a General Committee of twenty-four members was formed under the chairmanship of Marshal of the Royal Air Force Sir John Slessor and from this body an executive Committee of Management was appointed. In addition three subcommittees were formed under Sir Edwin Herbert, Professor H. H. Read and Sir Miles Clifford, to deal respectively with finance, the scientific program and the selection of personnel.

Now that the expedition has been successfully completed one can look back on those early days with an even greater appreciation of the faith and vision of those who gave their time and the prestige of their names to a venture which must have appeared more optimistic than capable of fruition. All of us who were privileged to take part in the field activities are deeply conscious of the debt we owe to the members of the committees, for it was their active and moral support which made it possible for us to set out.

Rear Admiral C. R. L. Parry became our Secretary and immediately set up an office organization which was to be the backbone of our activities in the United Kingdom.

On February 17, 1955, Sir Winston Churchill announced on behalf of Her Majesty's Government a grant of £100,000 and this was soon followed by financial support from New Zealand, South Africa and Australia. Later the New Zealand government was to do a great deal more by assuming responsibility for the Ross Sea Party and Scott Base. This entailed much work by government departments, in particular the Royal New Zealand Navy, which acquired and manned HMNZS *Endeavour* (Captain H. Kirkwood); the Royal New Zealand Air Force, which provided four men and an Auster plane; and the New Zealand Post Office, which gave us all the radio equipment and communication facilities. Many other departments also assisted in the planning and building of Scott Base, which was to house not only members of the Trans-Antarctic Expedition but also a number of scientists sent by the Department of Scientific and Industrial Research to form a part of New Zealand's contribution to the International Geophysical Year.

Together the four Commonwealth governments contributed a total cash sum of £187,000, but this still left over £300,000 of the estimated cost to be found from other sources.

Prior to the First World War private patronage was the normal means by which expeditions were launched, just as the various arts and sciences were assisted in their different fields. Now industry has assumed that role, and it is with the greatest sense of gratitude that I record the magnificent response of firms, large and small, both in the United Kingdom and New Zealand. The fact that some advantage might ultimately accrue to our supporters if we were successful was regarded as only a small return for a very practical act of faith when the project was in its early planning stages and open to all the doubts and criticisms which surround any new venture. In the end hundreds of firms assisted the expedition with material and by financial contributions.

Besides industry, various trusts and societies generously supported us. The first gift of all came from the Royal Geographical Society, which was invaluable because it gave concrete evidence of the Society's interest. Later the Graves Trust and the Everest Foundation provided substantial sums to swell our slowly growing resources. When Sir Anthony Eden became Prime Minister he assisted the expedition by launching an appeal and recommending our cause to the public. The response was both generous and sustained. The schools too took an increasing interest and nearly four thousand of them contributed to the cost, raising money for us in many ingenious ways.

4

The expedition itself was formed as a limited liability company which was granted the status of a charity. This enabled it to earn money toward the cost by the sale of press, book, broadcasting and other rights. In all, the income from these sources amounted to about a fifth of the total required.

We were soon in the throes of selecting the men who were to take part. For some time applications had been pouring in, mainly from Britain, but including offers from Canada, New Zealand, Australia, South Africa, various European countries and even from Nigeria, Pakistan, India and Ceylon. Certain guiding principles controlled selection, and occasionally these were found to conflict. For such an enterprise each successful candidate must be physically fit and have that equable nature so necessary to the vicissitudes of polar travel. He must be particularly qualified in his own subject and at the same time able to carry out duties in other fields should the necessity arise. He must also be prepared to take his turn at cooking or scrubbing and cleaning, and indeed to take part in any of the heavy work or unpleasant duties about the base. The Selection Committee had also to take into account nationality, for this was to be a Commonwealth enterprise and representatives of all the participating nations must be included in the party which would ultimately cross the continent.

Previous polar experience was naturally a great advantage, as it would have been inadvisable to attempt such a task without a large proportion of experienced men. It can therefore be seen that the task of selection was no easy matter, but two categories of applicant could be quickly dealt with. First, those who had no scientific or technical knowledge to offer had inevitably to be left out, as our numbers would be too small to include anyone who had no more than enthusiasm to contribute. In this way we lost a great many potentially excellent polar travelers, for by far the greater number of applicants were untrained in the necessary fields. Secondly, the men with experience were known from the polar work they had already accomplished and there was little difficulty in allocating a number of places to some who had already proved their qualities.

We planned that as individuals were selected they should join the office and assist in the procurement and preparation of the materials required in their particular fields. In this way the men who were to use the equipment were themselves responsible for its provision and had the satisfaction of knowing that it was up to them to see that their own requirements were adequately met.

The first to arrive was twenty-eight-year-old David Stratton, who was to become my second-in-command, and to him fell the immense task of preparing the stores lists, discussing our special needs with manufacturers, and co-ordinating the whole complex of material with the Crown Agents for packing and shipping. His two years of field experience as a surveyor in Graham Land with the Falkland Islands Dependencies Survey now stood him in good stead, for he could appreciate the needs of the party and anticipate the difficulties which might arise with various items should they not be precisely suitable for use in the Antarctic.

He was shortly followed by David Pratt, aged thirty, who immediately took over the engineering section and became responsible for our transport and fuel requirements. He had served in France with a Royal Engineers tank squadron, was well acquainted with tracked vehicles, and had subsequently taken an engineering tripos at Cambridge. Tall, active and full of ideas, he had the happy knack of persuading unsuspecting people into doing far more than they intended when first confronted with a Pratt scheme, and it was undoubtedly due to his untiring and relentless energy that the immense amount of work on our vehicles, in England, Norway and the Antarctic, was completed in the short periods of time available.

The Royal Air Force had agreed to provide very considerable assistance in the form of four men, two specially prepared Auster aircraft, the main radio communication equipment and the radio beacons. The deHavilland Otter which was later flown to England via Greenland was bought by the expedition but handed over to the RAF for operational purposes. All this took a tremendous load off the shoulders of the London Committee.

In the office we were relieved when John Lewis joined us as chief pilot, for it was his task to act as liaison between the expedition and the Air Ministry and to co-ordinate the provision of aircraft, spares, radio equipment and the variety of stores required for our purpose. Thirty-three years old, he had had experience of Antarctic flying when at Deception Island and later at the Argentine islands in

1949–1950. He was unfailingly cheerful, and we shall never forget his delight when, being measured for his windproofs, he discovered his vital statistics and announced gleefully, "I'm 42–44–46. Call me Pear!" When he was flying the Auster on floats it seemed almost incredible that the small plane could become airborne bearing his large frame and a passenger as well. Indeed, when there was little water available he sometimes flew alone to avoid any risk of running into the ice at the end of the pool.

The second pilot was Gordon Haslop, who was thirty-two. Although serving in the Royal Air Force, he was a New Zealander with wide experience of flying many different types of plane in out-of-the-way places. Cheerful, liable to burst into tuneful Maori songs on party occasions, he was soon to inspire in us complete confidence in his handling of a plane in really uncomfortable situations, for nearly everything happened to Gordon.

The RAF contingent also included Peter Weston, aged thirty-four, who had already had experience of maintaining aircraft in the Antarctic with the Norwegian-British-Swedish Expedition in the 1950–1951 season. Weighing about 220 pounds, he was the heaviest member of our party and bore with unruffled calm the whole responsibility for the maintenance of our aircraft in very difficult circumstances. They never failed us.

The Air Ministry also seconded "Taffy" Williams, who was to go with the Advance Party as radio operator and then remain for the second season. Thirty-five years old, he was responsible for all communications, keeping our bases and field units in touch besides maintaining our contacts with the outside world. Rather short, perpetually smoking a cigarette except when in process of losing a bet that he could give it up, his lilting Welsh accents and characteristic way of introducing the base over the air to London became renowned and his opening gambits were eagerly awaited on the other end. Quite unperturbed by anything that went on outside the radio room, he was a great asset to our life, and finally flew across the continent to Scott Base.

After that they joined us one after another, each falling into place in the work and knowing that it would be largely from their own efforts at home that the expedition would succeed or fail in the field.

Our offices in London were on the top floor of 64 Victoria Street and consisted of five small and sparsely furnished rooms. With sometimes as many as nineteen members of the expedition working from them they were overcrowded and congested to the point of standing room only, and they were almost never empty, for work went on late into the night and continued throughout a great many week ends. Gradually they filled up with all kinds of paraphernalia — skis, dog whips, samples of windproofs, sleeping bags, and every sort of survival ration sent for us to test. The latter often proved their worth by keeping the week-end workers alive till the shops opened on Monday.

We were proud that the Queen had become our Patron and her signed portrait hung in the main office; but the walls of the smaller rooms became covered with cartoons, press cuttings, engineering graphs and photographs, and on the outside of David Stratton's door was a large bow made of red tape. To our delight our Secretary hung up over his door the Duke of Wellington's famous dictum: *"If I attempted to answer the mass of futile correspondence that surrounds me I should be debarred from all serious business of campaigning."*

From the beginning we were magnificently supported by the enthusiasm, capacity for concentrated hard work and bubbling high spirits of the girls who joined us, and who endured with patience and good humor a constant pressure and telephone barrage which would have daunted many. It created around us a strong "family" feeling and a mutual loyalty which was to develop, when we were in the field, into a very happy confidence in the home base and their understanding of our needs.

Ken Blaiklock, aged twenty-seven, with four winters' experience in the Antarctic, was appointed leader of the Advance Party. He had been one of the two surveyors with me at Stonington Island in 1948–1950, and with two more years at Hope Bay, where he and David Stratton were together, had all the necessary experience to look after a party newly established in difficult conditions. Although appreciating the necessity for vehicles, his heart was with the dogs. With them he was to survey the Shackleton Mountains and finally he and Jon Stephenson were to drive the only teams to reach the Pole since Amundsen in 1911.

His deputy was Ralph Lenton, thirty-two, who had traveled to the Antarctic with me in January 1948 and since then had spent five winters at various bases. He was primarily responsible for the construction of the buildings at Shackleton, but his ability to turn his hand to anything was an enormous asset, and among other things he was our best cook. A keen radio ham, his distinctive keying has been easily recognizable at all Antarctic bases for many years. He took a share of all the radio work at base, and, as Taffy Williams flew across to Scott in the plane, Ralph was our only operator on the transcontinental journey.

There were to be three meteorologists with the Advance Party. Tony Stewart, thirty-two, took charge of the program, joining us from the Nautical College, Pangbourne, where he was an instructor in physics. He had had experience with upper air balloon work in the Atlantic weather ships. Short and well-built, he seemed to fit as naturally into a pair of overalls or windproofs as into an immaculate town suit.

Peter Jeffries was lent by the Air Ministry Meteorological Office. Lightly built, quiet, and a little withdrawn, he was always dependable in anything he undertook. Twenty-four years old, his service in Atlantic weather ships had given him experience of life in small isolated communities, and, disappointed that he could not carry out the upper air meteorological program with the Advance Party because of the loss of stores, he joined the Royal Society Base at Halley Bay and was able to make full use of his talents the next season.

South Africa sent us our third man. Hannes La Grange, twenty-eight, came from the Weather Bureau in Pretoria. He was a "blind date," but we need not have worried, for he was as solid in character as he was tall and heavy in build. His service at South Africa's Meteorological Station on Marion Island had prepared him for our way of life, and being meticulous and painstaking in all he did, he took the work in his stride.

Roy Homard, seconded by the Royal Engineers (Electrical and Mechanical), was going as the Advance Party engineer. Aged thirty-four, he had spent a year with the British North Greenland Expedition in 1953–1954, where he proved himself an adept at vehicle maintenance in very low temperatures. Undeterred by changing

Weasel engines in −50°F on that expedition, he was determined to try his hand in the Antarctic as well. Small, well-built, a very light sleeper, he worked indefatigably, and though his particular experience was with Weasels, his affections clearly became concentrated on the Sno-cat *County of Kent,* so christened as a tribute to his Kentish origins, which he finally drove the whole way across the continent.

The eighth member of the Advance Party was Rainer Goldsmith. Inevitably known as " Rhino," he was a large young man of twenty-eight with a tendency to look for new ways of doing things. As medical officer he not only cared for the health of the wintering party and started the physiological program, but joined Ken Blaiklock on several sledge journeys in the spring.

Another New Zealander was George Lowe, aged thirty-one. Originally a schoolmaster and later a member of the Cho Oyu and successful Everest expeditions, his ability with cameras won him a place as our official photographer. His beautiful pictures have since delighted many, but regrettably there are few photographs of his tall lanky figure in those unbelievable double-jointed postures he so casually assumed at unexpected moments. He and Gordon Haslop singing Maori songs in parts were a favorite double act when they could be persuaded to perform.

During the summer negotiations were completed in New Zealand for the organization of the Ross Sea Party. The Ross Sea Committee was formed in Wellington as the counterpart of the London Committee of Management, with corresponding subcommittees to deal with specialized subjects. Sir Edmund Hillary was appointed leader of the Ross Sea Party, which was to establish the reception base at McMurdo Sound and to lay the supporting depots toward the Pole.

By the beginning of November stores were pouring into the hands of the Crown Agents for loading into the Canadian sealer *Theron* (Captain Harald Marø) which had been chartered to carry the expedition to the Weddell Sea. Now our months of thought, persuasion, listing and letter writing took concrete form in the thousands of packing cases that began to fill her holds. Her deck space was taken up with hundreds of barrels of fuel, two airplanes, a Sno-cat, twenty-four dogs, oxygen and acetylene cylinders, stovepipes and a hundred other items. Moving from one end of the vessel to the other entailed climbing over all this assortment, while every cabin bulged with personal belongings.

It was time to say good-by — to our families and to "Number 64" where everyone had labored so hard to see us fully equipped. We hoped that for them there would be some relaxation from the turmoil and late hours they had endured in the past months. So closely had we all worked together that it seemed as though a part of the expedition itself was being left behind, and indeed, the strong unity of purpose which had been forged between the field parties and the office at home was to prove a great strength in times of unforeseen stress during the next three years.

11

The Voyage of the *Theron*

As THE *Theron* moved down the Thames from Millwall Docks on Monday, November 14, 1955, isolated groups or small crowds waved and shouted farewell and good luck from wharves and jetties, while tugs and steamers hooted their good wishes. When our astonished captain understood what was happening, our siren began to reply. It was then, I think, that all of us, expedition and crew alike, realized that we had the good will of the country and in return owed a debt we could only repay by our utmost endeavor.

Three miles below Gravesend we took on board a ton of explosive and a few last-minute items, then sailed for St. Vincent in the Cape Verde Islands where we could take on fresh water before the long trip across the equator to Montevideo. Arriving there on December 9, we were joined by Sir Edmund Hillary and Bob Miller, who was to be his second-in-command. Together with Squadron Leader John Claydon, RNZAF, who was already on board, they would accompany us to obtain a summer's experience in the Antarctic before setting about their own tasks on the far side of the continent.

From Montevideo we sailed for South Georgia, our last port of call before plunging into the Antarctic ice. By 5 A.M. on December 16, the *Theron* was edging her way into Grytviken, where the government station is situated on King Edward Point. There the resident magistrate was Mr. Robert Spivey, who had spent two years with me on Stonington Island in the Antarctic from 1948 to 1950. Half a mile away at the whaling station, Mr. Kenneth Butler was the manager and he had spent two years at Stonington Island before Spivey and myself. A number of my party were also well known to these two and our arrival gave the opportunity for a reunion in which all the expedition and many of the ship's officers joined.

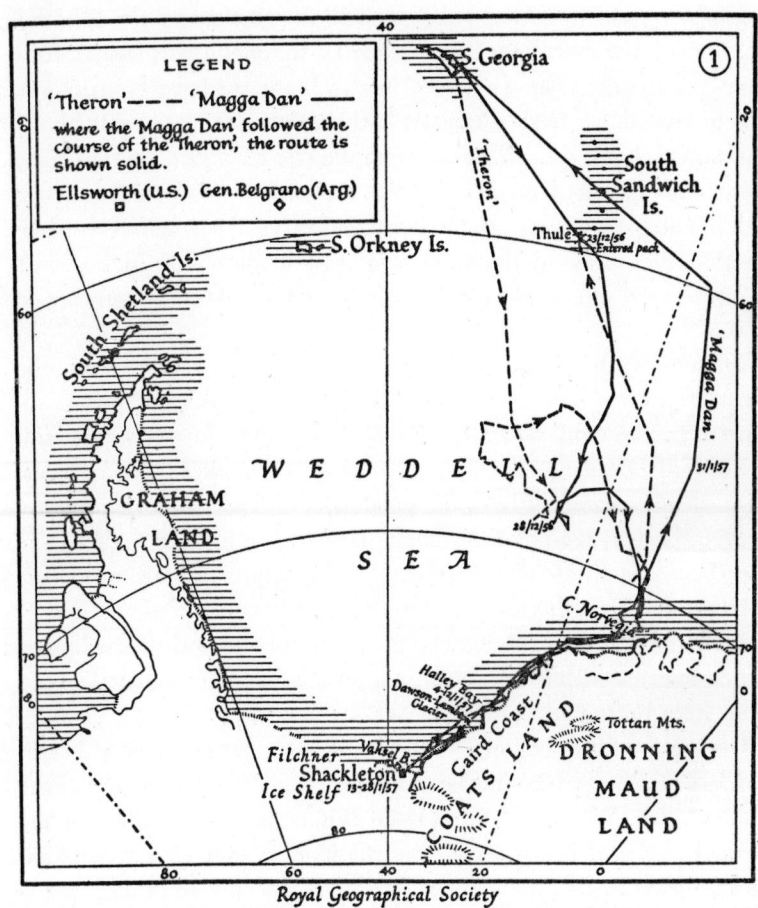

The Voyages of the *Theron* and *Magga Dan*.

Our main task at Grytviken was to fit the wings to one of the two Auster aircraft we were carrying, and to test fly the plane so that it would be ready for ice reconnaissance when we entered the Weddell Sea. During the morning of December 18 the plane was successfully flown and the next day we moved first to Leith Harbour for fuel and then to Husvik for fresh water. At both stations we were most kindly entertained, but it was clear that everyone was surprised we had come so far with our deck cargo of aircraft, vehicles, dogs and barrels of fuel. Though they were far too polite to say so it was perfectly obvious that they thought it would be purely a matter of luck should we ever reach our destination with all that we were attempting to carry.

The day we left South Georgia a few tall icebergs were seen, the largest standing 250 feet above the water. They were quite unaffected by the swell which was making the ship plunge heavily and drove many of our number to their bunks. December 21 saw us steering a steady course of 163°T, passing occasional icebergs and recording the first temperatures below freezing point. Throughout the ship there was an air of expectancy — everyone was waiting for the ice! Captain Marø because he loved to work his ship through it, I and others because of the interest it would provide and the feeling of getting to grips with the problem, many because of the relief it would bring from rolling and pitching.

During the afternoon of December 22 we entered a belt of brash, growlers and bergy bits that lay scattered over the water as far as the eye could see. We rightly interpreted this to be the beginning of the Weddell Sea ice, but it was not until 6 P.M. that we encountered the real pack in 63°50'S, 30°20'W. Now working from the crow's-nest, Captain Marø took a winding course along the open leads at a steady speed of 10 knots for the first few hours. The ice, though four to six feet thick, was very rotten and much of it showed the yellow staining of diatoms that flourish in the summer season.

As we progressed during the next days the ice gradually became thicker and more solid, the floes more extensive, until some of them were several miles across. In addition the leads of open water tended to run almost north and south, forcing us to take a more southerly course than we intended. Sometimes a huge piece of ice would become wedged beneath the bow of the ship, extending perhaps twelve or fifteen feet down into the water, slowing our speed and upsetting the steering. To dislodge these inconvenient and recalcitrant masses Marø would brush them off against a convenient floe.

From time to time we killed seals to provide food for our dogs and to build up a reserve for the coming winter. Most of these were Weddell or crabeater seals, but here and there were the rare Ross seals with their curious thick blunt heads and slightly brownish appearance. Of these we took one or two specimens, as only about twenty have ever been seen; the rest we left basking on the ice.

Frequently we encountered emperor and Adélie penguins, the former stately and uninterested in us or our doings, the latter hastening to satisfy their curiosity about our every move. For David Pratt, and indeed for many of us, it was the first time he had seen an Adélie, and he determined to catch one. To his surprise he found it far too nimble as it moved round and round an ice hummock with him in close pursuit. Quickly it learned to climb up a soft snow slope, pause at the top for David to flounder after it, and then scoot down the far side on its stomach at great speed. Unable to emulate the last maneuver David fell flat on his face time after time, much to the entertainment of another Adélie, which joined us in admiring this gymnastic display.

It was on December 26 that our troubles really began. First the promise of the wide pools of open water through which we had been passing ended when we reached an area of large and old hummocked floes through which it became increasingly difficult to penetrate. The day itself was, for the first time since we entered the ice, one of clear visibility and bright sun. How exasperating, therefore, when we became immovably held at midday. It took four hours to free the ship from the accumulation of upended pieces of ice, three feet thick and twelve to fifteen feet across, which had been forced alongside and beneath her. There they stood, jammed by the pressure of the floes and cemented by a mush of broken fragments and slushy snow, holding the ship in a vise. It was important that we should break free, for a few yards ahead lay a pool of open water from which we hoped to fly our Auster. When we finally succeeded in reaching this pool and John Lewis was making last-minute preparations for the flight, a low

15

mist formed around us in a matter of a few minutes. Flying was out of the question, so we settled down to wait until next day, thankful that the plane had not taken off before the mist closed in. Within two hours the whole ice situation had changed. Two large tabular bergs appeared to be bearing down on the ship, the pool had altered its shape and become reduced in size, while narrow leads of water began to appear in various directions. With the ice moving so fast, we could not fly the plane from so small a pool and decided to return along our route, where we found the narrow channels had opened, allowing us an easy passage.

By nine o'clock that night the mist had cleared, leaving a bright sun to cast long dark shadows over the coldly lit ice. Soon the aircraft was on the water warming up, while its attendant motorboat fussed about clearing all the floating ice fragments from the runway. On board, the bridge and chartroom hummed with activity. John Claydon was flying controller with radio, Aldis lamp, signal equipment, different colored Very lights, smoke candles and other "fireworks." The radio room stood by with Ralph Lenton working communications, Taffy Williams the radio beacon. In the chartroom Gordon Haslop was plotter, recording the position of the aircraft, while David Stratton and Ken Blaiklock were ready to plot the ice reports on special sheets as they were received.

The reconnaissance lasted an hour, during which time John Lewis, flying at 5000 feet, observed a long series of open pools extending to the southeast and reported that they were connected by wide leads. It seemed that they extended for thirty miles and probably led into more open water, as shown by a "water sky" some sixty or seventy miles distant. Within ten minutes of landing, the plane was back on board and we were hastening along the new course.

At first progress was good, but soon we were halted by really heavy ice, while the weather became overcast, making it difficult to see the way ahead. From this time onward the story of our progress was repetitive of hope and disappointment — the momentary opening of the ice, movement of fifty yards, then suddenly the ship's being held tight again half an hour later. All the time the *Theron* remained heading for the south, while we had long since determined to extricate ourselves northward. Yet the ice was so close that nowhere was it possible to turn her, nor were there navigable leads that would enable us to follow a circuitous route to the north.

Day after day, time after time, for hours on end, everyone was over the side with axes, shovels, boards and boat hooks, to clear the ice from the side of the ship. Some would hack at the huge piled-up floes and prize them free with crowbars, others poled the loosened pieces back into the wash of the propeller, thus clearing them into the small pool of water which always lay astern. Sometimes electrically fired charges of explosive were used to break up the ice or to dislodge the ship from some position in which she had become perched, unable to move forward or backward. All the time the combination of southeasterly winds and a southwesterly current was moving the whole mélange of pack ice, bergs, and ship to the west and north. I became convinced from our drift of fifteen to twenty miles each day that the ice of the central Weddell Sea is constantly turning in a clockwise direction, a certain quantity of floes and bergs being continually delivered to the open water along the northern edge of the ice while the remainder continues to rotate as a hard core for many years.

With our voluntary movement measured in yards per day and the short summer season rapidly passing, patience was a virtue hard to retain; as Hillary remarked, "All you need here is a timepiece that tells the days." Yet every day we were busy not only in moving ice but in bringing at least a ton on board to maintain our dwindling water supply. We also spent many hours discussing the unloading of the ship and planning the layout of the base stores dumps and buildings. In addition talks were held on vehicle maintenance and the use of specialized equipment, while outside we always had the dogs to feed and exercise.

By January 8 the course of our drift was changing from west to north and on that day we steamed a few miles, at least in the right direction, but still the bergs we had come to know by name in the last two weeks were clearly visible and we longed to see the last of them. In all this time we had become accustomed to the noise of steel on ice, of the propeller thundering against the floes. At first it seemed impossible that blades, or shaft, or engine could stand the strain when, from full speed, the spinning propeller was stopped in two turns and the whole vessel canted, turning about the shaft.

One day I wrote: "It is impossible to describe adequately this forceful butting of the ice. The ship runs up through crowded brash forcing three- or four-foot plates of ice many yards in extent, beneath the keel, or upending them alongside the hull. Then with a shuddering bump the bows rise on a floe — up and up we seem to go — when suddenly she subsides and cracks go shooting across the ice. Other times she hangs there with her bows up and we go astern to try once more. Over and over again the process is repeated, gradually breaking away the obstruction, while the ship jars, twists and shudders till one feels she will fall apart. The most frightening noises are when the propeller strikes the ice and a thundering hammering shakes us from stem to stern, or when going astern the rudder butts a heavy floe and the hydraulic release valve screeches in apparent agony."

Two hundred miles to the east another ship, the *Tottan,* had been working her way southward carrying the stores and the Advance Party of the Royal Society's International Geophysical Year Expedition. During our long battle with the ice the *Tottan* had reached South Georgia on Christmas Day, picked up the engine spares we had brought for her from Montevideo, and pressed on southward to enter the ice far to the east of the area where we were finding so much trouble. By January 6 a landing site had been found in latitude 75°36′S, and Surgeon Lieutenant Commander David Dalgliesh, in command of the party, began to unload the ship and build the Royal Society Base. Later the break in the ice shelf where the base was established became known as Halley Bay. At this time we were in daily radio communication with the *Tottan* and it was during one of these schedules on January 15 that HMS *Protector* broke in to ask, "Can you give me position of yourself and *Tottan* with courses and ice conditions?"

To this we replied, "*Tottan* unloading 75°36′S, 26°45′W. *Theron* drifting WNW from position 57°43′S, 30°30′W. Speed about fifteen miles per day. Local ice close heavy pack with leads now under temporary pressure. Hope we may be nearing ice edge to north or west. We cannot fly our seaplane as no water here. What is your position?"

The *Protector* was in the vicinity of Port Lockroy in West Graham Land, but Captain John Wilkinson offered to sail for the ice edge to the north of us as soon as he had refueled from a whale factory ship then operating in the Bellingshausen Sea. He would then be able to report the nearest open water and to use his helicopters to reconnoiter the easiest passage for us through the ice.

On January 18 we moved forward about two and three-quarter miles and were then stopped by two floes about fifteen feet thick below water. While charging these repeatedly to break them up, the ship became lodged on top of the ice. This in itself was not very serious because by digging and blasting we were certain to free her, but unfortunately while trying to haul some huge blocks clear with the after winch, a sudden give of the ice allowed the three-inch steel cable to be picked up by the spinning propeller. In spite of all our endeavors four turns of cable could not be freed from the shaft and finally we had to leave twelve feet hanging. From what we could observe, peering through the clear water, it seemed that the cable had forced its way between the stern gland and the propeller. What, we wondered, would be the result? Perhaps the cable would damage the gland or weaken the steel as it continually scoured its surface; but we hoped, and there was nothing else we could do, that the cable itself would disintegrate and fall away. For some time after this the loose end thrashed against the hull, making a most alarming clatter as the propeller turned, but this was at last torn away, the noise ceased, and we forgot to worry about the screw as other problems presented themselves.

Work on the ice continued all through that night, but the narrow lead we were following between the heavy floes turned so sharply that the ship could not easily follow round. As she went continually ahead and astern the rudder hit the solid ice and was so much twisted that when Captain Marø took over the ship next day in easier ice conditions he found that she answered to only about six degrees of port helm. All day he attempted to navigate in this condition but found it almost impossible, and it became clear that with the ice situation as it was we should not make any progress at all. Late that night Marø decided he must take a course once adopted by his father in a much smaller vessel many years before. This was to attempt bending the rudder back into position by purposely going astern against a solid floe. Three times he gently tried this maneuver without effect, then, risking all, he forced her hard into the ice.

Looking back one realizes that this was one of the occasions when the fate of the whole expedition must have hung in the balance. Certainly his only alternative to taking this risk was to move almost helplessly about in the ice hoping only that we should come clear before the freeze-up, but with no chance of establishing our base. As it was, his courage was rewarded by the rudder's being returned to an almost normal position (actually overcorrected five degrees to starboard), enabling him to reach the first pool of water we had seen for three weeks.

This pool proved to be about 350 yards long; just, but only just, long enough for the Auster to take off. It was not going to be easy, for the pool had a dogleg in the middle which would itself make the take-off run difficult. It was John Claydon's turn to fly and he told us by radio as he motored round and round warming up the engine that he would make a dummy run in the first place so that he could find out how the plane would behave on the curving take-off.

We watched him make the run and it suddenly became apparent that he was going to make his attempt. As the plane took the dogleg the wash from its floats curved out across the still water. Nearer and nearer he approached the ice at the end of the pool — it seemed impossible that he could clear it and the airmen among us, I am sure, hardly dared to watch. Then, at the very last moment, feet rather than yards from the ice, the plane lifted and he was airborne. Afterwards he told us, " I had to make it on the first run as I would never have dared to have another go."

For over three hours Claydon flew at 5000 feet, first to the northwest, then east, then north. All the time his radio reports were plotted, first disappointingly gloomy, then as he flew south towards the ship, increasingly encouraging. Fifty miles north of us he had found light open pack with a belt of navigable ice extending south to within twenty miles WNW of our position. Soon he came in to land, sharing the available water with a number of whales that rose to "blow" in apparent protest at this visitor from another world.

As soon as the plane had been taken aboard we started working westward toward the reported promise of easier conditions. Presently we had butted our way clear of the heavy floes into an area of thin ice only two feet thick and normally quite easy for the *Theron* to break, but the Weddell Sea was to make a last effort to hold us, for we found the whole area under pressure which prevented the ice parting before the ship. Too thick to work easily by hand, too thin to blast successfully, for the explosive merely made round holes in the ice and did not crack it, we worked away until 3:30 in the morning to clear one side of the ship. Then suddenly the ice closed again and in five minutes it was once more firmly pressed against her sides.

In such conditions it would be a disadvantage to continue freeing the ship, for the pressure would move the ice in again and again, building up thicker and thicker masses against the vessel and making it even more difficult to escape. Behind us not only our track but the pool from which the plane flew had closed. Everywhere small cracks were opening and closing and crumpled heaps of ice built up to the level of the *Theron's* decks. Then suddenly in the afternoon of January 22, the pressure eased; the ice, smeared with rust from the steel against which it had pressed, parted like a shell and left us free to edge gradually forward into easier conditions.

That night we were happy as we moved steadily northward, butting and pushing the floes out of our way at three to five knots. By now the *Protector* was approaching at the end of her thousand-mile voyage from Graham Land. Every hour we were putting on our radio beacon to guide her toward us and soon she would be able to tell us about the ice edge to the north. As neither we nor the *Protector* had seen the sun for a week our relative positions were somewhat doubtful, but on the morning of January 23 one of her helicopters flew 50 miles south in search of us. No contact was made and we realized that we must be separated by a greater distance than we thought. A second flight in the afternoon was successful and we were soon waving to the men in the helicopter and talking to them by radio. We learned that we were still some 50 to 60 miles south of the ice edge

I I I

Base Site Reconnaissance

HALF AN HOUR after midnight on the morning of January 24 the *Theron* parted company with HMS *Protector* and began again her assault on the Antarctic continent. Our intention was to follow the ice edge eastward in the expectation that we should find the area of more open water which had allowed the *Tottan* to reach the coast three weeks before us. All day we steamed steadily at 12 knots over a calm sea. A few hundred yards south of our course the clustered floes of the outer ice edge heaved and jostled one another in the gentle swell, while we, unwilling to enter the ice until really open conditions appeared, were gradually forced farther and farther to the north.

That night the ship pushed her way eastward through lonely belts of open pack ice and then headed southeast, directly toward Cape Norvegia, where we hoped to make our landfall. The chief reason for taking a course close to the land was to make use of the lead of open water which, in the summer, forms along the coast under the influence of current and offshore winds. Once we had found this "land water" we could expect to follow it for a long distance southward, perhaps even to the head of the Weddell Sea itself.

On the morning of January 26 we rose eagerly, expecting our first sight of the coastal ice cliffs. Conditions seemed almost ideal for flying, visibility was ten miles, there was no swell and just sufficient ruffle on the water to help the plain rise onto the steps of the floats. As we approached the coast, visibility became reduced to two miles and soon it was impossible to recognize Cape Norvegia through the squalls of snow sweeping across the water. Flying was definitely off, and as we could not afford the time to wait for better weather, we turned onto a southerly course along the edge of a wide strip of un-

23

broken sea ice attached to the invisible coast. For ten days the overcast skies had prevented us from fixing our position by the sun, and now that we had failed to identify Cape Norvegia we could only accept the fact that we did not know our true position within 30 or 40 miles.

At first we could only plot the coastal cliffs by radar, for they could not be seen through the snow, but soon the ice still fast to the coast forced us farther and farther from the cliffs until we were steaming down a 20-mile-wide, ice-free channel some 15 miles offshore. Everywhere huge stranded or floating tabular icebergs were scattered along our course. A particular concentration of these occurred where the great Stancombe Wills ice promontory, discovered by Shackleton in 1915, had extended 50 miles into the Weddell Sea. As we sailed across the site of this once enormous ice tongue we felt sure that the many grounded and tilted bergs represented its disintegrated remains.

By the evening of January 27 the *Theron* was some 40 miles north of Halley Bay. That night, in perfect weather, we sailed along a magnificent ice cliff coastline with a broad belt of unbroken sea ice still lying before it. In our imagination it seemed like the white cliffs of Dover, the sandy beach bleached by a perpetual sun, the holiday-makers represented by basking seals.

The ice cliffs were in fact the front of an ice shelf, a mass of floating ice attached to the land and varying in thickness from a few hundred to perhaps fifteen hundred feet. The surface of an ice shelf is normally level or gently undulating, and at times large or small masses break away from its edge and move out to sea as tabular bergs.

As we approached Halley Bay, a series of small embayments or clefts began to appear in the regular front of the ice shelf. Each of these had preserved its own small area of sea ice, from which drifts of snow extended almost to the top of the ice cliffs behind, but it was not until we reached Halley Bay itself that a way could be seen leading to the very top. At last, beyond a headland of 90-foot ice cliffs, we saw two small black figures waving from the sea-ice edge. David Dalgliesh and one of his party, George Lush, had come to guide us to the base site some two miles inland and invisible from the sea.

24

Soon a boat was lowered to put out ice anchors and to bring them both aboard. While we were exchanging greetings, the Auster was being lowered over the side, a second party was preparing to go sealing, while yet another set about the usual collection of ice for our water supply.

It was clearly of the first importance to establish from the air whether we also could use Halley Bay as a site for our base in case it should prove impossible to reach the Filchner Ice Shelf at the head of the Weddell Sea. At Halley Bay we were certain of a good landing place and the co-ordination of the two expeditions at one site would have advantages, as had been recognized by both committees at home. On the other hand, by establishing ourselves here we should be adding at least 200 miles to our transcontinental journey. Although I fully intended that we should continue our voyage south in the attempt to reach the planned position for our base, it was desirable to establish at this time whether there was a practical route inland from Halley Bay. Should this prove to be the case, we would at least know that there was a satisfactory base site to the north of us. On the other hand, if the air reconnaissance showed the hinterland to be impassable then we would have to make use of even the most difficult landing place to the south.

Owing to low cloud, John Lewis and I were forced to fly 800 to 1000 feet above the surface, our course being directed southeast toward the northern margin of the great Dawson-Lambton Glacier. This we knew reached the sea to the south of Halley Bay and I suspected that it would bar our route to the south. At the same time I hoped to see the junction of the floating ice shelf with the inland ice, for there too an impassable crevassed area could be expected.

As we flew in from the coast it was just possible to distinguish the sastrugi on the level surface below, while the distant horizon was periodically blotted out by trailing wisps of the cloud beneath which we were flying. Presently some disturbance of the surface could be seen in the distance and soon we were flying over a heavily crumpled and crevassed zone which extended eastward across our flight line. In the hollows between the high ridges of ice, pools of water had accumulated during some period of melt and now lay, blue and frozen, emphasizing the impassability of this tract which separated the smooth ice shelf surface from the higher ground beyond. Nowhere was a rock visible.

Away to the east we could see the inland margin of the ice shelf marked by a belt of wide crevasses running from north to south. In the distance these joined with the east-west belt over which we were flying. Although it was possible that closer investigation might reveal a route through the north-south crevasses, it was clear that to establish our base here might prejudice the transcontinental journey at the very beginning. I therefore decided, while still in the air, that only in the very last resort would Shackleton Base be set up at Halley Bay.

Even though we were flying at only 800 feet, cloud continually blotted out the surface below. Soon the ship began to report patches of mist over the sea with deteriorating visibility, so we reluctantly abandoned the idea of looking more closely at the inland crevasses and flew back to Halley Bay. There a low cold mist lay on the ice shelf and poured like a quiet waterfall over the ice cliffs to spread out on the surface of the sea.

I decided to stay until the afternoon of the next day in the hope of getting better visibility for a useful flight inland. Not only would this provide decisive information, but it would be useful for the Royal Society Expedition to have more knowledge of the ice shelf upon which they were to live for three years. For this reason Dalgliesh, the leader of the expedition, was given a short flight in the immediate vicinity of the base, but by the time our deadline arrived the next afternoon the weather showed no signs of improving sufficiently for a longer flight inland, so the project was reluctantly abandoned.

After entertaining the Royal Society party to breakfast and lunch on board, for they were living in tents and eating a monotonous diet of sledging rations while they built their hut, we put them ashore and sailed south in search of a more suitable landing place. The weather inland remained impractical for flying, but the sea was blue and glassy, and the sun became increasingly hot as we steamed past the gleaming cliffs, sculptured by the washing of the sea and ornamented above by many curved cornices of drifted snow. Nowhere could sea ice be seen and only a few large bergs floated on the shining water. Presently our straight course carried us away from the cliffs which receded eastward to form something of a bight. There we could see that for about forty miles the constant ice cliffs gave way to crevassed and undulating areas, which often appeared to slope gently to the surface of the sea. Any idea of landing at these points was prohibited by the heavily crevassed nature of the rolling inland ice which clothed the whole area. This was the region described by Shackleton as the Dawson-Lambton Glacier. To us it seemed that inland there was a high, snow-covered dome from which the ice was descending over a number of terraces to north, south and west. No rock was visible through the ice cover, although the latter had the appearance of a thin blanket through which rocks might appear at any time.

South of the Dawson-Lambton in the vicinity of latitude 76°32'S, we came upon an area of very active calving, where icebergs lay floating or stranded in scattered confusion. It was within four or five miles of this point that Shackleton's ship, the *Endurance,* became beset and began the long drift to west and north until she was finally crushed in the ice. By working a little farther out from the coast the *Theron* was able to wend her way through the western edge of this iceberg complex. Beyond, the wide reach of open water which we had been following gave way to an area congested with floes but through which it was still possible for the ship to force her way. Finally only one open lead led to the south and toward this Captain Marø forced his ship through a maze of interlocking floes. On reaching the lead we found it to be about three miles wide and trending somewhat to the southwest away from the coast. On either side of the open water the ice appeared unbroken but its contorted nature revealed the tremendous forces which had been exerted upon it in the past. No smooth areas existed, the whole consisting of crushed and tilted blocks, their angular corners standing four or five feet above the general level of the surface. The scene resembled nothing so much as a ploughed field after a first harrowing, but magnified twenty times.

By midnight the lead had narrowed to a mile and later to a hundred yards in width, the water, glassy smooth under the slanting rays of the sun, rippling with the movement of the ship at full speed.

Soon we had been steaming for two hours between the solid field of ice still attached to the coast 20 miles away and the equally massive area which extended to the western horizon. Never had I seen such thick or such universally crumpled ice, impassable to a ship, impossible to cross with any form of transport; even a man on foot could not have traveled more than a mile or two in a day over such a chaotic surface. Had the wind and current which forced the ice apart allowed it to close again not even the stout build of the *Theron* could have withstood the pressure. Despite this knowledge Captain Marø pressed on southward, determined to accomplish the task he had undertaken.

By 5 o'clock next morning we had completed this dangerous passage and were once more in an area of relatively small and light floes, but these were under pressure and it was some time before the turn of the tide released them and allowed the ship to make headway toward the coast. In the distance we could see two or three points where the snow slopes seemed to descend to sea level, and toward these we slowly made our way. We believed the ship's position was now 77°37'S, and we knew that we could not be far from Vahsel Bay and the Filchner Ice Shelf at the head of the Weddell Sea. John Claydon now flew Captain Marø on an ice reconnaissance, and to their surprise they found that we were only about 20 miles from Vahsel Bay and that ice conditions were very good. Even so we decided to examine the nearby landing places and edged the ship close in to the lowest part of the ice cliffs. At this point the snow slope reached almost to the level of the *Theron's* deck and it would have been possible to put our vehicles and material ashore. However the slope was inconveniently steep and above us the upward route wound between a number of dangerously crevassed areas. Altogether it was an uninviting spot.

While this investigation was taking place, John Lewis had taken off in the Auster with David Stratton to examine the inland terrain. They reported by radio that above 500 feet the crevasses ceased and a broad uncrevassed ice piedmont lay before what appeared to be a distant snow-covered mountain range. The air reports on the sea ice and the inland topography together with our close examination of the ice edge clearly indicated that we should push on south to examine the edge of the Filchner Ice Shelf. We therefore told Lewis to meet us at Vahsel Bay and lost no time in setting off on the last lap of a journey which had taken us through 2000 miles of ice in the Weddell Sea.

Ever since the first days of planning, the name Vahsel Bay had come into daily use as representing the objective for the first stage of the expedition. Although we knew that our base would be built somewhere on the vast expanse of the Filchner Ice Shelf, Vahsel Bay was a more precise indication of the position we aimed at reaching. Thus, for me at least, and I think for all my companions, it was a magic name representing accomplishment, a veritable "promised land." How disappointing, therefore, when increasing cloud and decreasing visibility gave us our first view of it in bad light and little contrast.

It was exciting to see the small nunataks, the first rock that we had seen, and indeed the only known rocks visible on the coast from Graham Land 500 miles to the west and for over a thousand miles to the north and east. But even these nunataks were only small slabs of rock, at most a hundred yards in diameter, which appeared as little dark patches against the white haze which merged sea ice and glaciers, snow and sky. On many later occasions we were to see more clearly the rusty rocks standing bravely against the grinding pressure of the interminable ice: ice which descends the steep slopes in perpetual frozen cascades to merge again into an ice tongue relentlessly pushing its way into the sea ice of the bay. There, at intervals of years, it breaks away and floats steadily westward in the form of small bergs.

Immediately after our arrival, sealing parties were put over the side onto the fast sea ice, while Gordon Haslop and I flew westward along the front of the Filchner Ice Shelf in search of a suitable landing site. From the air we could see that the ship was still several miles from Vahsel Bay itself, for a wide area of unbroken sea ice filled the bay and extended northward for some distance. The seaward edge of this ice swept round to the west in a long curve which brought it nearer to the front of the ice shelf. Evidently the ice had lain in that position for many years, for a number of old and eroded icebergs could be seen firmly frozen into it. At first the appearance of the Filchner Ice Shelf was not impressive, for the constant presence of the sea ice at its foot had allowed the ice cliffs to become drifted up. Indeed, it seemed that everywhere a gentle slope led from the sea ice to the top of the ice shelf.

As we flew west, the edges of the sea ice and the ice shelf gradually converged until the blue sea lay against the foot of the shelf and once more high cliffs extended into the distance. Turning back we flew low over the sea along the edge of the shelf attempting to estimate its height and the steepness of the slopes, for this would largely influence the ability of our tractors to haul the stores to the selected base site. The height appeared to range between 25 and 100 feet, but we were to learn later that this was something of an underestimate. I also selected several possible landing places, of which the most suitable appeared to be at a point on the sea ice about half a mile from where it ended against the front of the ice shelf. Very much later this was to prove an unfortunate choice.

At the time, however, I was well satisfied, and we flew on over the ice shelf in an easterly direction, intent on discovering the nature of the junction between the land and the floating ice shelf. As we approached the true coast a chaotic belt of broken ice lay revealed below, and from this a number of great chasms extended westward for three or four miles into the ice shelf. Though these were at least a hundred feet deep they could easily be bypassed; it was the crevasse belt, one to three miles wide between the ice shelf and the land ice, which seemed to be the most serious barrier to our movement southward. The farther we flew the more worried I became, for it seemed that there was no hope of breaking through this continuous and complex zone. At last, when 30 miles inland, I caught sight of a gleaming white line to the south. With binoculars it was possible to see that this was an ice cliff running from east to west and apparently joining with the crevassed zone over which we were flying. Clearly we had to continue our flight to the point where these two features met, for it was possible that in the angle between them an unbroken zone might exist.

We were now nearing the end of our outward fuel endurance, but Haslop flew on till we were over the western end of the great cliff which we had seen from a distance. We could see that it formed the south wall of a tremendous chasm extending westward for at least

20 miles before being obscured by low cloud. To the east, wide curving crevasses replaced the deep trench of the chasm, but at one point a smooth snow area seemed to bridge the crevassed zone and it seemed reasonably certain that we could break south through this composite barrier which otherwise threatened to make the whole of the ice shelf an impossible situation for our base. On the return flight we sent a message telling Captain Marø to sail westward along the ice edge. Three quarters of an hour later we were circling the *Theron* as she steamed in a wide lead of open water, and soon we alighted safely on the choppy sea.

Not long afterwards the ship drew alongside the selected landing site and made fast. Almost immediately David Stratton and others went ashore to reconnoiter a route across a small strip of very old sea ice and up the drifted slope of the ice shelf front. Stratton reported that the site seemed ideal, although there were crevasses at the top of the ice shelf twelve to twenty feet across, but it seemed that they were all old and solidly filled with snow.

Ken Blaiklock was to remain in charge of the base for the coming year and would be making the first southern ground journeys in the following spring. Clearly it was important that he should see for himself the obstacles which he would have to negotiate. John Claydon therefore flew him to the south, enabling him to examine the crevasse and chasm area.

Next morning, January 30, unloading began in a temperature of +7°F with a south wind of 20 knots. There still remained the selection of the final position for the base. This was to be called "Shackleton" in memory of Sir Ernest Shackleton, who had set out in 1914 with the same object of crossing the continent and who had intended to establish his base at or near to the very spot at which the *Theron* was now lying.

As the work began David Stratton and I set off on foot to climb to the top of the ice shelf and walk inland in search of a suitable base site. After crossing the half mile of sea ice lying before the ice front, we began to search for a possible route which our tractors might follow to the top. From the air it had seemed that the drifted slope was not only low but had only a gentle incline. Now we found it much steeper and it was some time before we found a reasonable gradient.

At the point we chose, the slope was of the order of one in eight with a somewhat steeper pitch toward the top. On the way up we encountered a number of crevasses, but these were deeply filled and only revealed themselves as broad depressions with narrow blue clefts along the edges. Arriving at the top of the ice shelf we judged our altitude to be about 120 feet above sea level (later it was found to be 150 feet). There the even snow surface bore a thin hard wind crust through which we trod at every step. Below, the coarse granular snow was loose and soft; by shuffling the feet one quickly sank to the knees. To the south the surface rose very gradually for about three quarters of a mile and then fell away into a hollow only to rise to a crest again half a mile beyond. This ridge and valley system seemed to extend indefinitely to the south.

Our requirements for the base site were a firm foundation in an area free of crevasses and in a position from which certain distant and recognizable features would be visible. We also wished to be able to see the sea so that the formation, movement and dispersal of the sea ice could be observed daily.

To test the solidity of the surface we probed the snow with long thin aluminum poles. This showed the depth of loose granular snow on the tops of the ridges to be about three and a half feet, whereas in the hollows it was some ten feet. By the time we had reached the crest of the third ridge, the sea had disappeared from view to the north of us, and the prominent landmark formed by the white wall of a higher portion of the ice cliff 20 miles to the west had also vanished. Twenty-eight miles to the east we could still see four dark patches of rock which outcropped on a vertical face not far from Vahsel Bay. Gradually we retraced our steps until both the white cliffs and the sea came into view.

By this time we were back to the crest of the first ridge and it was necessary to decide whether this was not only a suitable position for Shackleton, but also whether it was a safe place. Icebergs fifty to a hundred miles long are known to have calved from ice shelves, and in 1912 Filchner, who was the first to reach the head of the Weddell Sea, had to dismantle his hut when it floated away on just such a mass of ice. Our air reconnaissance had shown that the first part of the ice shelf to break away would probably be that in the vicinity of Vahsel Bay. Even this, it seemed, was unlikely to occur for a long time, so we felt certain that our selected area would remain undisturbed for a number of years.

It was therefore decided to build our base near the top of the first rise south of the ice shelf front and at a distance of about one mile from the sea. Later we were to find that the site was 195 feet above sea level, and that the ice beneath us was 1300 feet thick and afloat on 3000 feet of water.

So we completed the base site reconnaissance. The next task was to unload the ship as rapidly as possible and to start building the hut before the lateness of the season forced the *Theron* to depart.

I V

Shackleton

WHILE Stratton and I were searching for a suitable building site on top of the ice shelf, unloading had been going on apace. On our return we found the dogs picketed on the ice not far from the ship and it was delightful to see them enjoying their proper environment once more. Although the first transports of excitement had subsided, they were clearly overjoyed to be on firm ice once more and were eating, digging and rolling in the snow. Throughout the voyage we had washed out the kennels daily and generally made conditions as easy as possible for them. Even so the heat of the tropics, the constant rolling of the ship and the confined space must have been very unpleasant for dogs whose lives had been spent among the snows and rocks of Greenland. In spite of the long time that they had been confined on board we were proud to know that they had come through the experience in fine condition.

Besides the dogs from Greenland we had bought four puppies born at the Whipsnade Zoo. As these grew older one of them developed into a fine husky, but the others showed signs of dubious ancestry: long thin tails with short hair, quite unsuitable for curling over the nose, rangy bodies, legs too long and, worst of all, thin coats with little of the close wool so necessary for protection against the cold. Now that they were to spend their lives in the open in strong winds and with temperatures permanently below freezing, it seemed cruel to force them to such a life, and we reluctantly felt compelled to destroy them.

During the night the air party had spent many hours replacing the Auster's floats with skis so that the plane could be put over the side out of the way of the unloading operations. Once it was on the sea ice beside the ship John Lewis started the engine, and with Gordon Haslop and Peter Weston clinging to the wings to balance the plane, motored away to previously prepared pickets on a smooth stretch of ice about 300 yards from the ship. We had been extremely lucky to find this level expanse so close to the *Theron*, for throughout the weeks she was in the ice we had looked for an area from which the plane could operate with skis and had failed to find any floes without embedded blocks of pressure ice.

Besides the plane, dogs and other equipment, two Ferguson tractors and a Weasel were already over the side when Stratton and I returned. Our next task was to prove the route to the top of the ice shelf with a vehicle and to make safe the open cracks along the edges of the wide crevasses. For this purpose six of us set off with a tractor towing two sledges. On one was an eleven-hundredweight diesel generator, on the other, timber, tools and marker flags. All went well crossing the sea ice, but as soon as we began the steep climb up the drifted slope of the ice shelf where the snow was soft, the sledge runners sank deeply and the tractor began to dig itself in. Finally we left the generator at the foot of the slope and went on with only one sledge. Near the top the tractor tracks began to break through the thin crust at the crevasse edges leaving holes through which we could peer into the blue depths. Once on top of the shelf the surface was more or less level, but the tracks churned deep into the soft granular snow below. In spite of this it was possible to keep going and we decided to lay out our "beachhead dump" a short distance back from the edge of the shelf in order to save the time involved in hauling all the equipment direct to the base site.

To do this we began marking out the various circuit tracks, at the same time indicating the dump sites with poles and flags. On the very first circuit the tractor broke through into two concealed crevasses running at right angles to those which we could see. This showed that the apparently innocent area was far from safe, and although it was unlikely that a vehicle would drop into these relatively narrow subsidiary crevasses it would be impossible for men to move about safely on foot in such a place.

To establish the dump farther inland meant that it would be so close to the base site that we might just as well run the tractors the whole distance and avoid double loading and unloading. We therefore pushed on to the position which Stratton and I had selected for the base and there laid out the lettered marked flags at appropriate points. On our way back to the ship the route was marked with stakes driven into the snow at intervals, so that in bad visibility there would be some guide for the drivers.

On the way down to the sea ice the tractor again broke through some crevasse lids and in the evening a party went out to build wooden bridges over the open holes.

Next morning the temperature was +2°F, rather low for the time of year, in fact unpleasantly so, for in calm conditions the sea can freeze very rapidly at such a temperature. All day, owing to the difference in temperature between air and water, frost smoke rose like steam from the sea and drifted away in the wind. The scene was fascinating to watch, the sea resembling nothing so much as the surface of some gigantic boiling cauldron.

Captain Marø had been somewhat concerned both by the possible freezing of the sea which could quickly have imprisoned the ship, and by the westerly wind which could have closed the narrow channel through which we had made our way before reaching Vahsel Bay. Fortunately during the day the wind changed to the south and Marø agreed that if conditions remained as they then were it would be reasonable for us to stay at Shackleton until February 14. By that time we should not only have unloaded the ship but we should also have been able to aid the Advance Party in building the foundations, and possibly the skeleton, of the main hut. This then was our intention on January 31, but we could not know the troubles that were to come to us very shortly.

On the morning of February 1 work started under an overcast sky, with a northeast breeze and the temperature very high at +26°F. Early in the day one of the Weasels developed a fault and the spare part which was required we knew to be deep in No. 2 hold, which we had not yet begun to unload. Until then unloading had been kept down to a rate which allowed all the material to be removed immediately from the sea ice to the safety of the ice shelf. However solid sea ice may appear to be, it is bad practice to unload and stack stores directly beside the ship. Now I had to decide whether to leave the Weasel out of use, which meant that we had only one vehicle capable

36

of moving material over the soft snow of the steep slope to the top of the ice shelf, or to take the risk of unloading more quickly from the ship and permit stacking of material on the sea ice, which was here twelve feet thick. Owing to the lateness of the season, the latter course was adopted and we went ahead fast with the unloading of No. 2 hold.

No sooner was this work in progress and a considerable pile of materials collected on the sea ice than the wind rose and heavy squalls of snow began driving over us from the north. By the afternoon a real blizzard was blowing, with the drift so thick over the sea ice that it was necessary to put markers every 50 yards so that the tractor drivers could find their way to the foot of the ice shelf. Soon the sea began to rise and waves burst over the ice, flooding the surface, until a snowy quagmire began to form around the piles of stores now stacked near the ship. The *Theron* herself was grinding against the ice and straining heavily on her after mooring cables. As more and more water poured over the slightly raised ice edge and flooded the stores area, it became clear that every man must be used to salvage all we could before the cases became saturated with sea water. Sometime before, I had sent a message up to the men working at Shackleton telling them to return to the ship, because it was plain that Captain Marø might be compelled to move her from the ice edge if the pack ice began closing in from the north.

Within an hour or two the water was two feet deep over a wide area, and at one time our dinghy was used to salvage material which was floating. It was not long before everyone had become so wet that there was no longer any need to avoid wading in the slush and water. All this time the tractors were removing material as fast as possible to the dry area near the foot of the ice shelf half a mile away. In spite of our efforts the battle was partly lost and soon some boxes were floating while others remained completed submerged. What many of them might contain we scarcely dared to think; tinned foods would of course remain undamaged, but wireless and other electrical equipment would certainly be destroyed. I know that at one time I found myself standing on two completely submerged boxes marked "BBC Recording Equipment."

It was at this moment that I saw the *Theron's* stern cables part and the ship began to swing slowly away from the ice edge. Immediately I shouted to the half-dozen members of the crew who were working on the ice with us to run for the ship and try to scramble aboard before a gap opened between the bow and the ice. Splashing and scrambling through the water and slush they raced over the hundred yards to the ship and just managed to clamber aboard with the aid of ropes and ladders thrown over the side. Happy to know that at least Captain Marø had a complete crew, the rest of us arrived at the ice edge in time to see the ship swing completely round, part her bow cables and slowly drift away from us. As the driving snow and drift gradually blotted her from our sight the captain shouted through a megaphone from the wing of the bridge. We could just make out his words, "We'll be ba-a-ck" — a long-drawn-out call that carried over the howling wind.

The men up on the ice shelf had still not returned but now there was an immediate problem, for there were twelve of us on the ice with soaking feet and legs, and we did not know how long it would take for the ship to turn and come back to pick us up. Indeed there was some doubt as to whether she would be able to come alongside the landing place again, for as we continued with our work of salvaging stores, huge crumpled masses of pressure ice could be seen drifting past with the wind and current, turning and heaving with the waves as they rolled their way along the edge of the fast ice. My chief concern was our wet state and the possibility that we should be isolated for some time in low temperatures without change of clothing. As it was, the temperature was still warm at 26°F, but had it dropped much we should indeed have been in trouble.

While my mind revolved about the problem of shelter and the whereabouts of spare clothing in the hundreds of cases now stacked ashore at the foot of the ice shelf, we kept reasonably warm by hauling sledges, digging out bogged-down tractors and heaving packing cases from the ever-deepening sludge of snow and water.

It was a quarter past five when the ship parted the last cable; at a quarter to six a shout drew my attention seaward where the *Theron* had suddenly loomed mysteriously and silently through the driving blizzard. First the bow and foremast, then the whole ship gradually emerged like a wraith from the tearing white wall that enveloped everything. After watching for a few moments, the men in the ice went on with their tasks as though uninterested in the ship and I found it necessary to urge them to hurry, for it was clear that Captain Marø would not be able to hold the *Theron* alongside the ice edge. Indeed his first shouted words were, "You'll have to come aboard while she's moving."

Carefully judging his time Marø nosed the ship in to the ice edge between two huge drifting masses, bringing her close alongside the old landing site. Over the side were hanging every rope and rope ladder that the crew could muster, and up these we swarmed as the *Theron* slid past. One rope was thrown from the bow of the ship onto the ice and was seized by Gordon Haslop. As he began to climb, the rope swung vertically from the overhanging bow and Gordon found himself suspended over the surging water below and quite unable to negotiate the overhang above. Fortunately two of us were able to grasp the end before it fell into the water, and succeeded in hauling his dangling legs back onto solid ice.

Another who found himself in a predicament was Roy Homard, who scrambled up the side of the ship only to find himself standing on the bulwarks with the sheer side of an aircraft crate towering above him. Perforce he remained precariously perched in that position with the ship moving away from the ice edge, until some of us could reach down to him from the top of the crate and pull him to safety.

We now had on board all the crew and fourteen expedition members, the remaining five being still up at the building site. These were David Stratton, Ralph Lenton, David Pratt, Bob Miller and Peter Jeffries. As it was now impossible to hold the ship alongside the ice, Captain Marø moved off to open water. All navigation was by radar, the drifting fields of ice and patches of open water being clearly visible on the screen. Although I knew that the men ashore would have an uncomfortable time, I was not unduly worried about them because they had a number of tents and vehicles in which to shelter, together with large quantities of food and fuel lying in the dumps. Indeed, there was nothing that we could do and I therefore encouraged everyone to get a meal and go straight to bed, which we were glad to do.

At quarter past ten I was awakened by Captain Marø, who told me that the ice was closing in from the north and we had either to move east or west. After studying the radar picture of the scene we agreed that it would be better to move into a large enclosed area of open water to the west and north of the immediately impending ice. As the ship broke through a narrow stretch of extremely heavy floes we were relieved to feel her rise to a strong swell, for this meant that there must be extensive open water to the north. All through the night we alternately drifted and went half-ahead to keep clear of the coastal ice where more and more floes were accumulating until two miles of pack ice lay between us and our landing site.

The next day the northerly wind continued until three in the afternoon when it swung first to the northwest and then suddenly began to blow from the south. By 4 P.M. we were nosing our way in toward the ice edge through a steady snowfall. Miraculously, it seemed, the great accumulation of pack moved slowly away and Captain Marø brought the *Theron* back to our old landing site. As we approached, what a relief it was to see figures moving about among the vehicles, dogs and piles of stores.

Before the ship had broken her moorings I had frequently examined the narrow cracks which extended into the ice from the edge but none of them were "working"; I had therefore been fairly confident that there would be no wholesale breakaway. But with only the radar to watch, its picture confused by the drifting and accumulating ice floes, unpleasant doubts had assailed my mind. True the ice was for the greater part twelve feet thick, while along the edge we had seen that it was as much as twenty feet thick and more, but even such old ice can be broken by a swell and gale like that which we had experienced. As we came within hailing distance we could see Bob Miller cranking an imaginary camera at the ship, set on a photographic tripod abandoned in our rush. The next minute David Stratton, who had been firing red recognition signals, called out, "Guess what we had for breakfast!"

In fact they were all in good spirits in spite of having spent a rather rough night. It transpired that the party had attempted to reach the ship, but even with the aid of the stakes along the route they had lost their way in the driving drift before reaching the edge of the ice shelf, and had very sensibly settled down to await clearer conditions. It is difficult enough for five people to arrange themselves in a Weasel together with radio and other gear, let alone try to sleep for several hours in freezing conditions. From time to time the heater was turned on but this they found made them too hot, only to become bitterly cold again when it was turned off. Every quarter- to half-hour the vehicle was moved forward a yard or two so that the big sledge behind would not become drifted up and immovable. After four hours conditions had improved sufficiently for them to find their way down onto the sea ice. Then they knew for the first time that the ship was gone and that they were on their own for an indefinite period.

For two or three hours they continued with the salvage work which had been abandoned when the rest of us left in the ship, but then they returned to the building site and crowded into a small caboose which had been made from some packing cases the day before as a tea-break shelter. Now they found this to be very cramped quarters for five men, and by the time they had rolled themselves in bulky strips of Fiberglas they seemed almost to be lying on top of one another. By three in the morning the cold and restless night no longer seemed bearable, so a hot drink of sugar and milk powder was brewed and for breakfast they made a hotchpotch of sardines, tomatoes and sugar, all stirred together in one tin! Feeling better after this sumptuous meal and finding that the wind had dropped considerably, they pitched three tents for future use before going down to the sea ice to continue once more the salvaging of stores. That was at ten in the morning; seven hours later they caught sight of the *Theron* as she emerged from the curtain of falling snow and moved slowly in to the old mooring site.

I have since learned that the needs and possible courses of action discussed by the shore party and by us in the ship followed almost identical lines of thought, but only the five men themselves know what their thoughts were when they saw the *Theron* had disappeared, for nothing was said and our return was taken for granted.

With the ship once more safely moored, we set to work in the snow morass using Weasels and tractors to recover the remainder of our equipment, which was already beginning to freeze into a solid mass. Each item had to be towed some distance to dry snow where it could be loaded onto a sledge. Not only were the cases full of water, but thick layers of snow sludge adhered to the outsides of each, substantially increasing the weight. That day work ceased at midnight.

During the next days unloading continued apace, the stores being put down in organized dumps at the foot of the ice shelf to save tractor time. After the storm wide fields of pack ice studded with bergs large and small drifted continually westward, fortunately leaving a mile-wide lead of open water between them and the ship. This westward movement of the ice remained constant in spite of variable winds, most of which blew from the southeast or southwest. It therefore seems that the current sweeping down the east coast of the Weddell Sea and along the edge of the ice shelf is strong enough to overcome the usual drift of the sea ice with the wind.

On February 5 it became apparent that the shore lead was narrowing and that the ship might have to leave at an hour's notice. Therefore, with only half the hutting and 25 tons of coal remaining to be unloaded, the tempo of work increased to a maximum and the members of the Advance Party who were to stay behind were warned to pack all their belongings ready for an immediate landing.

As the tractors moved to and fro from the ship the drivers could be recognized by their characteristic attitudes as they perched on the bouncing metal seats. On at least one occasion George Lowe was observed to be driving with his legs lying along the bonnet of the tractor while in some remarkable way he managed to recline on the precarious seat in a carefree manner. Singing happily he disappeared into the distance, the tractor and sledge apparently looking after themselves.

During the afternoon John Lewis flew Captain Marø to Vahsel Bay and northward along the coast. On his return Marø seemed happier about our position, for he had seen plenty of open water to the north and west, at the same time observing that the very heavy and apparently close pack ice passing the ship toward the west was in reality broken up by a number of leads in all directions. By quarter to two in the morning all the hutting and 12 tons of coal had been stacked ashore and I knew that if the ship did have to depart suddenly we were in a position to leave the Advance Party at a moment's notice.

Next day, February 6, unloading was completed and stores once more began to go up to the Shackleton site. There Ralph Lenton started reconstructing the substantial Sno-cat packing case, which was intended to serve at first as an emergency shelter and later as a workshop. At the same time the weather had improved and in the evening I flew with John Lewis to Vahsel Bay, then in a southeasterly direction to see what country lay inland from the coast. I had always considered that the mountain belt which lies some 200 miles inland from the Queen Maud Land coast and more than 800 miles northwest of Shackleton probably continued southward more or less parallel to the east coast of the Weddell Sea. If this was the case it seemed possible that the small rock exposures at Vahsel Bay might represent the most southerly extension of these mountains, but it was equally possible that they continued toward the interior of the continent or swung to the west around the head of the Weddell Sea. It was therefore of the greatest importance for our future journeys that we should determine the topographical situation.

As we took off from the airstrip on the sea ice beside the ship, the 200 feet of ice shelf fell away below and a number of black specks in the distance sprang into view. These were the growing stores dumps at the Shackleton site and from them the tractor trail could be seen stretching back to the edge of the shelf and winding its way down the steep slope to the sea ice and the ship.

Turning onto an easterly course we headed toward Vahsel Bay, climbed steadily to 3000 feet. Below, the already familiar scene of sea ice and ice shelf passed beneath us. In less than half an hour we were circling over Vahsel Bay examining the few small rock exposures which seemed to be almost inaccessible on the ground. Then heading away to the southeast, we climbed to over 6000 feet as we flew over an almost level expanse of snow at an altitude of about 2000 feet. At 30 miles from Vahsel Bay, John Lewis suddenly said, "What's that on the horizon?" Seeing a low dark line, I replied, "Cloud," and cloud it undoubtedly was. A minute or two later, gazing through binoculars, I saw what John had tried to indicate: a distant ridge-like line of white and dark; certainly a far-distant range of mountains

43

lying due south of us and apparently extending in a general east-west direction. We judged the mountains to be several thousand feet high and at least 75 miles distant. The highest point on the range seemed to be at the western extremity beyond which we could see another spur farther to the south. To the east the dark patches of exposed rock were more isolated, and broad snow slopes appeared to descend through the mountains to a lower level, perhaps offering a vehicle route to the higher ice beyond.

So we experienced the excitement of our first discovery. The natural instinct was to set course for the mountains and find out what sort of barrier they might present to our southern traveling on the ground. Unfortunately radio contact with the ship had already been lost and we could not tell them of our new course, nor had we enough fuel to continue our flight as far as the position in which the mountains appeared to lie. Sadly we turned back to the ship. There we discussed our discovery and all that it meant to the expedition. On the one hand a new obstacle to our journey had been proved, on the other the surveyors and geologists could now look forward to a definite task instead of being faced with the prospect of interminable featureless snow fields.

That night it was decided to fly direct to the mountains next day. For this trip Blaiklock accompanied Gordon Haslop so that he could make a sketch map of the area which would be helpful to him when he started southward to reconnoiter the first part of our route in the following season. In the morning the temperature was −3°F and the mile-wide lead of open water around the ship was covered with half an inch of new ice. Fortunately there was little wind and the day was clear and sunny. Haslop and Blaiklock took off and set course for the new range which we were already calling the "Theron Mountains." An hour later they were circling over the highest point, which they reported to be at about 4500 feet. They observed that the mountains ran in a general northeast to southwest direction, forming a rocky wall facing to the north. At many points glaciers swept down between the mountains or tumbled over the precipitous escarpment, only to merge with the level ice at its foot.

Immediately to the south of this rock escarpment the mountains were buried beneath a smooth snow dome. Beyond this dome a wide

Coastal cliffs ninety feet high at the approach to Halley Bay.

M. V. *Theron* at the edge of the fast ice in Halley Bay.

M. V. *Theron* unloading beside the ice edge at Shackleton.

Supply dumps on the sea ice at the foot of the floating Filchner Ice Shelf.

Frost smoke drifting away from the shore lead at Shackleton.

Part of the great east-west chasm forty miles south of Shackleton. The picture shows about fifteen miles of the chasm. The left wall is probably a hundred feet high.

Incipient break-up of the floating ice shelf in the vicinity of Vahsel Bay. In the background the ice sheet masks the coastal hills.

Seven of the advance party in their Sno-cat crate. Left to right: Peter Jeffries, Roy Homard, Rainer Goldsmith, Ken Blaiklock, Tony Stewart (*standing*), Hannes La Grange, Taffy Williams.

The framework of the main base hut with the Advance Party's
Sno-cat crate on the right.

Snow filling the half-built base hut to the roof joists after a blizzard.
The Advance Party had to remove eighty tons of snow.

A view of the Tottan mountains discovered on a flight 230 miles east of Halley Bay in Norwegian territory. The name "Tottan-fjella" has been proposed.

Fitting a wing to the Otter at Halley Bay.

Icebergs breaking away from the crevassed edge of the Dawson-Lambton Glacier.

The *Magga Dan* lying in the dock cut in the sea ice to protect the ship while unloading. Shackleton Base lies in the distance on top of the ice shelf.

Looking west over Shackleton, with its lines of fuel drums and stores.

David Pratt and Hal Lister measuring snow density at Shackleton.

glacier flowed from east to west, its southern wall formed by a second range of more extensive mountains, which they believed to be 6000 or 7000 feet high.

On board the *Theron* the arrival of the aircraft had been anxiously awaited, owing to a change of wind to the northeast which was driving the pack ice toward the ship and every minute narrowing the lead in which she lay. As the pack closed in, it compressed and over-rafted the thin skin of ice which had formed during the night. It was fascinating, but ominous, to see the ice breaking into many-tongued plates, which slid silently one over the other like loose playing cards, somehow animated to rebuild themselves into a pack. Ever moving, always thickening, buckling, sliding, advancing on the ship, it seemed that the ice was alive and moving with the silent purpose of our destruction.

By half past twelve Captain Marø had decided that the ship must move within an hour, but the plane was still airborne and we had to wait for its return. As the minutes passed, the new ice continued to thicken around us, for the southern movement of the heavy pack gradually closed the mile-wide sheet of thin ice to a width of a hundred yards or less. At half past one when the Auster landed, the sludge and over-rafted ice was already eighteen inches thick around the side of the ship, and away to the east we could see a tongue of pack ice approaching the coast, threatening to close our escape route in that direction.

Haste was now imperative; the eight members of the Advance Party had already stowed their belongings on a sledge ready to go up to the building site. It only remained for us to hoist the plane on board and say a hasty farewell to those we were leaving behind. We knew that they had an enormous task ahead of them — a task which had become far greater than had been intended, owing to the lateness of our arrival. We had expected to complete at least the framework of the living hut before the ship left. As it was, all that had been done was to re-erect the Sno-cat packing case, which would serve as an emergency shelter until the main hut could be built. We little knew that it was to provide quarters for the entire party throughout the Antarctic winter.

They had also to face another major task which had not been foreseen: that of moving nearly 300 tons of stores from the sea ice at the foot of the ice shelf up 200 feet to the site of Shackleton Base. For this purpose they had one Sno-cat, two Weasels and two Ferguson tractors with special tracks. On the brighter side we were leaving them with sufficient stores and fuel to last three years should we find difficulty in returning the next summer.

As soon as the plane had been lifted on board we all congregated on the ice to say our good-bys to the eight we were leaving behind. Handshakes and badinage, some laughter and a little awkwardness, all played their part. No one liked to feel that the expedition was dividing into two, and many of those who were going home to prepare the next stage must have felt that in some way we were leaving our companions in the lurch.

Then the *Theron* slid slowly away from the ice edge, turning in a wide sweep onto an easterly course. Three long blasts of the siren drowned the final shouts of farewell and we found ourselves silently waving to the tiny cluster of men which seemed so quickly to dwindle in size, until individual figures could no longer be distinguished.

As the ship pushed forward, the floating ice sludge parted and re-formed again behind us as if we were sailing in some gigantic pool of white mud. Soon we approached the point where we had seen the pack ice closing in toward the fast ice. At the narrowest point the gap was now only twelve feet wide, but it still seemed that the ship could force her way through. When the bow nosed into the gap it quickly became apparent that, in her light unloaded condition, even under full power she could neither break nor move the very heavy ice. Had we been five minutes sooner there is little doubt that we should have passed easily through the gap to the open water beyond. As it was we had now to extricate ourselves from this point of increasing pressure. To go astern was no easy matter, because of the sludge of rafted ice that lay behind us and held the individual floes like a liquid cement. If this "cement" were to freeze solid the *Theron* would be as immobile as if she were set in concrete.

At last the ship moved slowly astern and Captain Marø was able to start making his way through the complicated maze of closely packed floes to the north. In less than half an hour we became immovably jammed and were compelled to settle down to wait for the easing of the pressure. At this time the tension on board could be felt, for everyone knew that we had to free ourselves soon or follow the drift of Shackleton's ill-fated *Endurance* to the west.

Two hours later we began to make slow and laborious progress toward the north, but it was apparent that we had only left Shackleton Base just in time. For many hours we could see the stores dumps we had left behind, and later the base itself came into view, appearing from the distance to be on the very edge of the ice shelf. During the night we gradually worked our way north and east to reach easier conditions near the Caird Coast. On the evening of February 8 we reached Halley Bay once more, where we picked up the Royal Society Expedition's final mail and headed north along the coast. By the evening of February 10 we found ourselves in the open sea and the following message was sent to our Patron, Her Majesty the Queen:

> Expedition vessel Theron now clear of Weddell Sea ice on return voyage having established Shackleton Base in latitude 77°57'S, 37°17'W. Wintering Party will examine mountains discovered to the southeast. Loyal greetings to our Queen and Patron.
>
> FUCHS

The following reply was received:

> Thank you for your message. I have been following your adventure with great interest and we are all delighted at your success. Please send my best wishes to all members of your Expedition.
>
> ELIZABETH R.

V

The First Winter

EIGHT MEN watched the *Theron* sail away, and as they watched, with the ship still less than a mile distant, the pack ice closed solidly against the beachhead where she had been lying. They turned to face 300 tons of stores stacked at the foot of the ice shelf. Broadly divided into groups, 25 tons of anthracite, 350 barrels of fuel, hutting and boat gear, food, clothing, sledging rations for men and dogs, it must have presented a picture of utter confusion and raised gloomy thoughts regarding the labor of transporting all this material to Shackleton, almost two miles distant.

Already the temperature was falling below zero and their first need was to establish themselves securely and organize their daily existence. There were tents to pitch, sleeping bags to unpack and personal gear to be stowed. Presently there was the first brew of tea and something to eat in the Sno-cat crate, which had been erected as a temporary shelter but which was in fact to become their home throughout the winter. This was by no means finished inside, nor had the outside been made drift-proof — tasks which were to occupy Ralph Lenton and Hannes La Grange for the first few days. That evening Taffy Williams twice attempted to contact the *Theron* using the small vehicle transmitter, but with no result. The first day ended half an hour after midnight when they retired to their two-man tents with their thoughts, and to sleep.

For the next ten days the main task was to move the stores from the sea ice up to Shackleton: days when they came to realize how small their working force really was. Mechanical troubles occurred one after another and on the second day Roy Homard and Rhino Goldsmith spent all their time repairing vehicles. With Taffy install-

48

ing radio equipment and cooking, Ralph and Hannes working on the crate, this left only three to load and transport the stores. With the available manpower varying from day to day, the amount moved seldom exceeded 15 tons and was frequently less than 10 tons. Yet at the end of ten days all the food, the timbers for the hut, and 50 barrels of paraffin oil and petrol together with a quantity of general stores and scientific equipment had been moved up to the base.

Now they turned their attention to laying the foundations and then to the construction of the heavy trusses which would form the main framework of the hut. Each truss was built in two halves and when, with difficulty, those on one side had been hauled upright in a row, they stood curiously like a line of the Queen's Beasts. When their counterparts were erected they would be bolted together to form the complete frame.

As February advanced the temperatures continued to fall and work was usually started in the morning with 30 to 50 degrees of frost. Occasionally blizzards blew for a day, covering the working site and the timber, causing much waste of time while everything was dug out. To handle nuts and bolts it was necessary to work with bare hands, and frostbitten fingers became a problem.

With the beginning of March the weather deteriorated considerably, blinding drift obliterated everything — conditions which were repeated day after day in the weeks and months to come. Wind was the great enemy. Relentless, unremitting wind, driving a torrent of snow like a horizontal waterfall, to fill every nook and cranny, burying everything in its path and making what would have been bearable temperatures almost impossible to endure.

On March 4 they carried out "Operation Dog-span" to move the twenty-four huskies from the sea ice up to the base. To walk each animal the two miles individually would have taken much time and effort and they were not yet trained to run as teams. So Blaiklock decided to leave them chained to their steel wire spans, and attaching a vehicle to each end, drove with them gaily to the top of the ice shelf, bringing the dogs to Shackleton in a chorus of excitement. There they were picketed close to the building site. An attempt to bring up the seals, which were the winter food supply for the dogs, was prevented by huge drifts of snow which had formed on the steep slope to the top of the ice shelf. So, during the first weeks of March the work continued. On March 1, regular meteorological observations were started, by the 19th the main framework of the hut was up, the gable ends were being completed, and Peter Jeffries and Tony Stewart began to haul the crates of wall panels into position beside the building.

March 20 began as one of the better days, cloudy with continuous snow and a light wind, but this gradually increased to 30 knots and the party was forced to retire to the shelter of the crate. By this time they had settled down to a routine in the confined space available and life was not quite so uncomfortable as it had been. The crate measured 21' by 9' by 8' and at one end a small kitchen bench had been built on which were the three Primus stoves used for cooking. Down the center was a table with forms on either side, while at the other end, near the door, was a workbench and the radio equipment. In this restricted space they now sat out what became known as "The Great March Blizzard," which lasted for seven days, only going outside to feed the dogs and to sleep in their tents at night. Writing, reading, playing chess or Scrabble, the time passed slowly for them, the snow building up outside the door and having to be dug away every hour to prevent their being completely buried. Ventilation was a constant problem and at different times all the party suffered from sore eyes and headaches from fumes.

For the first six weeks menus were governed by their inability to bake, and once the bread provided from the ship was finished they lived on biscuit. In time, however, the inventive Roy Homard constructed an oven from an empty British Petroleum oil drum insulated with Fiberglas. This stood on a Primus and became a challenge to the cook's ingenuity, for now it was at least possible to make bread and cakes, and if at first standards were not very high, appetites were keen and burnt offerings were overlooked.

Each night they retired to their tents, but comfortable sleep was now a rare thing, for the temperature ranged down to −45°F and the sleeping bags were becoming heavy with frozen condensation, cracking and creaking as they crept into them. In the crate a lining of Fiberglas gave some insulation and prevented the drips which had been such a bother at first, when the heat from the stoves had melted the ice on walls and ceiling. Now they could thaw out and dry their socks and clothing which hung in festoons from the roof, but only the duty cook was able to dry his sleeping bag during his "four days on" when he slept in the crate.

This task came round in rotation once a month, but in spite of the prized opportunity to dry out sleeping bags, cooking was undoubtedly a burden to most. Yet public opinion had become a taskmaster that ensured a certain standard, occasionally enhanced by an individual bright idea for some change, such as Roy Homard's surprising ability to provide tinned peas with a pleasant flavor of mint. It was only after some time that he divulged the secret of his success, which was achieved by adding half an inch of Mentasol toothpaste to the boiling pot!

At last, in the evening of March 26, the wind died down and they were able to move about outside and survey the changed scene around them. The tents were nearly buried and had to be dug out and repitched. On the north side of the hut a huge drift seventy yards long stood fifteen feet above the surface, and under it lay buried all the wall panels which had so laboriously been dug out the day before the blizzard began.

Ken Blaiklock and Tony Stewart went down to the sea ice to collect more dog food. As they approached the stores dump, they found clouds of frost smoke rolling away to the north. Coming nearer their worst fears were confirmed — a large part of the ice which had looked so solid had broken away through the middle of the various piles of stores, and gone were 300 drums of fuel, a Ferguson tractor, all the coal, the timber for the workshop, the boat and boat gear, besides many engineering stores and most of the seals. All that was left was dog pemmican, the sledge ration boxes, a case of detonators and a few drums of cement, one literally teetering on the very edge of the ice.

Returning to base, Blaiklock called a council of war to discuss the situation. The first thing was to assess the quantity of fuel which had already been taken up to Shackleton. They found that for cooking and heating there would be three gallons of paraffin a day for the remainder of the year, together with sufficient petrol for the amount of vehicle work that they would be doing. As all the food had been moved up to the base, they would have enough for three years; only fuel would have to be conserved and so they settled down to a new routine of careful economy.

Among the stores lost were all the chemicals needed for making hydrogen, and to the great disappointment of the three meteorologists, this meant abandoning the radiosonde program they had hoped to carry out.

April saw the daylight getting shorter and shorter, but work continued on the hut; the two gable ends were completed, the floor was laid and the roof began to take shape. Tunneling for the buried cases was a tremendous task, but better than digging down through fifteen feet of snow only to have the hole filled in by the next day of drift. These tunnels, which soon assumed the appearance of catacombs, were later used to house the dogs during the long winter nights when temperatures and winds were to become too severe for them to remain outside.

On April 20 the sun set for the last time for four months, but work continued by the light of Tilley lamps, each man setting out to his roof paneling or tunneling carrying his own lantern. The rays of the sun, hidden by the horizon, would color the clouds with red, orange and green that faded into the pale, moonlit sky. Aurora too appeared as curtains of wavering light, changing their form, intensity and color from minute to minute. Usually these displays were white, but sometimes they were tinged with red and green, colors that pulsated against the dark background of the polar night.

May was the coldest month, when the temperature really began to fall. The average was −35°F, which meant that on many days it was in the minus fifties and sixties. At the beginning of the month there was another blizzard lasting ten days, during which nothing but essential work could be done outside. The dogs had to be fed, meteorological observations continued, and food and fuel had to be brought into the crate, but for the rest of the time they could do little but read or write. Roy Homard had now rigged a wind generator and so at last they had electric light and ample power for the small radio set.

On May 7, twelve weeks after the ship had left them, Ralph Lenton at last succeeded in making his first radio contact — with the

Falkland Islands Dependencies Survey Base on Horseshoe Island, 1000 miles to the northwest. He jumped up waving his arms and shouting, "I've got him! I've got him!" Returning to his key he called again and kept repeating, "He's calling us!" Everyone was spellbound with excitement and Ken Blaiklock hastily composed a message to the London office reporting that they were all well. It was a great moment, and from that day communication was maintained at frequent intervals with Horseshoe Island or Port Stanley in the Falkland Islands, though it was many months before they were able to talk to their nearest neighbors at Halley Bay, who had been "listening out" regularly. After this first message it was possible to send a full report of their situation, demands for replacement stores, and as communications continued to improve, exchange messages with families in Britain.

So May ended, and they went on digging their way into June as the drift poured into the hut almost as fast as they could remove it. On the 6th they experienced their strongest wind, of 80 mph, and though the month was surprisingly warmer than May, there was much snow and constant high winds. By the time they had cleared 80 tons of snow from the east end of the hut, another 40 tons had filled the west, and — it was hard grueling work, but they were getting somewhere.

Midwinter Day — June 21 — is traditionally an Antarctic festival. Taffy Williams produced for the occasion all the radio messages that had accumulated, while Ralph Lenton prepared a special meal consisting of turtle soup, ham with Brussels sprouts and other vegetables, followed by strawberry shortcake and cream. He had even baked some excellent bread rolls. The table was graced with a cloth and decorated; a small clockwork train, presented by the Scott Polar Research Institute, ran on rails round and round a Dundee cake in the center, while above it two angels revolved endlessly in the warmth of the candles, merrily tinkling tiny bells. They had made each other presents and Peter Jeffries, who was never seen without a book, received a bookmark inscribed "Here you were interrupted . . ."

There were paper hats, balloons, games, sweets and cigars, besides numerous musical instruments that added to the air of gaiety and made them forget for a time their isolation and the perpetual battle with wind and the ever-encroaching drift.

Next day, perhaps a little later than usual, they were outside with shovels digging away snow from the framework of the hut, so that Ralph Lenton could follow behind setting up the interior partitions. Roy Homard walked south to search for the remains of a Dexion mast he had built but which had been blown away by a storm even before it was erected. He found various bent and twisted pieces up to three miles from the base, together with fragments of wood which lay as a long line of wind-blown debris.

By the end of the month the eastern half of the hut was taking shape and had been sealed off with snow blocks so that work could continue inside irrespective of the weather. During July conditions remained generally bad, but building continued.

The dogs were now all under cover in the tunnels, which became too warm for them at −18°F since the heat of their bodies melted the snow on which they lay. This was due to their own accumulated body heat, and a vent had to be cut in the roof.

Toward the end of the month the men began to tell each other that the faint light on the northern horizon was a little brighter — a thought prompted rather by hopeful anticipation than justified by reality. On August 2 they recorded their lowest temperature: −63°F, or ninety-five degrees of frost. In London it was David Stratton's wedding day and the Advance Party were determined to share in the celebrations, but their toast was considerably delayed because the carefully conserved whisky was frozen and even the paraffin had turned into a thick jelly.

On August 7, exactly six months after the departure of the *Theron,* the first two occupants, Blaiklock and Goldsmith, slept in the hut. Many of the bunks had now been completed but there was some disinclination to move in, as it was still easier to warm the tents than the two-man cabins. From then on work was concentrated on making the interior more habitable. The Aga cooker and heater stoves were erected, and tables, chairs and mattresses unpacked.

Slowly a partial daylight began to appear, which gave a new impetus to outside work. Roy Homard got one of the Weasels going, which then helped to move heavy material about the base site. Peter

Jeffries was building a new Dexion lattice mast for the meteorological instruments, while Ken Blaiklock and Rhino Goldsmith were preparing the sledges for dog-training. On August 18 the first tiny portion of the sun's rim was seen winking with the refraction over the northern horizon, then on the 23rd the sun truly returned to Shackleton.

By the beginning of September all the self-recording meteorological instruments had been installed and a full 24-hour program was instituted, which continued without interruption until the base was abandoned fourteen months later. With more and more hours of sunshine it really felt as if winter was passing and spring was on the way, but even when the whole party finally abandoned the crate which had been their home for eight months and moved into the hut, the outside temperature was still −40°F. The first fire was lit in the stove, using waste wood, and everyone rushed outside to see the smoke coming from the chimney.

To prepare for the first sledge trip the dogs were picketed outside again and were taken for training runs. On September 29 Blaiklock and Goldsmith left for Vahsel Bay to collect seals, for only a few weeks' dog food remained. They returned with some meat and had seen enough seals to know that with a vehicle they could fetch in sufficient to feed the dogs until the ship arrived in January.

Returning to base after ten days they found preparations going ahead to install the diesel generators and the main transmitter. All this heavy equipment was buried deep in drift, making it necessary to dig a huge hole six feet deep and twenty-five feet across before the cases could be hauled out with a Weasel and towed over to the hut. At the same time Taffy Williams, with occasional help from the others, was erecting the four 52-foot masts for a rhombic aerial, and Peter Jeffries was finishing off the new 33-foot Dexion meteorological mast. On October 17 this was erected, but seven days later a high wind broke one of the guys and it crashed to the ground. When mended it was re-erected but always retained an individualistic twist.

By the end of October the generators and radio were working and on the 29th the first voice contact was established with the BBC in London. Reception was excellent and several tests were made on consecutive days before the first radio program on the expedition was broadcast. During these tests the BBC allowed several of us to be in the studio and talk to the base; these opportunities of discussing our problems and exchanging news were greatly appreciated at both ends.

On the same day Roy Homard, Hannes La Grange and Ken Blaiklock had left with a Weasel and a dog team to hunt more seals in Vahsel Bay. They covered 32 miles in less than nine hours and were back at Shackleton the following night with one and one-half tons of meat.

At last the hut was weatherproof and the men were in daily radio contact with London, Port Stanley or Halley Bay. The weather was becoming almost too warm, and perpetual sun enabled work to go on at any hour of the day or night. The time had come to start the southern dog sledge journeys which would prepare the way for the vehicles later on.

In November two short trips were made to establish a small depot 50 miles south of Shackleton. On these journeys Blaiklock took with him Rhino Goldsmith and Peter Jeffries, who had yet to learn the technique of travel. Soon they found themselves crossing wide well-filled chasms up to thirty yards across, but saw no sign of the great chasm that had been observed from the air. After 50 miles they knew that they must have passed its eastern end, which was most encouraging, for we had feared that this might prove a serious barrier to our journey south. After putting down the depot in 78°40′S, they turned back to base where they arrived after three days, having traveled light in rather bad conditions.

Later the same party made a second trip with more material for the depot. Then on December 7 Blaiklock and Goldsmith set out on the long run to the Theron Mountains which had been discovered from the air in February. In the first two days they traveled 45 miles. On the third they picked up additional food at the 50-mile depot before continuing southwards over the flat and monotonous ice shelf. Here and there were large holes and some crevasses but nothing to trouble dog sledges. Until reaching 78°57′S their route was governed by a wide crevassed area lying along the foot of the snow-covered hills to the east of their course. These were later to become known as the "Touchdown Hills" and between them and the Theron Mountains a wide embayment of the ice shelf extended to the east.

Across this the party now drove toward a single rocky peak that peered above the horizon. For days a familiar sight, always ahead of them, never seeming to come closer, they called it "Mount Faraway."

The weather was fine with brilliant sunshine and temperatures in the plus twenties. In these conditions the snow became so soft that they were compelled to change to night travel, for then the cooler conditions provided a harder surface for the sledges. Traveling 15 to 16 miles daily, they reported their position to Shackleton every third day. Slowly Mount Faraway was joined by other dark masses that came peeping above the horizon, until a great rock wall intersected by steep glaciers could be seen extending out of sight to the east. On December 17 they camped about four miles from Mount Faraway and next day found some difficulty in negotiating a wide stream of melt water rushing into a small lake that had formed on the surface of the ice some miles distant. Ultimately they found a way across and camped close to the rocks. Above were small waterfalls pouring off the precipitous rock and ice slopes to feed the river running along the foot of the mountains. It was surprising to find all this water in so high a latitude and it testified to the amount of heat absorbed by the rocks when the sun was high in the sky. As the day advanced and the sun sank it seemed that an invisible hand slowly shut off the supply of water, reducing the spouts and rushing torrents to mere trickles that gurgled their way beneath screes or dripped slowly from hanging masses of the tumbling ice falls.

High against the 2000-foot rocky cliffs hosts of snow petrels wheeled about the crags among which they had their nests. In the lower fastnesses, waiting to feed their young upon the eggs and chicks of the snow petrels, lived their dark enemies, the skua gulls.

At the foot of Mount Faraway, Blaiklock took sun observations to fix the southern end of the outward traverse, then after collecting many interesting rock specimens that showed the range to be composed of sandstone, shale and limestone, they turned back with eight days' food and 120 miles to go before reaching their depot. There they arrived on Christmas Day after a difficult run in soft snow and bad weather. Christmas fare encouraged both men and dogs; for the dogs there was an extra block of pemmican, for the men a "believe-it-or-not meal" of soup, smoked salmon, asparagus, pineapple *glacé* — and a single tot of brandy.

The last 50 miles they covered in two days, while sun halos and mock suns heralded a deterioration of the weather from the south. Fortunately the following wind was no hindrance to their progress and they reached Shackleton at nine in the morning after traveling 360 miles in twenty days.

By now there were a number of ships in the Weddell Sea, and the American icebreaker USS *Staten Island,* and the transport *Wyandot* were approaching Halley Bay on their way to establish a new base somewhere along the Filchner Ice Shelf. On December 31 these two ships sailed past Shackleton in the open-water lead that had formed along the edge of the ice shelf. The base was visited by Captain MacDonald, who commanded the *Staten Island,* and Captain Finn Ronne, who was to remain in charge of the new base. They brought with them fresh fruit and Christmas presents, which were greatly appreciated by the eight men who had been so long isolated in conditions more severe than anyone should expect to endure, even in the polar regions.

In spite of the difficulties of living in cramped quarters, of sleeping a polar winter in tents at 78°S and of being deprived of a great part of their stores, the Advance Party had performed their tasks. They had built the hut, and the first part of the route to the south had been reconnoitered. Now they would be reinforced with more men, more vehicles and new stores with which to face the second winter and prepare for the crossing of the continent.

V I

The Return to Shackleton

ON THE RETURN VOYAGE to England the *Theron* called at South Georgia, Montevideo and Madeira, arriving in London on March 23, 1956. The next six months were spent in preparing for our return to Shackleton at the end of the year. The office in Victoria Street once more became a hive of industry. Expedition members in charge of different sections busied themselves procuring stores and equipment; where possible, persuading the various firms to give us the material or reduce the price; and right nobly did industry respond.

There were factories to be visited all over Britain, Sno-cats to be tested in the snows of Norway, the Otter aircraft to be flown from Canada via Greenland and Iceland. Presently an endless stream of stores was once more pouring into the hands of the Crown Agents who had undertaken to handle the packing and shipment of our equipment.

During the summer the last four members of the expedition joined the office. Hal Lister, aged thirty-three, had spent two years with the British North Greenland Expedition as glaciologist, and this provided him with practical experience which he was to put to excellent use in the Antarctic. Keen on his scientific work, commander of South Ice, his cheerful Yorkshire accents represented the well-being at that inland station throughout the winter. His propensity to write poetry and read it over the radio to Shackleton was a frequent source of entertainment to our American friends also listening in on this frequency.

Allan Rogers, aged thirty-eight, and a physiologist, was to replace Rhino Goldsmith as medical officer for the second season. He joined the expedition from Bristol University, where he was a lecturer in

59

physiology. With little medical work to do he was able to concentrate on his scientific program and delighted in making or repairing instruments of all kinds. His services were also constantly in demand for dental treatment and many a tooth was to be saved by his meticulous and careful work.

Jon Stephenson was Australia's representative. Aged twenty-six, he was a geologist just completing his thesis at London University. Short, strong and indefatigable, he quickly and enthusiastically took to dog driving, was never happy out of sight of mountains, and was constantly thinking of ways to reach new rocks, however inaccessible they might appear to be.

Lastly the British Petroleum Company lent us Geoffrey Pratt, a geophysicist, aged thirty-one. Tall and heavily built, he had worked in Papua and Canada and now became responsible for our seismic work and the gravity traverse across the continent. Capable of sleeping at any time, impossible to rouse when once asleep, he was nevertheless always on the job when the time came.

All through the summer and autumn the tempo increased until, at the beginning of November, the newly built Danish polar vessel the 1850-ton *Magga Dan,* arrived to load at Butler's Wharf, Tower Bridge, in the heart of London. On November 13 Her Majesty the Queen was shown over the ship by Captain Hans Christian Petersen, and all the members of the expedition were presented.

Finally, on November 15, 1956, the great day of departure had arrived. The *Magga Dan,* bearing the stores and the main parties of the Trans-Antarctic Expedition and the Royal Society's Antarctic Expedition, sailed down the Thames on the beginning of her 10,000-mile voyage to Halley Bay and Shackleton.

Steaming via Madeira and Montevideo, it was not until December 17 that we reached Grytviken in South Georgia. There we again test flew our Auster seaplane before visiting the whaling station at Leith Harbour, where, at the request of the British Petroleum Company, Messrs. Salvesen had once more undertaken to bunker our ship before we finally sailed south into the Weddell Sea. At 6 A.M. we went alongside to fuel from the tanker *Polar Maid,* which had arrived the previous evening. As the captain was an old friend from the previous season, Stratton and I went aboard and sat talking until we suddenly realized that it was the time set for *Magga Dan* to sail. Dashing out on deck we found that she was in fact under way, and as soon as we were spotted climbing into a motorboat shouts of derision could be heard across the water. However we were soon aboard and the expedition, once more complete, at last set out on the final leg of the return to Shackleton.

We were putting the Auster over the side at Leith Harbour when a derrick cable had swung sideways fouling the rudder of the plane. This would take several days to repair and it was doubtful if the plane would be ready for ice reconnaissance by the time we reached the Weddell Sea. Now, on the evening of the day we sailed, the sea rose considerably and suddenly a heavy wave came inboard on the starboard side, smashing the rudder of our cocooned de Havilland Otter. Peter Weston was still in the process of repairing the Auster, but here he had a more formidable task, for the Otter's rudder was ten feet high and had a stressed metal skin, which was far more difficult to mend than the small fabric-covered rudder of the Auster. In the end he repaired both planes successfully, and throughout our subsequent flights no trouble was experienced as a result of these incidents.

It was on the evening of December 22 that we first met ice in position 58°38'S, 30°00'W, but this was mostly brash, with a few floes in the last stages of disintegration. As darkness fell we reduced speed to await the morning light before deciding upon our point of entry into the pack ice proper.

From first light on the next day Captain Petersen worked the *Magga Dan* to the southeast with extensive areas of thin ice floes on either side of the wide lead along which she was steaming. As the day wore on, Southern Thule, the most southerly island of the South Sandwich group, gradually disappeared over the northern horizon. This was the last land we should see before reaching the Antarctic mainland. On we went through a vast area of rotten floes with open pools and leads of water. Away to the east the American icebreaker USS *Staten Island* and the transport *Wyandot* were held up by heavy pack ice to the north of Cape Norvegia. This we learned from Shackleton, where they were in daily contact with the *Staten Island*. In the light of our experience the previous year with the *Theron*, we had intended to enter the ice much farther to the east than in 1955, but this news did not encourage us to do so. Accordingly Captain Petersen maintained a general course of 160°T, heading directly for Cape Norvegia. In this way we hoped to avoid the heavy pack entering the Weddell Sea from the east, and to make our way through an area of rotten ice which could be expected to have come from the west.

During the day the repaired rudder was being fitted to our Auster so that the plane could be used for ice reconnaissance. Suddenly John Lewis noticed a smell of burning, and looking round, saw wisps of smoke rising from beneath a tarpaulin lashed over one of the ship's electric winches. While someone rushed away to find the chief electrician, Lewis and others tore off the tarpaulin and found the entire winch smoking hot, owing to some electrical fault. That this was noticed in time was a lucky escape indeed, for firmly lashed to the winch were six barrels of aviation petrol and had these caught fire, the other 650 barrels on deck would almost certainly have been ignited, with serious if not disastrous results.

By noon on Christmas Eve our position was 61°04′S, 24°32′W. The ice floes remained generally thin but had increased considerably in area. All the time I was watching for the really heavy floes which, we had learned in the previous season, marked the solid core of the Weddell Sea pack ice. Although individual floes were now many acres in extent, none of the really heavy floes had yet appeared.

As it is the Danish custom to celebrate Christmas with festivities on December 24, we had decided that the two expeditions should join in the celebrations rather than upset the ship's routine twice in a few hours. Indeed we all felt it would be a much happier occasion if we could celebrate as one large party. Accordingly, at 5 P.M. the engines were stopped in a convenient lead and everyone repaired to the various messes for a tremendous meal and a general jollification. Soon speeches and songs, the clink of glasses and roars of applause resounded from all quarters.

By 4 A.M. on Christmas Day we were on our way again rejoicing, not only because of the party but on account of the relatively easy passage through the ice. All that day the floes became larger, the greatest being some six feet thick and as much as ten miles long and it seemed that the ice was becoming unpleasantly like that which had held the *Theron* for so long.

It was Christmas Day, and although we had celebrated the previous evening the Expedition had saved their presents for this occasion. Special efforts had been made by David Stratton's wife, who had sent a brightly colored knitted cap and some form of musical instrument for each member. Rainer Goldsmith too, although still at Shackleton, had managed to provide a present for each of us in the form of a blue handmade pottery mug. These were ornamented with the name of the recipient together with some amusing emblem representing his particular occupation. Before long a motley crowd of figures with multicolored headgear could be seen on the afterdeck, where the welkin rang to the tune of many untutored instruments. The concert over, we crowded into the lounge to hear the Queen's Christmas Day broadcast. To complete our day, the ship made wireless contact with Shackleton and everyone was able to talk to the Advance Party by radio-telephone. The new members were introduced over the air and chatted at great length with those at the base.

On Boxing Day, Bill Petersen, the *Magga Dan's* first officer, flew with John Lewis on our first ice reconnaissance, which was immediately successful in showing the way out of the congested floes which were holding us up. Thereafter we progressed steadily, and on the morning of the 28th, a huge area of open water appeared before us in about latitude 68°22′S, longitude 16°44′W. Soon we were astonished to find that except for a gleam of ice to east and west there was only open water in sight, and Captain Petersen set the automatic pilot: probably the first time that this has ever been possible in the Weddell Sea.

In 1823 Weddell sailed south through this sea which now bears his name to latitude 74°15′S. His course was uninterrupted by ice and he only turned back owing to the lateness of the season. Since that time such open conditions have never been seen. Were we now about to enjoy a similar easy passage, perhaps to the very head of the Weddell Sea itself? Hour after hour we maintained a steady 12 knots into the teeth of a 45-knot southerly wind, yet it seemed impossible that we should reach Shackleton without encountering more than the occasional icebergs we could see drifting in our path.

Shortly after 6 P.M. our rising hopes died. The hundred-mile stretch of open water we had been following was closed by solid and impenetrable pack ice at 69°43′S, or 275 miles north of the point reached by Weddell. At first we attempted to push our way south-eastward, but after a few miles it was clear that we might be running into real trouble and the ship was stopped in a pool beside a small iceberg. An hour later Gordon Haslop flew off with Bill Petersen to reconnoiter the conditions ahead. Visibility was poor, with low cloud down to 500 to 1000 feet, but after two hours' flying it was clear that we had no alternative but to retire ignominiously northward and attempt to break eastwards toward some areas of dark "water sky" which indicated more open conditions. First we had to extricate the ship from the closely packed floes, a task which proved more formidable than we expected. For the first time everyone was over the side chopping and poling the ice, just as we had done so often from the *Theron* the previous year.

On the morning of December 30 John Lewis took off in the Auster and made three separate runs from the ship, to southeast, east and northeast. It was only to the northeast that he could see any hope of progress, all the ice in the southern area being under pressure. When trying to leave the pool of open water from which the Auster had taken off, we found the floes at all the possible exits to be under pressure, and for the second time in twenty-four hours we had parties over the sides of the ship, digging, levering, winching and poling. At last a huge ice block came loose, followed by many over-rafted floes which floated to the surface. Then as the mass heaved and wallowed the *Magga Dan* pulled quickly astern while we skipped nimbly clear of the tumbling ice.

Freed once more, we pushed on in icebreaker style through close but thin pack ice two feet thick. Here and there it was necessary to crack floes up to twelve feet thick, but these were exceptions. Progress was well maintained for the next three days. Our noon position of 70°50′S, 13°19′W, on January 2, 1957, showed us to be only 25 miles from the *Tottan,* which was also on her way to Halley Bay, carrying additional stores for the Royal Society Base. Captain Jacobsen of the *Tottan* reported considerable difficulty with very heavy pack and asked if we could make an aerial reconnaissance to assist him. This suited us excellently, for in spite of our progress, we our-selves were now encountering increasingly heavy ice.

On reaching the next fair-sized pool of open water just before midday, John Lewis took Bill Petersen on a triangular flight, first to the *Tottan,* then southwest to look for the open "land water" lead, finally returning direct to the *Magga Dan.* This flight confirmed the presence of a wide stretch of clear water close to the coast and en-abled both ships to free themselves from the clutches of the ice. Dur-ing the flight communication was maintained between the aircraft and the ships in English, Danish and Norwegian. The *Tottan* was seen to be jammed between two immense floes and heading away from the open water, which could be seen from the plane about twenty miles to the southeast of her. On being told to go about and make for a certain gap between floes, she was able to reach the open water in four hours.

Conditions for the *Magga Dan* did not appear so good, for her course to the nearest large lead opening into the "land water" was through some 25 miles of very close and heavy pack. That evening the scene from the crow's-nest was magnificent, if discouraging. In all directions to the horizon nothing could be seen but grotesquely hummocked pack, its ruggedness emphasized by a brilliant low sun that picked out every irregularity with sharp, elongated shadows. In many places the hummocks stood six or eight feet above the general level of the surface, but fortunately there was no pressure on the ice and the ship could force her way through the areas of smaller floes at a speed varying from one to four knots. By next morning we had reached a wide lead which took us into the open land water. From that time our ice troubles were over and the ship steamed steadily at 12 to 13 knots past the well-known ice cliff coastline. Here and there we observed a number of low places where landings could be made, if such should be needed, by future expeditions. We reached Halley Bay (75°31′S, 26°36′W) by 6 P.M. on January 4, just two hours after the *Tottan.*

The next week was spent in unloading, transporting all the ma-terial up to the Royal Society Base, and in preparing the Trans-Ant-arctic Expedition's Otter. For these purposes everyone from both ex-peditions turned to, and the work went with a swing. By January 10 some 300 tons of stores had been transported to the base site, the Otter was test flown and local seismic sounding and gravity observations were completed. Next day, while the remaining stores were coming out of the ship, we took the opportunity to fly east from Halley Bay with the object of investigating the possible existence of mountains in that direction.

In October 1956, David Dalgliesh had reported their possible existence, for he had seen a tiny black speck on the distant horizon which he thought could only be the miraged top of a high mountain. At six minutes after midday the Otter, piloted by John Lewis, took off with David Dalgliesh, Robin Smart (leader of the Royal Society's relieving party), George Lowe and myself as passengers. Our set course was 96°T, but subsequent calculation indicates that our actual course was 110°T.

Fifteen miles out we began to pass over crevasses in the ice shelf; here and there were sunken areas of ice where pools of water could be seen. Some of the tilted edges of the ice were stained a light yellow, which seemed to indicate the presence of marine diatoms and that therefore the water we could see was probably sea water.

About 90 miles inland we flew over a chaotic area of ice cliffs and one huge, tumbling glacier so heavily crevassed as to be quite impassable. A quarter of an hour later a distant jagged range of snow-clad peaks appeared momentarily through the horizontal layers of cloud ahead. Then we sighted two dark rocky nunataks on the port bow, and another great range with outlying ridges appeared to the north. It seemed to us that these ranges must be the southern extension of the known mountains of Dronning Maud Land to the north. By 2:17 P.M. we were flying at 6800 feet and rapidly approaching the most easterly range, which we judged to be some 50 miles long and from which two large glaciers descended to the west, both of them seeming to offer a suitable surface route to the high ice beyond. By 2:30 P.M. we had climbed to 9600 feet and we thought the highest rock peak to be about 9200 feet. The mountains themselves appeared to be formed of old volcanic rocks intruded by diorites, while here and there basic sills and dykes occurred. The general trend appeared to be in a northeast-southwest direction, but away to the south the rock exposures disappeared beneath a mantle of ice. To our surprise, just before we turned back toward the coast, George Lowe saw two snow petrels flying around the top of a 7000-foot peak. We could only presume that these birds were nesting in the mountains 230 miles from the sea where they normally feed.

When we had been flying about an hour and a half on the return journey, we began to watch for the crevassed area which we had previously crossed, but the surface remained even and unbroken. We had been out of radio touch since half an hour after leaving base and still could make no contact with the ship, nor even hear the radio beacon for which we were continually calling. Presently it became apparent that our drift had been greater than we expected and we were considerably off course. Certain that we had drifted to the south, Lewis turned on to a NNW course with the intention of hitting the coast and following it back to the ship. After another hour with still a limitless white plain below, dappled with deceptive shadows, I began to envisage a rather awkward situation; especially with that incredible crevassed area between us and Halley Bay.

Two and a half hours after leaving the mountains we began to see a low cloud bank which we hoped lay over the open water along the coast. About this time the engine coughed and stopped, but picked up again as Lewis switched to another tank which was already nearly empty. A few minutes later the same thing happened again as the remains in that tank were used up. This was scarcely encouraging to Lowe, Dalgliesh and Smart, who were in the back of the plane unable to know properly what was going on. Smart asked George Lowe if anything was the matter.

"Oh," replied George, " I don't think they know where we are."

"In that case," said Robin, "I don't think there is anything I can do to help," and reclined to admire the view.

Presently we could see on our starboard bow what appeared to be a confused mass of broken ice blocks, but these merged into the low cloud and it was difficult to determine whether we were seeing cloud alone or masses of ice mixed with cloud. Lewis thought it was the Dawson-Lambton Glacier. If that were so we were some 60 or 70 miles south of Halley Bay. Ten minutes later we were flying over the cloud where we hoped the coast would prove to be. Then, suddenly there was a small gap through which we could see two ice floes floating on dark water. Down we went through the gap and found ourselves over heavily crevassed ice cliffs. From the previous year's knowledge of the coast, we knew this could only be the front of the Dawson-Lambton Glacier. Lewis's guess was proved right and all we had now to do was to fly north along the coast to the ship.

A few minutes later we heard Halley Bay calling and we were able to tell them where we were. Little more than half an hour later we landed safely at base. There we found that they had been able to hear us calling most of the time and had switched on the radio beacon every quarter of an hour, although we had only heard this a few minutes before reaching base.

Next morning on January 12, George Lowe, Donald Milner (the BBC correspondent) and I left Halley Bay for Shackleton in the Otter, piloted by John Lewis. Before long we ran into low cloud and went down to 200 feet to get under it. Everywhere the fast ice was so hummocked that there was scarcely a place where it would have been possible to walk. Frozen into it were countless icebergs, most of them only about fifty feet high. As we flew it became apparent that the ship must keep to the edge of the fast ice, where a water lead extended most of the way. Where there were floes they were heavy, but it seemed that there were sufficient narrow leads to enable the *Magga Dan* to progress.

By the time we reached Vahsel Bay the cloud had cleared, and flying in brilliant sunshine at 2000 feet we could see Shackleton when we were still 20 miles distant. Circling the base we saw that a flagged runway had been marked out for us. A few moments later, after two and a half hours in the air, we touched down and taxied up to the small group of waiting figures. There was a great handshaking all around; then we unloaded a year's mail, potatoes, oranges, apples, coal and various other items brought for the base. All of us then repaired to the hut where the remainder of the day was spent by the Advance Party in reading their letters or exchanging Shackleton news for news of the outside world.

After a late meal Ken Blaiklock took me round the site to see the stores dumps and general layout of the base. The Sno-cat crate in which the party had wintered was now derelict and buried to the roof in snow, but it was very easy to visualize the appalling conditions in which they had existed.

It was late that sunlit night when we went to bed, and late too when we rose the next morning. From the *Magga Dan* Stratton reported that the ship was making good headway and would arrive that afternoon. As she came into sight Roy Homard lit a bonfire he had prepared at the top of the ice shelf. Then, as the black smoke drifted away across the dazzling snow background, we all went down to the ice edge to greet her. Everywhere the edge of the fast ice had been hummocked by the pressure of passing floes and bergs, in places to a height of fifteen feet. Choosing the lowest pressure area with smoother-looking ice beyond, Captain Petersen began cutting out a small "dock" for his ship. A second line of pressure proved obdurate, but ultimately huge pieces began to float to the surface, some of them like small icebergs as much as thirty feet thick. For hours this process of attrition continued until the ship was sufficiently far into the firm ice to be protected from all but a direct northerly blow, and even then only small floes would be able to follow her into the "dock," which inevitably became known as "Pete's Cove."

After the first hour of this work the Advance Party who were waiting on the ice were able to scramble aboard; the shouted greetings changed to handshakes and everyone repaired to various cabins or the saloon to exchange news over a drink.

So at last all the members of the expedition were together again, ready to complete the building and storing of Shackleton before the ship left. To aid us in this we had the ten members of the Royal Society Expedition's Advance Party who were returning to Britain in the *Magga Dan*. They had declared their determination to work as hard as anyone while the ship remained at Shackleton, and this they most certainly did.

VII

Preparations and the Establishment
of Scott Base

While we who had returned to London in the Theron *were preparing to go south again and later were actively engaged in consolidating Shackleton and establishing South Ice, the Ross Sea Committee had been very busy implementing the plan for the establishment of Scott Base. Men and material, planes, dogs and tractors were found and a ship procured in which they would go south to McMurdo Sound.*

Because five scientists provided by New Zealand as part of that country's contribution to the International Geophysical Year were to join the New Zealand section of the Trans-Antarctic Expedition, both the accommodation and the quantities of supplies and equipment were considerably increased. The responsibility for the control of both parties would rest on Sir Edmund Hillary and I leave it to him to describe, in the next two chapters, their preparations and successful progress.

THE ORGANIZATION of the Ross Sea Party of the Trans-Antarctic Expedition took on a new sense of urgency when Miller, Claydon and I returned from our trip to the Weddell Sea in the *Theron*. The establishing of Shackleton Base had been a most useful experience and in particular made us realize how important pre-expedition training and planning would be to our own party before we left New Zealand. Although a great deal of work had been accomplished in our absence by our controlling body, the Ross Sea Committee, through its Secretary, Mr. A. S. Helm, and the various executive

70

subcommittees, yet there was still much left to be done and time was rapidly going.

Our task for Bunny Fuchs didn't seem an overwhelming one. We had to find a tractor route from the polar plateau down to the sea and establish two depots of fuel and food for the crossing party — one at 80°S and one at 83°S. But the scope of our expedition had grown enormously since its early days. Our party was now to include a group of five scientists who would be carrying out the research programs of the International Geophysical Year. As well, I was determined to have sufficient strength in the field to enable us to carry out a wide program of survey and geology. This meant that our wintering party had grown from a modest total of twelve men to a more impressive twenty-two, and our base huts and equipment had expanded in a similar manner. Later on I decided to keep Murray Douglas down with us as well, so twenty-three of us finally spent the winter at Scott Base. We no longer regarded ourselves only as a support party to the Trans-Antarctic Expedition, but also as New Zealand's first major effort to explore its own Ross Dependency, and we intended making the most of every minute.

We were now in possession of much firsthand knowledge of McMurdo Sound where we intended putting our base. While some of us had been away with Fuchs in the *Theron*, another party of three New Zealand observers had gone south into the Ross Sea with the United States Navy's "Deep Freeze I" operation. Two of these men were members of our wintering party — Dr. Trevor Hatherton, a geophysicist and the senior scientist in charge of our I.G.Y. party, and Bernie Gunn, one of our geologists and an experienced and forceful mountaineer. The third observer was Lieutenant Commander W. J. L. Smith of the Royal New Zealand Navy; as the first officer of the expedition ship, HMNZS *Endeavour*, his task was to report on suitable unloading places for his ship. The main job of this party was to examine the west side of McMurdo Sound with a view to finding a suitable location for Scott Base. Fuchs's original plan had envisaged the use of the Ferrar Glacier as the route to the polar plateau. Scott had used it on his western journey and although his reports indicated that it was rather rough, he had been successful in getting up it, so it was a promising first line of investigation.

There were enormous advantages to us in the Ferrar route, as it was a very direct one and if no great problems were met on the plateau it would prove a very easy way to the southern depots. There were several places to investigate as possible base sites. Two members of Scott's party, Professor Debenham and Sir Charles Wright, had each recommended investigation of an area — the former the Dailey Islands and the latter Butter Point.

Our McMurdo Sound observers showed considerable determination and resourcefulness in carrying out their task. No transport was available, so they hauled their food and camping gear behind them on Fiberglas sledges over several hundred miles of rough sea ice and glacier. They had considerable difficulty in getting onto the Dailey Islands, which were surrounded by a formidable belt of ice pinnacles and thaw pools quite impassable for vehicles. Each of the islands was encompassed by a deep moat of running water and their steep rubbly slopes offered few flat sites for a single hut, let alone the half dozen we wished to build. The examination of Butter Point and the Ferrar Glacier was much more promising. Our men were landed on the lower portion of the glacier by an American helicopter and they then manhauled up it for some sixty miles. They reported it as hard and icy but reasonably smooth. At their farthest point they climbed a mountain peak and examined the route ahead, and were encouraged to find that the glacier merged into the polar plateau without any obvious major difficulties. They reported, too, that at the foot of the mountain spur behind Butter Point there was ample room for our base and the extensive radio aerial system we planned. Access to the site appeared reasonable and there was suitable landing for our aircraft either on the sea ice or on the Bowers Piedmont Glacier.

Gunn made one very useful flight with the Americans. The four-engined Skymaster flew south across the Ross Ice Shelf, keeping close in to the mountains of Victoria Land. Gunn, with his mountaineer's eye, was able to assess the possibilities of the various glaciers as routes up to the polar plateau. Most of them appeared quite unsuitable, but he took note of the easy sweep of the Skelton Glacier and filed it away for future reference — information that was to be of great value to us later.

With this background knowledge of McMurdo Sound we in New Zealand were able to plan much more accurately. We knew that the 900-ton *Endeavour* would be incapable of carrying south our enlarged expedition, but to aid us with our International Geophysical Year commitments the Americans had offered us a great deal of assistance with the transportation of men and materials, so the scale of our activities was governed more by the equipment we could afford to buy than by the problem of getting it to the Antarctic. Finance is always a severely restricting factor in an expedition that is depending largely on public support and subscription, and although we made every attempt to obtain the best in every line we had to compromise severely on the more expensive items.

Perhaps this restriction on finance was most noticeable when it came to a question of transport in the field. Much as I would have liked to equip the party with the highly desirable Sno-cats or, to a lesser extent, Weasels, yet they were both beyond our financial grasp. In air transport, too, for our long-range freight carrying we had a single Beaver aircraft with its limited freight capacity of only half a ton but its proven sturdiness and reliability. Our second aircraft, the Auster, was suitable only for short-range flights and light loads. All of our depot laying would fall on the Beaver and in the event of any mishap our whole field program would, at the least, be seriously inconvenienced.

We therefore based our planning on the assumption that our field work would be carried out using dog teams supported from the air as Fuchs had originally envisaged. I was anxious to have at least sixty dogs to enable us to operate six teams of nine dogs each, and getting them together was quite a problem. Suitable huskies are not easily come by and it was a great relief when the Australians offered us thirty of their dogs. An expedition member, Harry Ayres, who in his private life is New Zealand's most famous mountain guide, traveled down to Mawson, the Australian Antarctic station, and looked after the dogs on their way back to Australia in the *Kista Dan*. The dogs were then flown across the Tasman Sea by the Royal New Zealand Air Force and moved into new homes at the foot of the Tasman Glacier in New Zealand's Southern Alps. From husky dogs in the Auckland Zoo we bred several litters of fine sturdy pups and then

73

made up our total with a dozen dogs obtained by the London Committee from Greenland.

For unloading the ship it was necessary, of course, to have vehicles. Our problem was overcome by the generosity of Massey Harris Ferguson, Ltd., in the United Kingdom, and their agents C. B. Norwood, Ltd., in New Zealand. These firms lent us five Ferguson tractors modified to operate in snow conditions. We had used two of these vehicles for unloading at Shackleton and they had given us very good service, being hardy and reliable, though really soft snow, we had found, proved to be their Waterloo. As we anticipated that most of our unloading work would be over icy surfaces, we thought that the "Fergies" should do the job. We were, however, more than delighted when Admiral Dufek offered us the loan of two U.S. Navy Weasels, for we now knew we could cope with all types of snow conditions. This gave us a total strength of seven vehicles — enough, I felt, to transport our 500 tons of stores across the possibly ten miles of rough sea ice from the ship to the base site. The large quantities of petrol required for the operations of these vehicles and, in fact, the many tons of fuels and lubricants needed both at Scott Base and by the *Endeavour,* were all contributed by the British Petroleum Company — certainly the largest donation received by the expedition and an important factor in making the venture financially possible.

The design, layout and construction of our huts was our biggest task. We were very fortunate in having as supervisor of the project Mr. Frank Pender, a senior architect in the New Zealand Ministry of Works. His enthusiasm and drive carried everything before it and enabled us to surmount every difficulty. We had six large huts and three much smaller ones, all constructed of 8' by 4' insulated panels fitting one into the other and held rigidly together by steel rods threaded right through them. This type of construction permitted very speedy erection, which was an important consideration to us, as we would have very little time available between the unloading of the *Endeavour* and its departure for New Zealand. In order to speed things up even more, we intended taking south with us a group of experienced tradesmen who would have already become familiar with the buildings in New Zealand.

Late in 1956 all of the huts were collected together in Wellington and the base was erected in a large open space by our five tradesmen under the direction of an experienced overseer, R. Heke. They corrected any mistakes and ensured that all the panels fitted snugly. Even the heating units and stoves were installed and the insides of the huts painted in tasteful colors. Each panel and piece was then carefully marked and the huts were dismantled and crated up ready for the voyage south.

A good deal of thought went into our food. From the London office we had obtained a list of the rations the United Kingdom party intended using. We also had a list of the rations used by the Australians at their Antarctic station and this seemed much more to our taste. We combined these lists and added various modifications to cater to the New Zealand palate. The manager of a large group of chain stores gave us his advice and the benefit of his experience in our selection of various brands of goods and this worked out very satisfactorily. Our basic sledging ration in 20 man-day boxes came out from the United Kingdom complete and was used by our autumn sledging parties. We had many criticisms of it and during the winter completely modified and repacked all the boxes for the main summer operations.

The selection of a party is a difficult business, especially when there are hundreds of keen and capable applicants. But before long, the Committee had produced a short list and then finalized its choice. The wintering party was as follows:

Sir Edmund Hillary	Leader
J. H. Miller	Deputy Leader and senior surveyor
Dr. G. W. Marsh	Medical officer and senior dog driver
M. R. Ellis	Engineer
Lieutenant Commander F. R. Brooke, RN	Surveyor and dog driver
H. H. Ayres	Mountaineer and dog driver
B. M. Gunn	Geologist
G. Warren	Geologist
R. A. Carlyon	Civil engineer and surveyor

M. H. Douglas	Mountaineer and dog driver
Dr. R. W. Balham	Meteorologist and biologist
J. G. Bates	Diesel-electric mechanic
E. S. Bucknell	Cook
Chief Petty Officer P. D. Mulgrew, RNZN	Senior radio operator
J. E. Gawn	Radio operator
Squadron Leader J. R. Claydon, RNZAF	Senior Pilot
Flying Officer W. J. Cranfield, RNZAF	Pilot
Sergeant L. W. Tarr, RNZAF	Aircraft mechanic

The I.G.Y. scientific party who were also to spend the winter at Scott Base consisted of:

Dr. T. Hatherton	Senior scientist and auroral observer
V. B. Gerard	Magnetic observer
R. H. Orr	Seismologist
H. N. Sandford	Ionospheric observer
W. J. P. Macdonald	Solar radiation observer

In July 1956, I gathered the expedition together on the Tasman Glacier with the intention of carrying out a training and familiarization program. It seemed likely that winter conditions in an alpine region would not be dissimilar to summer in the Antarctic. Our dog teams were already here under the control of two experienced dog drivers from the United Kingdom — Marsh and Brooke. All of the field party had a period under their instruction learning to drive the dogs and becoming proficient at handling the sledging equipment. Both the dogs and the men learned quickly. We established ourselves in the Malte Brun hut nine miles up the glacier at an altitude of 5500 feet and flew all our supplies in by aircraft. We installed a radio in the hut and maintained daily communication with Wellington, nearly three hundred miles away, where we had temporarily set

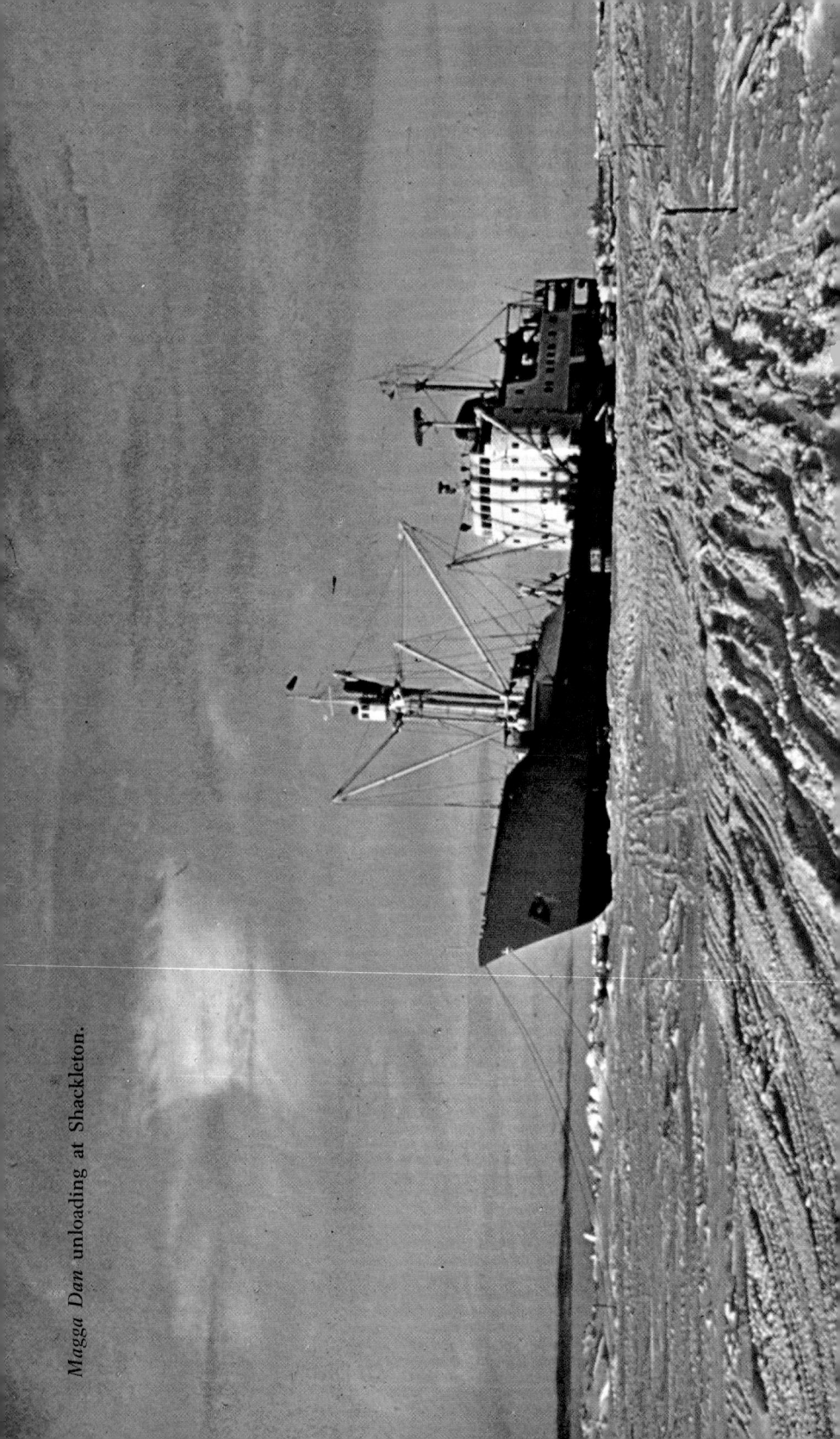

Magga Dan unloading at Shackleton.

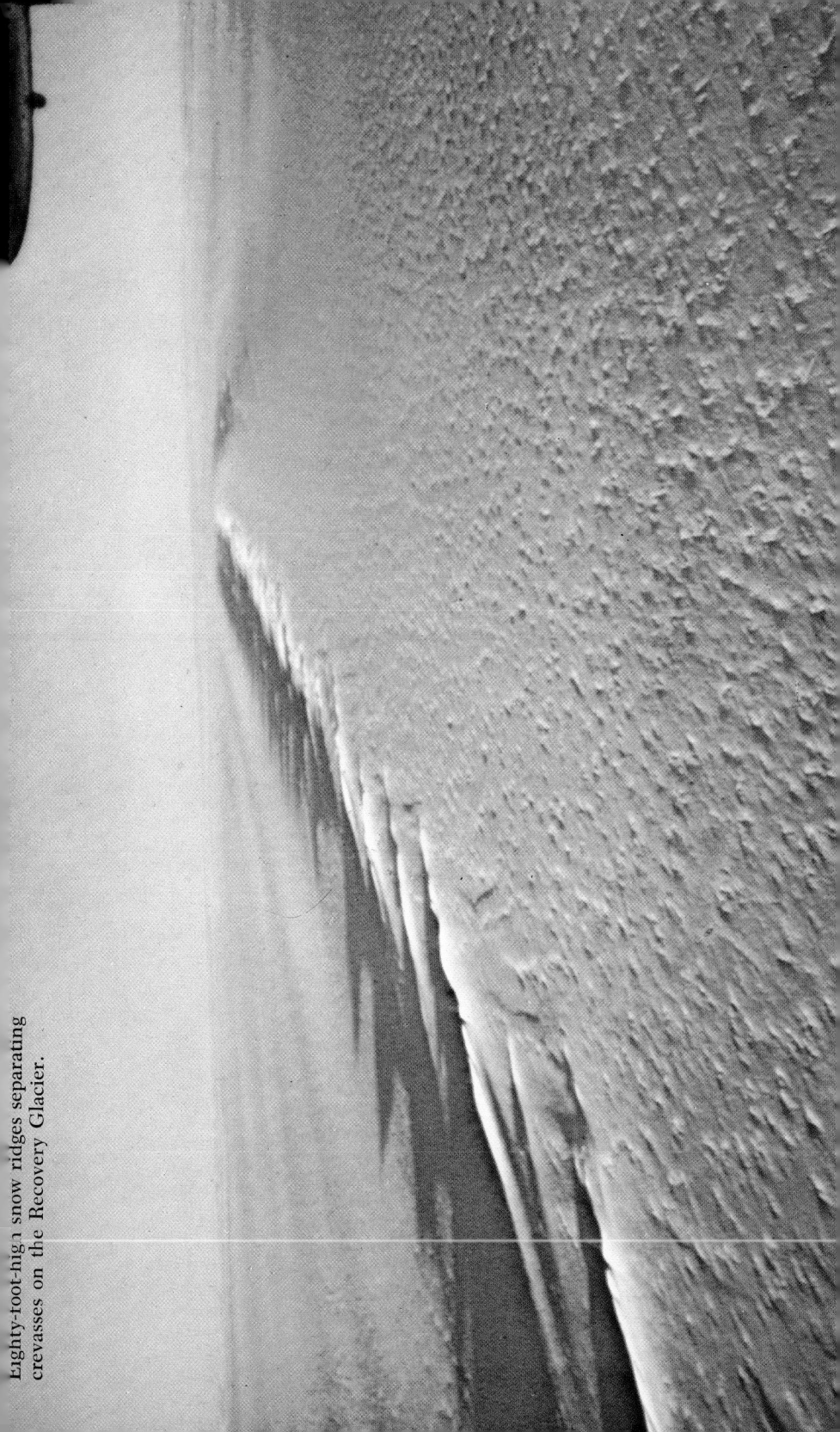

Eighty-foot-high snow ridges separating crevasses on the Recovery Glacier.

Looking over the Shackleton Range.

...ited up after the winter at Shackleton.

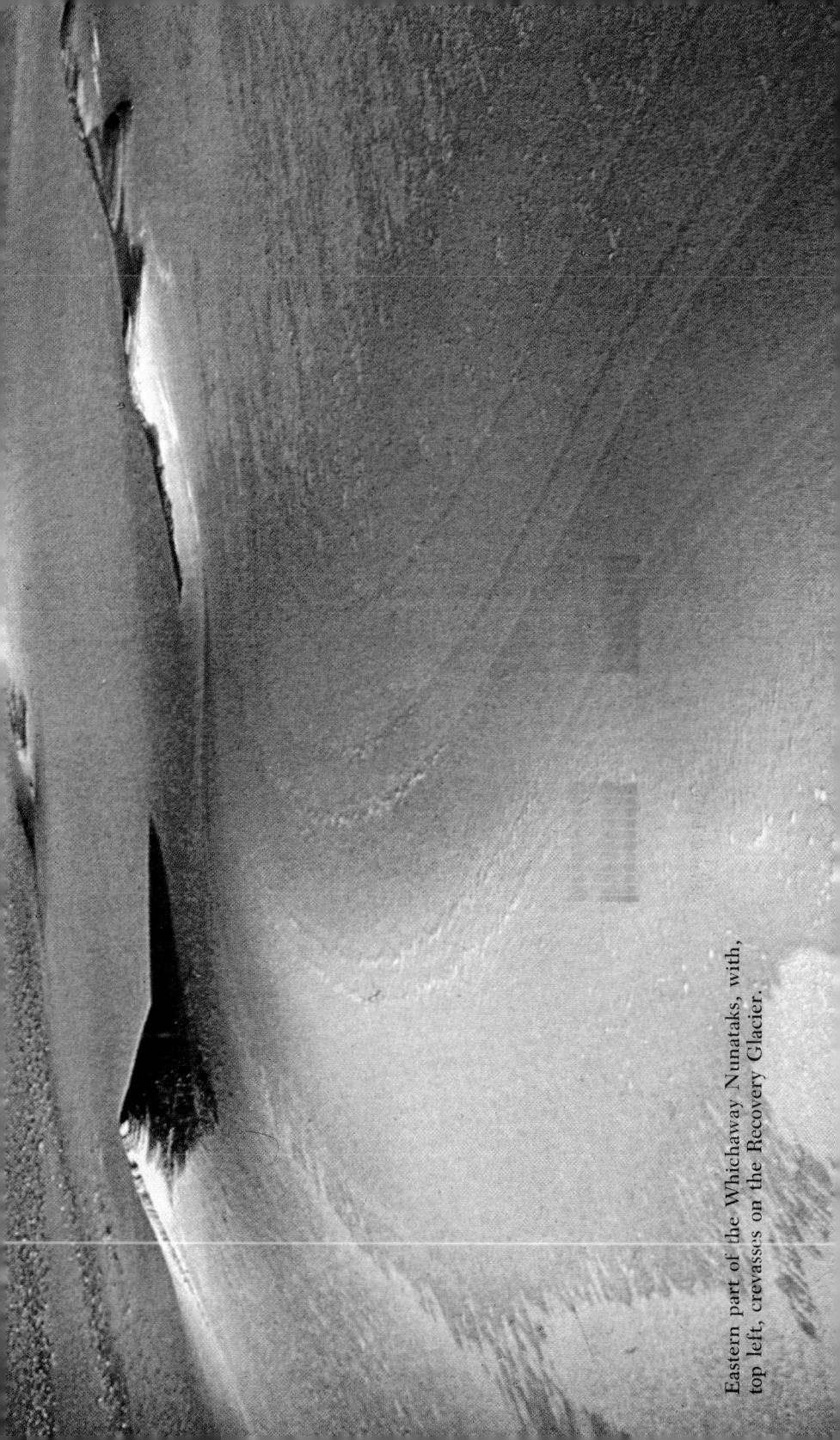

Eastern part of the Whichaway Nunataks, with, top left, crevasses on the Recovery Glacier.

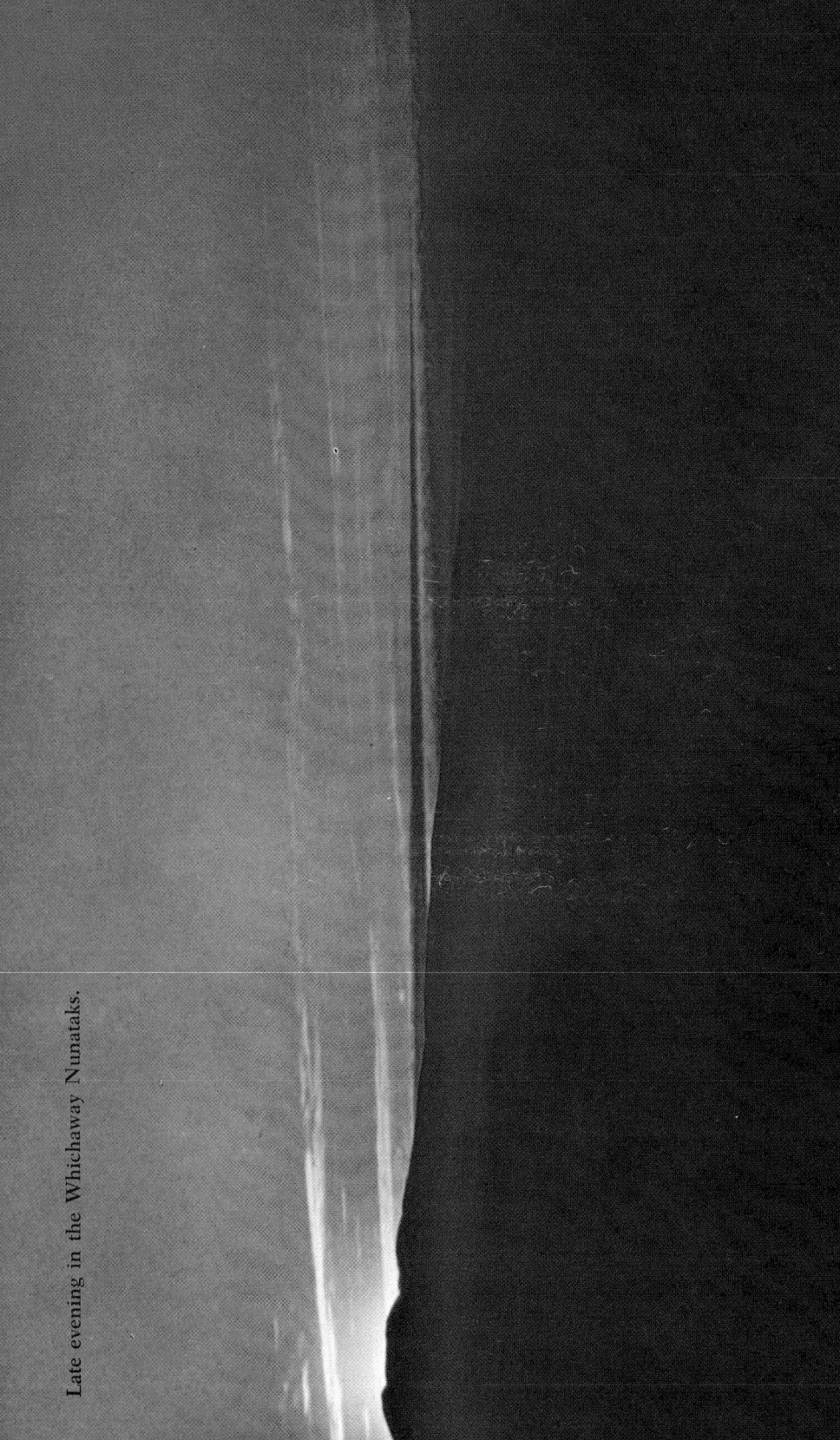

Late evening in the Whichaway Nunataks.

up one of the main Scott Base radio sets. This was excellent practice and resulted in various modifications being made to the sets.

The first ski landings of our aircraft on the glacier were not without incident. Indeed, the Auster's first landing was also its last. The ski-wheel combination specially developed for it proved quite unsatisfactory and John Claydon had the unpleasant experience of turning upside down in the aircraft when it tipped over and landed flat on its back. But even this setback had its useful side. The aircraft was uprighted and pulled to the edge of the glacier amongst some snow hummocks, where a protecting wall of snow blocks was built to shelter it against the prevailing down-valley wind. Here the plane was repaired despite blizzards and cold temperatures — an excellent introduction for our airmen to the rigors of operating aircraft in the Antarctic. When the aircraft was patched up the offending ski-wheels were removed and standard aircraft skis substituted. Claydon then took the plane off the glacier and skillfully landed it on some thin strips of snow which remained on the local grass airfield after a snowstorm. Wheels were then put on the plane and it was flown back to its home airfield for a thorough overhaul. It did no more ski flying until it reached the Antarctic.

The Beaver also had trouble on its initial landing, but the error was soon rectified and the plane then did magnificent service, carrying vast quantities of freight up and down the glacier. This was an admirable opportunity for the field men to gain experience in ground to air communication and co-operation, for a good understanding of the aircraft's problems and limitations would be essential when we were operating in the Antarctic.

Meanwhile all the members of the party were working hard at various expedition activities. Those with no previous mountaineering experience were given instruction in the use of rope and ice ax on the long steep snow slopes in front of the hut, and all of us did a lot of skiing. Our cook, Sel Bucknell, cooked magnificent meals for us on three Primus stoves, for the keen air and activity were giving us substantial appetites. Tractors were not neglected, for every man would need to be an efficient driver in the big task of dragging our equipment from the ship to Scott Base. Each man spent some hours driving Ferguson tractors over rough river beds and through soft snow. Roads were graded, piles of shingles flattened out, and ditches dug under the enthusiastic hands of our tractor drivers. By the end each man regarded himself as something of an expert.

By the time we had completed our training period, we were all a great deal fitter and in many ways a lot better prepared for the tasks ahead. Certainly we had learned something of each other's strengths and limitations and had started to weld ourselves into a compact and hard-working team.

The last months of 1956 were very hectic ones in the Ross Sea Office in Wellington, and with the date of our departure fast approaching there still seemed so much to do. Enormous quantities of food and equipment were gathered together in a large storage shed and then carefully packed in crates and boxes, with the contents clearly marked. Truckload after truckload of aircraft spares and scientific equipment, radio transmitters and diesel-electric generators, tractor attachments and sledging equipment, rolled into the store, and the last purchases were made to complete our lists of requirements. Each man was issued with all his clothing so that he could mark it with his name and check it for size. But then, to add to our burden, the *Endeavour* arrived in Wellington from the United Kingdom with much of the equipment and food in her lower hold damaged beyond recovery by salt water. Fortunately most of the material lost was obtainable in New Zealand, and in a high-pressure round of telephone calls we placed new orders and asked for maximum priority. Without fail we were given the fullest co-operation by the merchants and our requirements were delivered in time for loading.

The ordinary problems of organizing the expedition were not our only worry. Despite a good deal of assistance from the New Zealand government and some generous support from the public, we were still short of the necessary finance to cover our total costs. Throughout the country the members of our appeal committees were doing sterling work on our behalf, but although a few centers achieved excellent results, in general progress was slow. This need for keeping up pressure on the appeal for funds was a serious drag on our time and energy, but was in the tradition of Scott and Shackleton, who had had to do the same sort of thing — possibly one part of their great tradition which we could well dispense with nowadays.

By the middle of December the *Endeavour* had completed loading and a large amount of our gear had already gone south in the American cargo vessel *Private John R. Towle*. The warm farewells we experienced, not only at official functions but from everyone we met, made us realize that we were carrying the good wishes of New Zealand with us to the Antarctic. The culmination of it all was in Christchurch, when my whole party dined on board the Royal Yacht *Britannia* with His Royal Highness, Prince Philip. It was an experience to remember and gave us good heart for the tasks ahead of us. On December 21 we sailed away from the port of Bluff. The days of planning and preparation were now over and we were all conscious of a growing feeling of excitement when we thought of the trails and adventures still to come. But as the green headlands dropped below the horizon and the *Endeavour* rolled her way southwards, there were few of us without some thoughts of sadness at leaving our wives and children for so long.

As the *Endeavour* sailed steadily into the southern ocean, we were favored with a spell of weather quite exceptional for these notorious waters. The fine weather and smooth seas, combined with the fact that we were accompanied by two Royal New Zealand Navy frigates, *Pukaki* and *Hawea*, gave us a pleasant feeling of companionship and security. It was bright and sunny on Christmas Day, and we all gathered up on the bow of the *Endeavour* for Captain Kirkwood to conduct the Christmas service. It was a solemn and moving moment enhanced by the crisp clear air as we plunged on through the sparkling blue water. Already we were sighting large numbers of whales and the air seemed to be full of birds. On the morning of Boxing Day we ran into fog and had to reduce speed as we were in an area of icebergs, but we still progressed steadily over a smooth sea and a long swell.

Late on the afternoon of December 27 we were sailing in heavy overcast with a visibility of only a few miles. The mist lightened a little and two jet-black rock faces loomed up to starboard. It was Scott Island. By now we were in an area of light pack ice and the *Endeavour* was bumping off small floes like the veteran she is. The two warships continued on into the pack with us, but as the ice thickened they decided it was time to return. We exchanged shouts and cheers, and then to a succession of toots and the wail of sirens they turned and headed back into the mist toward warmer waters, while we continued slowly southward through easy pack ice.

By December 29 the ice was somewhat closer and almost covered the sea, leaving only small leads of open water. Some of the ice floes were enormous in extent and reminded me of the floes which caused so much trouble to the *Theron* in the Weddell Sea. But this was the only point of similarity and in general the Ross Sea pack lived up to its reputation of being the easiest in the Antarctic apart from the Graham Land peninsula. When the ice thickened up, we hove to and waited for leads to open up and invariably they did so. The ice was generally soft and rotten and soon gave way under a determined onslaught. We had plenty of time to enjoy watching the birds and seals and whales which were sporting on and around the ice floes, and to laugh at the antics of the Adélie penguins. As we forced our way southwards the *Endeavour* handled the ice well and our confidence increased in our "little wooden warship."

By New Year's Eve we had broken through the worst of the pack. A strong southerly gale was blowing and it was clear that we were in for some bad weather. At midnight the *Endeavour* was wallowing through huge waves and receiving some severe buffets from heavy ice floes that it was impossible to dodge. As we passed through the last band of ice, its damping effect on the waves was removed and we entered the open water of the Ross Sea into the teeth of a terrific southerly storm. Huge waves, a black lowering sky and frequent snow showers seemed to close around our violently tossing little ship and combined to give a most unpleasant impression to those on board whom either the call of duty or the benefit of a strong stomach permitted to be out of their bunks.

Around noon on New Year's Day, the storm reached a crescendo of fury and we were seriously concerned for the dogs and vehicles stowed on the forward deck. We were just maintaining steering way to limit the amount of water sweeping over the decks. One great wave crashed over the bow, demolishing several dog kennels, and in a somewhat exciting rescue operation we extricated the dogs from the debris and tethered them at the stern of the ship. They were thoroughly wet but none the worse for their uncomfortable experience.

The weather improved considerably by January 3 and we knew we must be approaching McMurdo Sound. Early in the afternoon the bridge reported that land could be seen ahead. We rushed up onto the flying bridge and with our binoculars readily picked out the volcanic cones of Erebus and Terror — still more than a hundred miles away. By late afternoon the Western Mountains of Victoria Land were assuming some prominence to starboard, but Erebus still dominated the scene with its long plume of smoke sweeping away to the east across the sky. In perfect weather we passed the steep cliffs of Franklin Island and then approached Beaufort Island at the entrance to McMurdo Sound. To our disgust we ran into more heavy pack ice and spent the night immobilized in its grip.

Time was now becoming very important to the expedition. The USS *Glacier,* probably the most powerful icebreaker in the world, was in the vicinity, so Captain Kirkwood asked for its assistance. In an impressive exhibition of power, the *Glacier* steamed toward us, seemingly unconcerned by the heavy pack and throwing great ice blocks aside like toys. We thankfully followed behind her out into open water in McMurdo Sound and then across the bay to the edge of the sea ice opposite Butter Point. Here we lay alongside, and went on board to visit Admiral Dufek and his staff. The Admiral offered us the use of one of his helicopters to make a quick reconnaissance of the route across the ice to Butter Point and a visit to the site itself. It was too good an opportunity to miss.

It was late in the evening when Miller and I took off from the *Glacier* in the helicopter and churned our way across the bay ice. We were not impressed with what we saw. The ice was soggy with thaw pools, and, being split with tide cracks and heavy pressure ridges, looked decidedly unpleasant traveling for vehicles. We landed on the shingle flats at the foot of the rocky spur and walked around. There was certainly room for our base on good solid rock well above sea level, but we couldn't see how we could get onto the site. The summer thaw had produced a small lake on the glacier side which would make access from that direction impossible, and the ice slopes behind were rather formidable for vehicles. We returned to the ships feeling somewhat pessimistic about our chances. However, we knew that an aerial reconnaissance could be misleading — the only thing to do was to make a thorough ground reconnaissance with dogs and vehicles.

The *Glacier* chopped an unloading bay for us into the heavy ice and then departed, while we commenced unloading at once. First off were the dog kennels and our dogs were soon staked out on a long line, leaping and cavorting in their delight at being back on snow again. Next followed four tractors, three of them with full tracks and the other with half-tracks and a fork lift. Tractor sledges followed and then dog sledges, tents, food, and all the equipment for the reconnaissance which we had carefully stowed on top of the cargo in New Zealand. Meanwhile I commenced reconnoitering a route with the half-track. It was a laborious business as areas of soft wet snow and thaw pools were interspersed with patches of firmer going, and the resultant track was a long and winding one.

Soon after midnight on the morning of January 7, our reconnaissance party set off. We were now experiencing twenty-four hours of daylight, but fog had swept down from the Ferrar Glacier and it was dim, cold and clammy. Our start was not a propitious one as the tractors bogged down in thaw pools and the sledges had to be relayed across. The pressure ridges were rough and bumpy and as the tracks were not properly adjusted on some of the tractors, they kept coming off. Altogether we were suffering from the inevitable teething troubles.

When we finally camped we were still several miles out from Butter Point, but were very glad to pitch our tents and crawl in for a sleep. We had a radio schedule with the *Endeavour* and I gave them news of our progress. I arranged with Captain Kirkwood for the *Endeavour* to cross to Hut Point on Ross Island and pick up the men and some of the material brought down for us by the Americans.

It was still foggy when we started again next morning, but the sun was attempting to shine through. Mulgrew and I went on ahead in the half-track Ferguson and found that the conditions were improving — the surface was firmer and we had no difficulty in finding our way through the lumpy pressure ridges. We found a seal lying on the snow beside its hole in the ice and we shot it as food for the twenty-seven dogs we had coming along behind. The mist cleared and we raced on past grounded icebergs, frozen in the sea ice. Then we struck an open tide crack and spent some hours throwing a bridge across it. The traveling now became increasingly rough and the route was frequently cut by water channels and thaw pools. Seals and seal holes were becoming much more common and the whole area gave a distinct impression of instability. We were still some distance from the prospective base site, and getting close to it was proving a much greater problem than we had anticipated. In fact, as we came opposite the site we found we were being forced farther and farther away. A party on foot investigated the route ahead. They reported an impassable chasm in the ice which completely blocked tractor access from this direction. We retraced our steps back to the smooth sea ice again, and then reconnoitered a different route. By crossing a tide crack and climbing a low ice cliff, it was possible to get out onto the Bowers Piedmont Glacier. The surface of the piedmont was rough but by crossing several miles of it we could arrive above the base site. However, the icy slope leading down to the rock was steep and difficult.

We camped the night out on the bay ice. It had been an interesting but a frustrating day and I had come to the conclusion that the difficulties of getting our 500 tons of supplies across the fifteen- to eighteen-mile route we had been following would make the establishing of Scott Base at Butter Point an unsatisfactory proposition. The soggy and dangerous nature of the sea ice would be a constant worry and access to the site with our vehicles a distinct headache. I went to sleep with the conviction that we would have to abandon our preconceived ideas and look elsewhere for a base site. The most suitable prospect seemed to be Ross Island, and although this would involve crossing McMurdo Sound in order to get to the Ferrar Glacier, this should not prove too difficult in the spring when the sea ice would probably give good traveling surfaces.

It seemed propitious that when we had our early morning radio schedule with the *Endeavour* there was a message from Claydon saying he had arranged to cross over to us in an American helicopter and report on the position at Hut Point. Claydon had never been happy about the possibilities of operating our aircraft from Butter Point and seemed much more enthusiastic about the other side of McMurdo Sound. The helicopter duly arrived and the pilot agreed to take Miller and myself back across the bay. I left the reconnaissance party with the task of establishing a route for the tractors and dog teams up onto the Ferrar Glacier. The dog teams would then continue on up the glacier and attempt to reach the polar plateau. Twenty minutes later we were landing on the ice beside the *Endeavour* and the *Glacier*. Once again Admiral Dufek generously offered us the use of a helicopter for further reconnaissance purposes and even suggested several likely spots for investigation.

Of these, Pram Point sounded the most interesting, so we decided to examine it. A few minutes later, we were hovering over a rounded rocky spur with the Ross Ice Shelf sweeping away to the south on one side of it, and the bay ice on the other. A short walk around was sufficient to enable us to make up our minds. It seemed an ideal position. There was ample room on several broad rock terraces for our huts and aerial array; access from the sea ice for vehicles was good; we had ideal landing grounds for our aircraft within a few hundred yards — and the views were magnificent. There was only one problem to be disposed of: was the surface approach suitable for our tractor trains? We returned to the *Endeavour* determined to waste no time in putting this question to the test. We filled up a tractor with fuel, hitched a sledge on behind, and then Miller and I set off from the ship. For the first few miles our trail followed the route used by the Americans in unloading their ships. It was in a frightful condition as their heavy tractors had churned out great holes in the surface of the ice and these had filled with water. It took us a long time to find a way amongst them and frequently we had to go straight through. This usually involved a rather frightening descent into several feet of water and some rapid mental calculations on the depth of sea ice that remained between the tractor and several hundred fathoms of cold sea water. We finally crossed this area and came onto untracked snow. It was rather soft and bumpy, but we had little difficulty in making a satisfactory route around Cape Armitage and across several miles of similar going to Pram Point. The nine-mile haul would not be an easy one, but it was certainly far preferable to the Butter Point approach and we returned to the *Endeavour* in a happy frame of mind. We would build Scott Base at Pram Point.

V I I I

Inland Reconnaissance, Local Journeys and the Completion of Scott Base

ONCE THE DECISION had been made to establish Scott Base at Pram Point we wasted no time. The majority of our tractors and sledges were still at Butter Point, but on the evening of January 9 we left with our remaining vehicles and equipment and crossed to Pram Point to commence the laying out and leveling of the base site. The *Endeavour* sailed back to Butter Point to pick up the tractor party, which had been rebuffed on the lower approaches to the Ferrar Glacier after a determined but hair-raising trip. At Pram Point we established a camp on a level shelf of shingle just above the tide crack, and pitched all of our pyramid tents. We then surveyed the area and marked out the position of the various huts on a broad ledge well above the bay ice. On the gentle slopes behind we measured out the approximate distances of our long rhombic radio aerial. When the *Endeavour* returned with the tractor party, we moved the remainder of our camping gear to Pram Point and the construction unit took up permanent residence in the tents. The tractor trains commenced running in earnest on a 24-hour basis and load after load was moved onto the site. By January 13, sufficient material had arrived for the construction unit to lay the foundations of the mess hut, and it was obvious that our unloading program was going along particularly well.

Bad news had come from Marsh, in charge of the dog party working over on the Ferrar Glacier. He reported that they had found the lower glacier virtually impassable for dog teams in its present condi-

85

tion and he recommended that their attempt be abandoned. This was most discouraging, as we had been relying to a considerable extent on using the Ferrar as our polar route. I decided to wait and do an aerial reconnaissance of the glacier before finally giving up all hope. We were working at high pressure now and sleep was at a minimum. Despite frequent crises, things were going very much according to plan as far as the base was concerned, but our field work was being frustrated in every direction.

January 14 started with a message from Hut Point that an American Weasel had broken through the ice and that one man had been drowned. This only confirmed our views that certain areas of the bay ice were getting dangerously thin. We tightened up our safety procedure, ensured that the tractors kept more rigidly to the marked routes, and made it a rule for the tractors to travel in pairs.

By midday the floor of the mess hut had been laid and the walls were going up. At 9 P.M. the hut was externally complete, so we now had effective shelter for the first time. At 3 in the morning there was a roar overhead and to our delight the Beaver aircraft swept across the camp. The Royal New Zealand Air Force contingent had worked furiously uncrating the fuselage, putting the wings on, and getting the plane operational. This was a big step forward, and it was no time to bother about sleep, so at 5 A.M. we set off in the Beaver for Butter Point, and twenty minutes later were beating up the tents of the dog party. Before landing we flew on to have a look at the Ferrar Glacier. It was an appalling sight with its rough, eroded surface and giant thaw streams, and certainly bore out the report of the reconnaissance party. There was a smooth stretch of bay ice beside the tents and Claydon came in for a perfect landing. In a few moments, we were greeting Marsh and his party and discussing the difficulties they had encountered. As a final check, we did another long flight up the glacier with Marsh and Brooke on board. The upper glacier appeared to have quite a reasonable surface, but once again we confirmed that the lower glacier was out of the question — certainly at this time of the year. We therefore made a rendezvous for the *Endeavour* to pick up the dog teams and then returned to Scott Base.

January 15 and 16 were days of storm and there was always the

86

constant threat that the sea ice would break up and go out. In bad visibility we struggled through wind and snow to get a few more loads off the ship. But despite the weather the hut construction went on as before, and it was quite apparent that the base would go up in very quick time indeed. My main concern now was to discover a suitable route to the polar plateau as I still regarded the establishing of such a route and the laying of depots along it as the first priority before the winter. Now that the Ferrar had proved unsatisfactory, we would have to look elsewhere. I remembered the report Gunn had given about the Skelton Glacier some miles to the south, and decided to investigate it.

Cranfield was the pilot on our first exploratory flight, and Miller, Marsh, Brooke and I were the passengers. We took off in the Beaver from Scott Base on the morning of January 18 and flew south between Black and White Islands, and then around the tip of Minna Bluff, where the pressure ridges and crevasses were very bad indeed. We then flew west into the mouth of the Skelton Glacier. The lower trunk of the glacier was broad and although heavily crevassed at the sides there seemed to be a relatively unbroken stretch running up the center. We commenced climbing up above the steep middle section, and the farther we went the more optimistic we became. There were large areas of crevasses, but it appeared, from the air at least, that by following a somewhat devious route it would be possible to dodge most of them. We emerged on a great glacier névé and in the distance could see the rock wall which we were convinced was the edge of the plateau. We had insufficient fuel to go farther so turned back to base, where we refueled and with Claydon as the pilot set off again to complete our examination of the route. This time we flew direct to the Skelton névé and then on toward a gap in the surrounding wall. To our delight, the névé climbed up in a wide gradual slope through the rock wall and merged without apparent difficulty in the vast featureless expanse of the polar plateau. It was certainly a most promising route.

The summer was quickly passing, so no time could be wasted if we were to carry out a ground reconnaissance. On January 19 three dog teams, with Marsh, Brooke, Ayres and Mulgrew, left Scott Base to cross the Ross Ice Shelf to the Skelton; but five days later they were all back in Scott Base again. Thirty miles out on the Ross Ice Shelf, Marsh had become very ill, and I had decided to evacuate him to Scott Base and also to recall the rest of the party. This delay in our reconnaissance called for more drastic action, and I determined to fly a party with two dog teams direct to the foot of the Skelton Glacier, and to let them start up the glacier from there. On January 25 we almost came to grief when we attempted a landing on high, rough sastrugi twenty miles up the glacier, and Claydon had to lift the aircraft off again after some nerve-shattering crashes from the undercarriage. The only really smooth area we could find was right back at the mouth, and here we finally touched down to initiate the Skelton Depot. Two days later Brooke, Ellis, Ayres and Douglas had been airlifted into the depot with their two dog teams, two sledges and all camping and living requirements and they started up the glacier the following morning. This was also an auspicious day back at base for we completed the unloading of our supplies from the *Endeavour* and *Private John R. Towle,* and were able to focus the whole of our attention on completing the buildings and their internal fittings.

The training we had done in New Zealand was showing substantial dividends. The sixth and last of our main huts was completed on February 5, only three weeks from the laying of the foundations of the first. Work was concentrated on inside finishing, the building of a covered way between huts as a protection against the weather, and the completion of three more small scientific huts. Several of our six 6-kw electrical generators were already operating and Bucknell was cooking for us all on the large oil-burning stove. There was a great deal of scientific equipment to be installed, but this was also well under way and it was now possible to release more men for field activities.

The route from Scott Base to the Skelton Depot had still to be established, and as all previous parties across this area had reported crevasse dangers, I considered it advisable to have the route investigated. Bob Miller had worked like a Trojan in the early stages of the base establishment, but he could now be spared, and accompanied by Carlyon he set off with one dog team on the 180-mile journey across the Ross Ice Shelf to the Skelton Depot. As neither of these men had run dog teams by themselves before, they were taking on a task of some magnitude and we didn't expect them to have a quick or easy trip. We were proved wrong. They quickly adapted themselves to the job and maintained an average speed across the Ross Ice Shelf of 16 miles a day. On their arrival at the Skelton Depot, they concentrated on the survey of the lower part of the glacier.

The Beaver had meanwhile been flying load after load of food and fuel into Skelton Depot to complete the stocking of it for Fuchs's party. On one of the first flights, the aircraft had as passengers a geological party consisting of our two geologists, Gunn and Warren, and A. Heine, an experienced mountaineer and a member of the summer party. These three men had no transport to assist them, so manhauled their camp up and down the Skelton on light Fiberglas sledges. They crossed the heavily crevassed edges of the glacier and visited every major rock bluff to examine the rocks and take geological specimens. The culmination of their trip was a fine ascent of the over 9000-foot peak, Mount Harmsworth — a climb done from their camp on the low glacier floor and a marathon effort of twenty-three hours up and down.

The Skelton reconnaissance party under Brooke had meanwhile been making steady progress. Soft snow in the steep middle section had slowed them up considerably, however, and they were forced to relay loads. As we had forecast from our aerial survey, their route proved to be a devious one, but almost completely dodged the bad crevasse areas. Once they reached the névé, the going was much more straightforward and in a couple of days they reached the long slope breaking through the rocky rim. Here the surface was rough and hard, and they were subjected to constant wind and drift and cold temperatures. In these uncomfortable conditions, they pushed on over the edge to reach the polar plateau at over 8000 feet on February 8. On this day also the Beaver completed the stocking of the Skelton Depot with seven tons of food and fuel. With these two tasks completed, the next morning was to be a critical one for the expedition, for we planned to make our first aircraft landings on the polar plateau.

Under a clear blue sky and in bright sunlight both of our aircraft took off from Scott Base and headed for the Skelton. We climbed steadily over the jagged ribs of the Western Mountains, sidled over the steep glaciers draining off Mount Huggins, and emerged over the Skelton névé. Still climbing, we crossed the last wall under Mount Feather and started searching the plateau for the tents of the dog party. At first we couldn't find them, and we had almost given up hope when we caught a glimpse of them out to the east. Claydon circled round several times before he found a suitable spot, and then brought the aircraft in for a perfect landing. The temperature was −27°F, with a strong wind, and when we stepped out of the aircraft to greet Brooke and his party their scarred and bearded countenances plainly showed the effects of the rigorous weather. We gave them their mail and discussed their future activities. Then we climbed back into the plane. This was the crucial moment — getting the plane off the ground again in the thin air at 8200 feet. We taxied laboriously to the point for take-off and then Claydon gave the aircraft full throttle. At first our progress seemed very slow, but then the Beaver gathered way and to our great relief leaped into the air without any apparent difficulty. The Auster had been standing watch overhead, but when we became airborne again, Cranfield brought it in to a smooth landing. At this altitude it was at its limit of power and from high above we anxiously watched its progress in take-off. It seemed to go on and on across the snow gaining no speed at all, but finally staggered into the air and circled up to join us. Delighted that such an important step was safely behind us, we returned to base to initiate the airlift of supplies to the Plateau Depot.

By flying twenty-four hours a day when weather permitted, our airmen were successful in completing the stocking of the Plateau Depot despite temperatures in the minus thirties and persistent winds of 20 knots or more. This meant we had two depots finished and ready for the crossing party. I asked the field party, who had been holding the fort on the plateau, to retreat down to the Skelton névé and to go on with their mapping until the end of the month. They were delighted to withdraw from such a miserable location and descended to the relatively salubrious conditions on the Skelton névé, where temperatures were 10 to 15 degrees warmer. All the outside work at Scott Base had now been completed: the huts were firmly tied to the ground with steel wire ropes; the covered way between huts was finished and was being used to store essential foodstuffs on packing case shelves; and our nine radio masts — two of them 80 feet high, and seven 60 feet high — made a most impressive array. We had regular twice-daily radio telegraphy schedules with New Zealand and had also initiated our radio telephone service and dispatched our first photograph by radio facsimile machine. Altogether our base was becoming a very comfortable home.

Early on the morning of February 22 the *Endeavour* sailed for New Zealand, taking with it the construction party and the rest of the men we had brought down for the summer. They left us in a strong position to face the winter.

With the departure of the ship, we entered a period of dull gray weather. Temperatures were appreciably lower and heavy cloud accentuated the shortening of the days. At the end of February the weather cleared for a day, and in a concentrated period of airlifts we evacuated all our men and dogs who had been sitting out the storms at the Skelton Depot. This meant that for the first time we had all the wintering party together at base, and it was possible to institute a regular routine of base duties. Although we concentrated on an active program of preparation for the winter, the onset of autumn conditions did not put an end to our field work, for we continued our journeyings until the coming of complete darkness.

Early in March the weather improved from its unsettled state, and we had a series of fine clear days. A number of long reconnaissance flights were undertaken in the Beaver with a view to gaining more knowledge for our spring activities. We flew south for several hundred miles from the Plateau Depot in the direction I was hoping we could follow towards the South Pole, but found extensive areas of crevassing and realized that we would have to strike even farther west with our land parties than we had anticipated. From our farthest point, we swung east to reach Mount Albert Markham, and then back to base over the Ross Ice Shelf. Several flights to the north along the mountains of Victoria Land were of particular interest. They showed great snow-free valleys, large lakes (frozen at this time of the year), and even extensive river systems — quite the contrary to what one expects in the traditional snow and ice of the Antarctic continent. These northern flights stimulated our interest in this area, and we resolved to send a party into them in the summer to carry out survey and geology. We had received several reports that an unknown island had been sighted some distance back from the edge of the Ross Ice Shelf several hundred miles to the east of Ross Island. We set off in the Beaver to look for it, and after a long search in which we covered many thousands of square miles of barren snowy wastes, split only by a few enormous chasms, we came to the conclusion that the island had either been a mirage or a figment of the imagination.

Although it had never officially been part of our plan, I had nurtured private hopes even before we left New Zealand that it might be possible to take some vehicles south on the trail with us. The excellent performance of our Ferguson tractors in unloading the ships had made this idea seem more realistic, and the various modifications to the vehicles carried out by Bates and Ellis had improved their performance in soft snow to a considerable extent. I was anxious to give the modified tractors a thorough tryout under conditions more comparable to a southern journey, so decided to repeat by tractor the route covered on foot by Wilson, Bowers and Cherry-Garrard reported in their amazing *Worst Journey in the World*. This would entail crossing the Ross Ice Shelf from Scott Base to Cape Crozier at the eastern tip of Ross Island, a round trip of about 100 miles. A satisfactory performance by the Fergusons would remove another burden from my mind, for it would give us a strong second line of support in our depot establishing operations and enable us virtually to guarantee their establishment even if something unforeseen occurred to the Beaver — always a possible risk when landings were being made in out-of-the-way spots, and where the aircraft was operating heavily overloaded in extreme weather conditions at maximum ranges.

On Tuesday, March 19, Ellis, Bates, Mulgrew and I left Scott Base with two tractors and four laden sledges. In bad visibility and deep soft snow we fumbled our way through the pressure ridges and crevasses, and then across the "windless bight" in the shadow of Mount Erebus. Our progress was very laborious, and it took us two days to cover the first 25 miles. We carried out various experiments with sledges and repaired and modified the track mechanism on our Fergusons. This enabled progress to be made under conditions that would normally have bogged us down. On the third day, we came to an end of the soft snow and reached much firmer going. We raced round Cape Mackay and along the trough between the walls of Mount Terror and the broken pressure ice of the Ross Ice Shelf. Our fears of large crevasses were fortunately not fulfilled, and at no stage did we break through the lid of anything more than two feet wide. In the dim light of evening we scratched our way up a long icy slope to a snowy shelf at the foot of the "Knoll" which crowns Cape Crozier. Here we established a camp and occupied it for several days in continuously windy weather with cold temperatures and drifting snow.

Our main interest was to look for the remains of the stone hut built by Wilson's party where they had spent so many hard and difficult days. After some unsuccessful searching, we finally found it: four low rock walls without any roof, half-filled with snow and ice. Thrusting above the top was the framework of a manhauling sledge chafed by nearly half a century of wind and drift, but still in excellent condition. We dug the ice out of the hut and uncovered many interesting relics — some of Wilson's drawing pencils, test tubes, thermometers, unexposed film, a blubber stove, a heavy pickax, and the skins and blubber from emperor penguins. As we worked, the wind whistled around us and we found it difficult to understand why they had chosen such an exposed spot when more suitable ones were readily available near at hand.

On March 24 we set off for home with the intention of covering the fifty-odd miles within the twenty-four hours. Heavy winds and drift delayed our departure and it was a long and arduous job digging away the piles of snow which had accumulated around the tents and tractors. We departed at 1:30 P.M. and made a cautious descent of the ice slope down into the trough where we rattled along at a good pace to Cape Mackay. The farther we went the better the weather became, but the temperature was steadily falling. As we struggled our way in the darkness across the soft snow of the "windless bight," our thermometers were showing −46°F. The lights on one of the tractors failed, and those on the others proved temperamental as the cold affected the batteries. Ground fog came up as we approached Pram Point, and we developed ice in a carburetor and a frozen fuel line. It was a long business finding our way through the pressure ridges near Scott Base, and we were a tired party when we finally drove into camp at 3:40 A.M. We had covered 47½ miles in a total elapsed time of fourteen hours, despite one holdup of two hours. Although we felt there was still much room for improvement, we were well satisfied with the tractors' performances. We resolved to work on them with a view to taking them south in the spring.

The first fortnight of April was cold and windy and temperatures were consistently between −30°F and −40°F. We made every effort to complete our main outside tasks. All the food was carefully re-stacked and sorted; our fuel drums, totaling a thousand of one sort or another, were laid in rows and marked with stakes; and every-thing required in the huts was moved inside and stowed away on shelves constructed as required. Each day that weather permitted, several of the dog teams would be run to keep men and dogs in good condition. Brooke and Gunn, who were a hardy pair, took a dog team across the Ross Ice Shelf in temperatures of −40°F and climbed White Island. They were only prevented by a deterioration in weather from climbing Black Island as well. On Sunday, April 14, the sun touched Scott Base for the last time before the winter. We were getting about ten hours of rather dull light, but there was a feeling of darkness in the air. Across the bay the high peaks of the Western Mountains were still a glorious sight, bathed in pink sun-light, but McMurdo Sound was freezing up except where frequent storms kept breaking the new ice out, leaving a broad open channel in the middle.

We still had one trip in mind before the winter. This was a pil-grimage to Scott's old hut at Cape Evans. It proved to be a large-scale operation. Ellis and Mulgrew manhauled their way across, towing their camping gear behind them. Claydon and Cranfield did the same, but took advantage of the opportunity to live off their special air emergency rations and to use the emergency tent and equipment they always carried in the aircraft. But the main trek occurred when eight of us crossed over with four dog teams.

As the direct route to Cape Evans involved traveling over the dan-gerous new sea ice, we had to try a different approach. We set off from Scott Base and sledged out through the pressure ridges onto

94

the Ross Ice Shelf, continuing along in soft snow until we reached the narrowest place on the Hut Point peninsula. We then headed our dogs directly up onto the saddle and reached its crest after a strenuous effort by man and beast. After a brief rest, we wound a dog chain around each runner of the sledge to act as a brake, and plunged down on the other side. In fading light and drifting snow we became involved in some lines of crevasses, so stopped and camped for the night. Next morning we reconnoitered a route through the crevasses and brought the dogs and sledges down onto the sea ice. There was a strong wind to harass us as we sledged over the very wet and sticky surface of the new ice, and we were glad finally to reach thicker ice and then climb up onto Glacier Tongue, which pushed its long snout out into the sea. Despite numerous crevasses, both large and small, we had no difficulty in crossing the icy surface of Glacier Tongue, although once again chain brakes were a necessity and our descent down the other side was a hectic one. We camped on some old and solid bay ice.

Bad weather kept us from moving next day, as the ice ahead was too fresh and thin to risk crossing it while an offshore gale was blowing. However, the next morning was fine, so we had a magnificent run across the bay, past grounded icebergs, with the last rays of the sun in a rosy glow on the summit of Mount Erebus, high above us. We crossed the frozen tide crack without difficulty, and drove our teams up a small ice wall below the rocks of Cape Evans, where we staked them out on a frozen pool well clear of the sea ice. We then crossed on foot to the Cape Evans hut. It was a saddening disappointment to all of us! The ground around the hut was a complete shambles with rubbish, empty tins, and the ancient carcasses of seals strewn in every direction. The bottom floor of the hut was filled with ice and only the top floor was accessible, but this, too, was an unpleasant mixture of disorder and dirt. Obviously no attempt had been made by the various parties who had wintered in the hut to keep it the least bit tidy. It seemed a poor memorial to a great man, and as there was little we could do, we were glad to go. *

* The situation is different now. In January 1958, Captain Kirkwood and the crew of the *Endeavour* spent some time at Cape Evans giving the place a thorough clean out and getting rid of the rubbish.

I X

The Establishment of South Ice

APART FROM UNLOADING the *Magga Dan,* the completion of the base hut and the building of various stores and workshops, our first need was to establish an inland station at a point some 300 miles south of Shackleton. During the planning stages this station was referred to as Depot 300, for in addition to using it as a winter meteorological and glaciological observatory, it was to be the depot from which the transcontinental party would finally set out. During the winter it was to be manned by Hal Lister (glaciologist), Ken Blaiklock (surveyor and meteorologist), and Jon Stephenson (geologist and glaciologist). Hal, who would be in charge, had already spent a winter at the icecap station of the British North Greenland Expedition which was known as North Ice, and it was due to his "home from home" feeling that Depot 300 soon became known as South Ice.

When we arrived at Shackleton we still thought it possible that South Ice would be put down by a ground party supported from the air, though we always knew that we might have to risk carrying out the entire project with aircraft alone. Before any decision could be taken long-range air reconnaissance was necessary, to select the site and determine a possible route to it. Perhaps fortunately, the first days after the arrival of the ship were unsuitable for flying and we were able to concentrate on the work at Shackleton. At first unloading required most of the available manpower and, using three Snocats, one Weasel and the Muskeg tractor, we were able to move 75 tons a day from the ship to Shackleton. In this the expedition party were greatly assisted by David Dalgliesh and his brother Robin, Dr. Stanley Evans and David Limbert, all of the Royal Society Expedition's Advance Party.

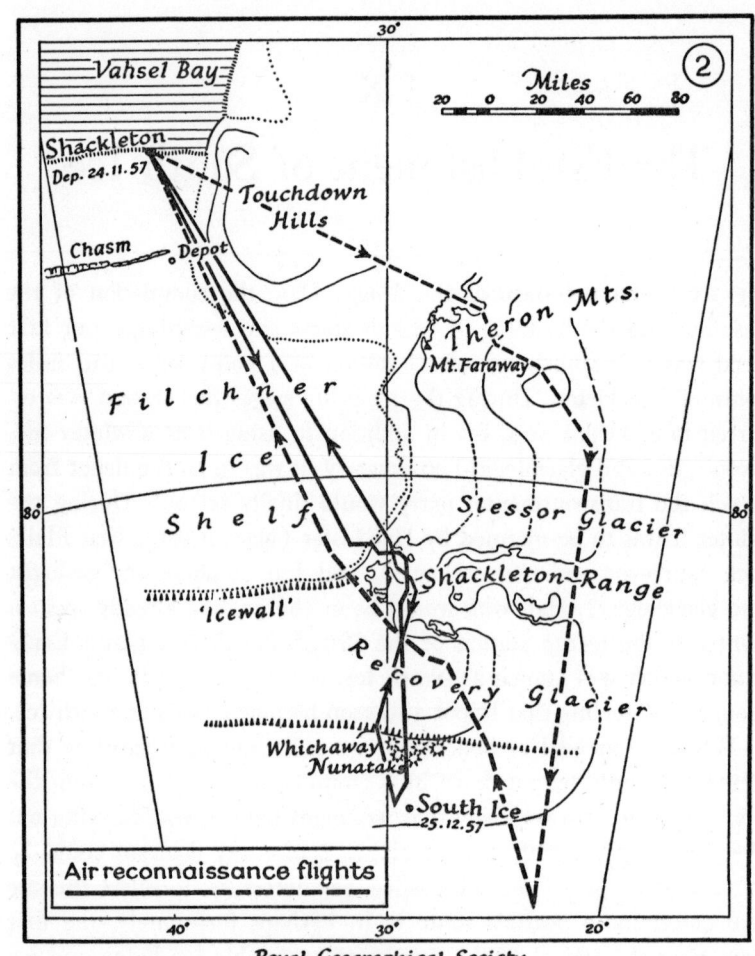

Air reconnaissance flights

Royal Geographical Society

Shackleton to South Ice (Air Reconnaissance).

Up at Shackleton final work was going ahead on the main hut under the direction of Ralph Lenton. Here again our own men were greatly helped by our visitors. Major "Gus" Watson assisted in suppressing the generators, Lieutenant George Lush and Sergeant Charles Le Feuvre installed the hot-water system and erected chimneys, while Kenneth Powell helped with the electric wiring. Perhaps our hardest-worked visitors were the two carpenters, John Raymond and Douglas Prior, who helped Ralph not only with the hut but in the construction of four separate buildings: the aircraft workshop, the vehicles stores hut, the hydrogen hut and our emergency stores hut. By the time all these had been built and the long lines of stores and fuel barrels laid out on the snow, the site of Shackleton was quite extensive. From east to west it occupied a distance of 800 yards, from north to south 400 yards.

When building an Antarctic base there is always the problem of what to do with all the material that cannot be brought under cover. In the past, expeditions have tried building tunnels of the actual packing cases themselves. When these become drifted over it is possible to walk inside the tunnel and obtain what is wanted by opening the end of the appropriate case. The disadvantage is that the surface of the snow is raised to the height of the tunnel and this drift tends to extend over a wider and wider area which can be very inconvenient. We had intended to build platforms of angled steel Dexion on which the stores would be raised above the surface, allowing the drift to blow beneath in the hope that no accumulation would occur, but so much of our Dexion had been lost when the sea ice broke up the previous year that we were unable to do this. However, it had been observed at Shackleton that where there was no obstruction to the wind, no snow accumulation occurred. Indeed when we returned in January 1957 the tracks made by the vehicles the year before could be clearly seen on the surface. We therefore decided to lay out all our stores and barrels of fuel in long, widely separated lines but nowhere must one case stand on top of another. In this way the tops of the boxes remained exposed at the surface and it was a simple matter to locate and dig up anything we required.

By January 18 unloading was nearly complete and the weather sufficiently good for local flying so John Lewis took John Heap in the

Auster to observe ice conditions and look for seals between Shackleton and Vahsel Bay. Heap, a member of the Falkland Islands Dependencies Survey, was occupied in making a study of sea ice in the Dependencies and had accompanied us in the *Magga Dan* to take the rare opportunity of observing the ice of the Weddell Sea. Seals were required as dog food to carry us through the winter and I had asked Captain Petersen to take the ship along the ice edge with a sealing party, to bring in forty-five more which would be enough to last us until the sledging season in October.

On January 20 it was possible to make our first inland reconnaissance flight. Just after eleven in the morning Gordon Haslop took off with Ken Blaiklock, George Lowe and myself as passengers. For this first flight I decided to leave the Theron Mountains to the east and fly direct to the larger range farther south which were later called the Shackleton Range. The Therons had been visited by Blaiklock and Goldsmith on the ground, and though we expected to find a route through them up one of the glaciers, it seemed of paramount importance to know what problems would be presented by the greater mass of mountains to the south.

Fifty miles from Shackleton we passed the depot left by Blaiklock and Goldsmith. Away to the west the great chasm we had found the previous season could be seen extending out of sight into the distance. From its eastern end a complex of huge crevasses curved away toward the land where they joined with the crevasse belt that marked the junction of the floating ice shelf with the coast. Clearly the whole shelf was heavily shattered and there would be no possibility of avoiding this area when we set out with our vehicles. After little more than an hour we could see the highest of the Theron Mountains, Mount Faraway, on the port beam and soon we were flying over the end of a great east-to-west glacier that pushed out into the shelf in three monstrously crevassed tongues. This we were later to call the Slessor Glacier, after Sir John Slessor, Chairman of the Expedition Committee. To the south lay the western end of the Shackleton Range and from it a highly crevassed area extended far to the west. This appeared to descend about a thousand feet as a tumbling fall of ice and it clearly marked the inland margin of the Filchner Ice Shelf. At this time these great cascades of ice seemed to form an impassable barrier on the ground and we therefore flew east into the mountains in search of a glacier route to the south.

Now we were flying low through the mountains on an easterly course, but climbing steadily as we followed the most likely looking glacier past the gray-black ridges and peaks. Here and there red and yellow rocks varied the scene while below the wind-swept surface of the glacier showed blue where the snow had been stripped from the ice beneath. We imagined the tracked vehicles with their heavily loaded sledges attempting to climb these steep and slippery slopes. True, the crevasses lay revealed and might therefore be avoided, but this also reminded us that where the snow still lay it must hide many a treacherous pitfall.

At 6200 feet we found ourselves about 1500 feet above a wide snowfield which fed the glacier we had been following and which also declined southward. Turning onto a southerly course we flew out over a huge east-to-west glacier which we were later to know as the "Recovery Glacier." This was 40 miles wide and at least as long as the Slessor Glacier, although the upper reaches have not been seen. While the north side is flanked by the length of the Shackleton Range, the south side is marked by a line of nunataks, rocky peaks which we called the "Whichaways," and a precipitous tumbling slope of ice which continues the line of the nunataks for many miles to east and west. Beyond the main line of the Whichaways, a few rocky outcrops thrust through an undulating and somewhat crevassed expanse of snow and ice. Circling the most southerly of these, which stood at about 5000 feet, we scanned the southern horizon with binoculars and saw nothing but rising, undulating snowfields. Here and there a white gleam seemed to indicate a crevassed area but no further mountains could be seen and we felt certain that we were looking over the high polar plateau itself. Satisfied, too, that in this area a suitable site for South Ice could be found and that the proximity of the nunataks would aid the location of the station from the air, we turned back to land at Shackleton after five hours and twenty minutes.

Although we had now chosen the approximate position for South Ice, it would lie beyond topographical obstructions which could prove to be formidable obstacles on the ground. It was therefore necessary to examine the various potential routes. We knew that the glaciers descending through the Theron Mountains probably presented an easy passage to the high ice beyond, but would it also be possible to negotiate the Shackleton Range so far to the east and what was the nature of the upper part of the huge Slessor and Recovery Glaciers?

The next good flying day was on January 22, when John Lewis took off with Ken Blaiklock, Taffy Williams, George Lowe and me, to investigate the area round the Therons. Arriving over Mount Far-away at the western end of the mountains we turned northeast along the high, imposingly stratified cliffs, then southeast up a seemingly unbroken glacier flanked by rocky outcrops. The upper snowfield merged smoothly with a broad snow dome on the south side of the mountain, but beyond this the surface began to decline steeply and we were soon flying over the marginal crevassed zones of the Slessor Glacier. Here, some 70 miles east of the point where we had crossed it on the 20th, the glacier maintained a width of 25 to 30 miles, with the northern foothills of the Shackleton Range flanking the southern margin. Along its length ran a number of complex corrugated crevasse zones like medial moraines which clearly made it an impassable barrier to ground travel. To the northeast we thought we could see the upper snowfields from which the glacier sprang but owing to shortage of fuel we could not visit the area and reluctantly turned once more toward Mount Faraway and our base.

As we flew along the vertical cliffs of the mountains we could see that the surface below was clearly good enough for a landing. Lewis brought the Otter down about a mile and a half from the escarpment to avoid the areas of rock dust blown onto the snow, for these could have made the surface soft, honeycombed and treacherous. Setting off for the rocks at top speed I arrived twenty minutes later at the edge of a small frozen stream running along the foot of some screes. At the height of summer this would, during the daytime, be a rushing stream of melt water formed by the heat of the sun's radiation on the snow and rocks above. Now it was easy to cross its frozen surface and I scrambled hastily fifty feet up the scree to the foot of the cliff. There to my astonishment and delight I found an alternating series of limestones, shales and coal. Both the limestones and the shales contained fossil plants which seemed likely to provide an age for the rocks.

By this time John Lewis had taxied the plane nearer to the cliffs and I was soon on board and we were heading back to base. It had now become clear that to establish whether or not a potential ground route existed through the Therons we must make a much longer flight over the upper reaches of the Slessor Glacier, across the eastern part of the Shackleton Range, and south to the selected area beyond the Whichaway Nunataks. For such a flight the range of the Otter had to be increased and Peter Weston therefore set about installing the auxiliary tank which would give us fourteen hours in the air.

All this time construction work had been continuing at Shackleton and it was now possible to bring the entire shore party from the *Magga Dan* up to the base so that the ship could go sealing. Rhino Goldsmith and Tony Stewart, who were returning to England, together with Peter Jeffries who was going to the Royal Society Base at Halley Bay, moved into the ship. We asked the two Royal Society Expedition carpenters, Raymond and Prior, to stay at Shackleton while the ship was away so that they might continue to provide assistance in completing the various buildings.

On January 24 John Lewis took Captain Petersen in the Auster to look at the sea ice along the return route to Vahsel Bay and northwards. During the next three days the ship's party obtained sufficient seals for our winter needs, and while this was going on, we attempted to make our final long-distance reconnaissance but found the Theron Mountains and the Slessor Glacier shrouded in low cloud. Forced to return early in the afternoon we flew over the *Magga Dan* and the sealing parties working on the ice. From the air it was clear that they were having difficulty in getting the seals they had killed back to the ship through the very heavy pressure ridges along the ice edge. Nearly everywhere these jagged ridges rose to twelve or fifteen feet, making it almost impossible to manhaul the carcasses, each weighing many hundreds of pounds. This difficulty was finally overcome by running out steel wire ropes from the ship over the ice and winching the seals by sheer power over the intervening pressure ridges.

Soon it would be time for the ship to leave and that night we gave a party at Shackleton which was attended by the members of both expeditions and about half the crew. Perhaps the highlight of all the hilarity was to see Doug Prior borne across the crowded room by several stalwarts who hung him by his braces on the corner of the door. Dangling like a spider from its thread his struggles finally released him, to fall in a confused heap.

Next day was "writing day." No work was done as all who were staying behind dashed off their last letters, but time was found to give several of the Royal Society Party and the ship's crew short flights to see the scene of their activities from the air. A return party was held on board the ship that night and in the morning we congregated on the ice edge to see her sail at 8:15 A.M. Slowly she pulled out of Pete's Cove and began to move along the ice edge, dispersing a school of killer whales as she went. Her high raking bow, now far out of the water, seemed to be carving miraculously through the heavy pressure ice that in reality hid the water from view.

When a party is finally left by a ship in the Antarctic there is a sudden brief feeling of intense loneliness. In our case, perhaps, that much maligned word "marooned" could have been applied, for as in the days of the buccaneers, we had been purposely set down on a desolate coast and no ship would return to pick us up again. Our way out was not even along an inhospitable coast, but 2000 miles across a continent.

We turned to the vehicles and dog sledges that had brought us down to the ship and hastened back to Shackleton. That day and the next we began shaking down as a single unit at last, and quickly found that our great problem was going to be manpower. So much to do, so few to do it, everyone competent to perform a number of specialized tasks, but all needing to be done at once. Sixteen pairs of hands were not enough.

On January 30 we flew south again, this time only Gordon Haslop, Ken Blaiklock and myself. First to the Theron Mountains, then over the previous route up the glacier to the snow dome, before turning eastward along the northern margin of the Slessor Glacier. Soon we reached the wide undulating snowfield which descends in two armlike tributaries, toward the deep channel of the main glacier, and turned south. Here and there crevassed ice knolls rose above the general surface and crevasses could also be seen in the hollows between, but it did seem possible to negotiate the area on the ground, although it would clearly be a difficult and slow task to pick a safe route. Scattered nunataks of the eastern Shackleton Range still extended across our path. These in themselves would be difficult to pass and beyond them came the upper reaches of Recovery Glacier to which the inland ice descended in a series of crevassed terraces. At last it seemed clear that this route would present at least as many problems as that we had seen to the east, and in addition it would add some hundred miles to our journey, possibly more.

Continuing to latitude 82°15′S we could still see crevassed areas and seemingly small ice streams extending across our path to the west. Suddenly the engine stopped and our interest was immediately concentrated on the surface 2000 feet below. Hardly had this happened when Gordon began telling base we were going down, at the same time trying his various fuel tanks. Five times the engine restarted and stopped as we descended rapidly toward an uncomfortably rough-looking surface. Then remembering the newly fitted auxiliary tank from which all the petrol had now been used, Gordon told me to close a valve which might prevent air from the empty tank reaching the remainder of the fuel system. Almost immediately the engine picked up and we were able to climb away from the all too near surface below.

Perhaps influenced by these events, we made this our turning point and headed for home by a slightly different route. We flew along the Recovery Glacier to pass the west end of the Shackleton Range and join our outward flight route of January 20. In this way we did not repeat the flight over the glacier we had followed through the mountains, but found what seemed to be an altogether easier route, if it should prove possible to travel past the most westerly point of the Shackleton Range. The most difficult place appeared to be the area where the Recovery Glacier descends to merge with the Filchner Ice Shelf. This was the tumbling area of crevasses which had, on the previous flight, made us turn our search into the mountains. Now from a height of 7400 feet we gazed west along the length of this steep descent which disappeared into the indefinite distance. Later we determined that the ice falls the last 1500 feet in two steps, the lower 700 feet being the steepest. In due time this was to become known as the "ice wall," but now it seemed likely that the best way to surmount it was to run in close under the mountains, where a seemingly smooth slope led upward a few yards from the rocks themselves.

Arriving back at Shackleton after seven hours in the air we settled down to assessing our acquired knowledge of the route, for we now had finally to choose when and where to establish South Ice and which surface route should be adopted. As a result of these deliberations we decided to travel past the western end of the Shackleton Range, and it was agreed that South Ice should be established in about 81°40'S, 29°00'W, or some six miles southwest of the farthest nunataks we had discovered on the 20th.

The next four days were devoted to the preparation of separate aircraft loads, each weighing 2000 lbs. First came camping equipment, food, fuel and the radio, which would go with the building party on the first flight. Next the hutting material and tools, which had to be selected to arrive in the right order, followed by furniture, generators, scientific equipment and a multitude of etceteras. To save weight every item was unpacked, then weighed and labeled before being allocated to its particular flight load.

At 11:15 A.M. on February 4 John Lewis took off with Lister, Blaiklock, Stephenson and Lowe, together with thirty days' supplies. Shortly after their departure an American Otter arrived bearing Captain Finn Ronne and Captain MacDonald, who were building a United States International Geophysical Year station called Ellsworth about fifty miles to the west of Shackleton. During their visit we heard that our party had landed safely at the appointed place and were busy unloading the plane. By 5:45 P.M. John was back at Shackleton and reported that although the position selected for South Ice was very suitable from a glaciological point of view the party had been disappointed to find that undulations of the surface hid all the nunataks from their view. This meant that for many months all they would see would be an endless expanse of snow.

From then onward every opportunity was taken to fly, whether by day or night, for the weather could not be expected to hold for many weeks and at any season the number of safe flying days was bound to be restricted. Even though we now had the advantage of weather reports from South Ice, we found that the distance of 275 miles between the two stations allowed time for conditions to change before the plane could arrive, sometimes making it necessary to turn back when halfway on the journey. At other times a South Ice report of excellent weather at their altitude of over 4300 feet coincided with drift or "whiteout" at Shackleton.

On every flight to South Ice one or another of us accompanied the pilot as observer. Sometimes a specialist had a task to perform such as the erection of the wind generator by Roy Homard, the installation of the radio by Taffy Williams or the making of gravity observations by Geoffrey Pratt. On other occasions one of us would go along for the trip since it was undesirable for the pilot to be alone with the plane if it should be forced down during a flight.

When I first visited the station on February 7 the hut was in the early stages of construction, only the foundations having been completed in the bottom of a pit five feet deep. This was dug in order that the whole building should be quickly covered with drift and so become protected from the winter winds. On the flights, too, I could study the potential surface route in considerable detail, but although we later followed the general line I then selected, we were to find many more areas of trouble than could be seen from the air.

By February 20 the outer shell of the hut had been completed and was already drifted up, with little more than the shining aluminum roof panels and chimneys showing at the surface. Inside, the partitioning had yet to be done and the building party were still living in tents. The entrance, which would ultimately be through a trapdoor, was then down a flight of snow steps. From beside the door a tunnel had been dug to a number of small chambers which would serve as storerooms, a snow crystal laboratory, the petrol generator room and a lavatory.

By February 22 the hut was ready for occupation and two tons of food and ten barrels of paraffin had already been flown in. This meant that the party of three, for George Lowe had returned to Shackleton, were safe enough for the winter, even if they had had to conserve the fuel for cooking and suffer the rigors of the cold. For their complete comfort they would require a total of 35 barrels of paraffin, each weighing 360 pounds, and in addition, petrol for their generator and a reserve of aircraft fuel. This would entail many more flights, but now a SARAH beacon was operating at South Ice enabling the plane to "home" in bad visibility. The operation of a more powerful transmitter provided consistent weather reports to Shackleton.

I had now determined to bring back to base each of the South Ice wintering party for a few days' change and to enable them to pick up last-minute personal items they might wish to have for the next six or eight months. The first to return was Ken Blaiklock, who flew back with Gordon Haslop on the night of February 23. They took off from South Ice at midnight in a temperature of −40°F. Conditions were not very good and Gordon was compelled to fly for the last 200 miles between two layers of cloud. The night sun was obscured, the light bad and this nearly led to a serious accident. While still 40 or 50 miles from Shackleton, Gordon reported receiving the SARAH beacon satisfactorily and said he was going down to find out the height of the lower cloud. A few moments later the Otter bounded upward as its skis hit the top of some snow-covered hills at 110 knots. In the poor light these had so merged with the cloud as to be invisible. Fortunately Gordon retained control and climbed away from this uncomfortable spot. Ever since this episode the hills which extend southward from Vahsel Bay have been known as the "Touchdown Hills."

While flying to South Ice continued whenever possible, we also had plenty to do at Shackleton, the major task being the building of the vehicle workshop. The foundations had been completed some time before, but the very heavy superstructure had still to be erected. Until this was complete neither the lathe nor any of the other power tools could be set up, and this seriously hampered the engineers in preparing the vehicles for the journeys we still hoped to make before the end of the summer. In spite of this they were hard at work with their limited facilities, and already the stores hut allocated to them was being filled with boxes, trays and piles of spares which must later be ready to hand when repairs and modifications would be in full swing.

On March 3 John Lewis flew Hal Lister and David Stratton to South Ice, leaving them to man the station while he took Ken Blaik-

The installations at Scott Base on Ross Island.
McMurdo Sound is frozen over.

The sea ice of McMurdo Sound is a highway in winter, but in the summer it is liable to break away with little warning.

The wintering party at Scott Base, which included five I.G.Y. scientists.

Left to right, front row:
Vern Gerrard
Bernie Gunn
Ron Balham
Bob Miller
Ed Hillary
Trevor Hatherton
George Marsh
John Claydon

Middle row:
Jim Bates
Herbie Orr
Neil Sandford
Harry Ayres
Selwyn Bucknell
Guy Warren
Peter Mulgrew
Murray Ellis

Back row:
Wally Tarr
Ted Gawn
Peter MacDonald
Roy Carlyon
Murray Douglas
Richard Brooke
Bill Cranfield

The route-finding dog teams had their troubles with crevasses.

A crevasse rescue of sledge and dogs.

Bob Miller and Jon.

The Northern Party met icy conditions and comparatively
high summer temperatures near Mount Suess.

Surveyors at work with the Northern Party between
Fry and Mawson Glaciers.

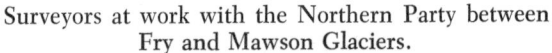

Part of the territory surveyed by the Northern Party
near Mount Suess.

One of the many "dry" (ice-free) valleys
found by the field parties.

The Mount Markham area which was surveyed
by the Southern Party.

View from the slopes of Mount Longhurst over the
Ross Ice Shelf to the east.

Ferguson tractor and the radio "caboose" en route
to the South Pole.

The depots, which were stocked by the Beaver, were usually
the meeting places between ground and air transport.

At all times Mount Erebus beckoned the field parties towards Scott Base.

HMNZS *Endeavour* established the base at Scott and after the successful completion of the crossing, withdrew the expedition.

lock and Jon Stephenson to the Whichaway Nunataks to do survey and geological work for two or three days before the plane returned to collect them. They had ten days' rations, a small sledge and a radio receiver, and as they were only 30 miles from South Ice they could, if necessary, walk back manhauling the sledge with tent, rations and equipment.

Two days later while having our lunch at Shackleton there was a sudden shout of "Fire!" in the living room and smoke could be seen pouring from the attic. While David Pratt leaped up the ladder to the roof the rest of us rushed to the workshop where a sheet of flame was shooting up the wall behind the bathroom boiler into the roof. As Roy Homard hurled a bucket of water onto the flames below, David let off a nitrogen-pressured powder extinguisher above. In a moment the fire was out, the air was filled with choking dust and we spluttered our way to open all the doors.

Fire at polar bases has been a common occurrence and is a particularly dangerous event because the huts are usually buried beneath the surface. As in this case, many fires have been due to hanging clothing too close to a stove chimney. But at least we were happy to find how efficient was our specially constructed Pyrene extinguisher, and indeed the only complaint came from Dr. Rogers who said he did not know what the powder was and might it not be toxic? However we all ate our lunch, powder and all, even the doctor, and no one was any the worse.

On March 6 Gordon Haslop and I took off for South Ice intending to pick up Ken Blaiklock and Jon Stephenson from the Whichaways, but forty minutes after we left, South Ice reported that the weather had changed again and we could only turn back to base. By the 9th we were talking to them every two hours hoping for better weather reports and on that day the Otter again left Shackleton only to be turned back after half an hour in the air. That night Ken and Jon had four days' rations left and I estimated that they would start walking to South Ice after another twenty-four hours.

It was clear that with the temperature now constantly below −40°F and winds of 15 to 30 knots a manhauling trip would not be a pleasant experience. They would also have the problem of navigation in the prevailing high drift. As they could pass within fifty or a hundred yards of the station in such conditions and never see it, I told South Ice to fire a recognition signal every night at 6 P.M. The field party could hear us talking to South Ice and they would know when to look out for this.

At last on the 11th, South Ice reported clear skies but very heavy drift on the ground. As conditions were reasonable at Shackleton, Gordon Haslop and I took off in the hope of being able to pick up the Whichaway party, or at least to drop them additional food and fuel. For this purpose the rations were sewn up tightly in sacks and red streamers attached to them and to a jerrican of paraffin. When we finally left at midday conditions were perfect as far as the Shackleton Range, but passing over the "ice wall" we could see the drift pouring down the slope in great ribbons that merged into a sheet on the level ice shelf below. Flying over the Recovery Glacier to the Whichaway Nunataks we saw that the whole surface was obscured by snaking, writhing streams of drift which seemed to have a stealthy, evil look.

Arriving at the nunataks we circled the spot where Ken and Jon had been left but could see no sign of them or their camp. Round and round we went searching the vicinity of every nunatak for half an hour before setting course for South Ice. Below was the rippling drift, but every moment we expected to see the shape of a tent or figures. Weaving from side to side to cover as much ground as possible we scanned the scene in vain. Soon we were over South Ice and circling to descend. From above, the station was clearly visible, but as we ran in to land the surface disappeared, then in a flash we were coming down through a driving torrent of snow which obscured everything as effectively as the blackest night. Down and down we went till the skis touched and Gordon brought us bounding gently over the sastrugi to a standstill.

Now we could see nothing at all and called for "two-star-reds" to be fired to give some indication of the direction of the hut. David Stratton told us that Hal was having trouble lighting the pyrotechnics in the wind but that he would be firing them, so I got out of the plane to see if they appeared behind us. Suddenly a trail of smoke could be seen blowing away high above the fifty-foot drift which enveloped us. This was ahead and to the left, but when we attempted to taxi forward we found the skis would not break free of the surface. Gordon then stopped the engine and we fitted the wind baffle and exhaust plugs to conserve as much heat as possible, for the temperature was −25°F and the wind speed 35 knots. To lessen the weight we unloaded 1500 pounds in the form of fuel barrels, which we had brought to replenish the depot, before I went forward in the hope that I should see the masts of the station. All the time it was necessary to watch behind to ensure that the plane remained in sight because once lost it would be only too easy to lose one's way altogether. After fifty yards she disappeared so I turned back.

After removing the wind baffles we climbed in again and Gordon started motoring cautiously forward for we did not want to run into masts, stores dumps, or the hut itself, nor did we wish to overshoot, as it would be impossible to turn the plane in such a wind. Presently a lumbering red figure stumbled out of the drift to the left. This proved to be Hal Lister who had ploughed over towards the sound of the engine. He shouted that he could not wait as his footprints would be drifted up and these he needed to find his way back to South Ice, two hundred yards distant. I therefore ran back with him, talking while making new footprints, until we found David standing within sight of the hut. Hastily we all three doubled back to the plane, held a hurried consultation and I handed over two frozen chickens before they had to chase their footprints back to base.

As soon as we heard David on the radio again Gordon made an instrument take-off. Just as we left the surface the engine coughed unpleasantly and continued to do so as we scraped a little height to see over the drift. After a few minutes she settled down and we began our long run home with just enough fuel to circle the nunataks once more and then reach Shackleton.

As we flew the sun sank below the horizon and for the first time we landed along a flare path at base. Everyone was concerned that we had been unable to find the wanderers, for now they had full rations only for two more days, but we presumed that as the bad weather persisted they would have saved a little day by day and would finally go on to half rations.

The weather made a second relief flight impossible until the 15th, two days after their rations should have been finished. Early that morning South Ice reported excellent conditions, and by 4:30 A.M. John Lewis, Geoffrey Pratt and I were airborne. Climbing away from Shackleton we found ourselves flying between two cloud layers, the surface was obscured, there was no sign of the Theron Mountains and as we approached the Shackleton Range only patches of rock could be seen merging with cloud above and below.

About this time South Ice reported that thin cloud had formed over the area and was lying right down on the surface, but we decided to fly on in hope of a clearance. Over the Recovery Glacier we flew at 300 feet above the surface but could see nothing through the thick low cloud. Then, far ahead, a small black peak appeared and this we knew must be the highest of the Whichaway Nunataks. Presently the cloud layer above us ended and by climbing we were able to see that by some miracle the lower cloud had dispersed around the nunataks which were now all clearly displayed before us. Then, even more miraculously, the cloud-free area extended a solitary arm to the south in the direction of South Ice while all the rest remained under a thick woolly blanket.

As we flew over the Whichaways and circled the place where Ken and Jon had been put down, the sun shone brightly on the snow enabling us to see the drifts and empty ration boxes left at their camp site. Thinking that they would have left a note we went down, John making a skillful landing on a surface torn by recent winds. In a ration box we found a tin containing the expected message. This gave precise directions concerning the route they intended to follow and told us that they had left at 11 A.M. on March 11, five days previously, with four days' full rations and two days' emergency rations. Gordon and I had been actually circling over them on the 11th but the combination of the drift and the noise of the wind had prevented them from either seeing or even hearing us.

Before leaving we put down ten days' rations for two and four gallons of paraffin in a 40-gallon drum so that if we did not find them they could be told by radio where to go for food. That small depot still remains in the Whichaways. Climbing back into the Otter we took off and started to search along the route they had given. Visibility was excellent but still we saw nothing by the time we were circling South Ice. Before landing to refuel we decided to make one more run. This time while scanning the snow with binoculars I saw, about twelve miles from South Ice, a tiny black triangle set in the vast white expanse. It could only be their tent! In a moment we were swinging east toward it.

It was the tent all right but there was no sign of activity and I had visions of two incapacitated men, for the temperature at South Ice had recently been in the minus fifties with winds of 30 to 40 knots. Soon we were bounding over the snow and came to rest fifteen yards from the camp. Just as we were landing I saw Ken's figure come out and quickly go back inside. Leaping out of the plane I went over to put my head into the tent, where I found them both well and drinking a cup of cocoa which they wished to finish before dressing to come outside. Not surprising perhaps, as the temperature was −35°F.

While they got ready Geoffrey and I stowed all their camping gear and sledge in the Otter. We had landed at 8:10 A.M., and fifteen minutes later were winging our way to South Ice where Hal and David Stratton had prepared breakfast for all. We now had time to examine our two wanderers and found that Jon was frostbitten on nose, cheeks, both heels and one finger. Some were unpleasant but not serious. Ken had got off more lightly with minor frostbite of the fingertips. Deciding to take them both back to Shackleton I asked Geoffrey to stay with Hal at South Ice until the others could return.

Safely back at base there was much to talk about. We learned that each day they had marched for six hours towing their sledge in conditions of severe drift, the temperature ranging from −25°F to −47°F and the wind varying from 20 to 35 knots. Each day they had traveled five to six miles over steeply undulating country navigating by compass and the sun. When we found them they still had half rations for one day and one fill of paraffin for the Primus. They had determined to go on that day to South Ice regardless of the time it might take. We were all glad that that had not been necessary.

On March 22, 23, and 25, the last three flights to South Ice were made, a total of twenty trips in all. On the first of these Blaiklock and Stephenson returned to join Lister for their winter sojourn. On the last we could only think of three mapping nibs, a bottle of ink, a bottle of developer and a 12-inch ruler to add to the main load of five drums of paraffin. Now the station was fully equipped for eight months and we had provisioned it with sufficient stores to last until it was abandoned by the transcontinental party in the following November.

X

The Second Winter

THE FINAL FLIGHT to South Ice was made on March 25, yet we had already been experiencing the onset of winter weather since the beginning of the month. At Shackleton our activities were directed to preparing ourselves, our dogs and our vehicles to face the conditions we knew must come. Peter Weston's task was to ensure that the Otter would withstand the winter. First he removed the tall rudder from the tail assembly and closed all the gaps through which drift might find its way inside the tail fin; then, inhibiting the engine and protecting it with a canvas cover, he made and fitted a wooden shield in front of the nacelle and behind the propeller. A wide shelving pit about four feet deep had been dug and into this a tractor towed the plane so that the skis and undercarriage stood in the deepest part, while the tail ski still rested on the original level surface. In this way the attitude of the plane's wings was brought horizontal with the surface to prevent undue lift by strong south winds. North winds might also cause damage or metal fatigue through "flutter" of the ailerons and elevators, and to reduce this danger Weston constructed sloping timber windbreaks about a foot in depth, close behind the trailing edges of the wings and tail plane. These proved extremely effective by breaking up the air flow and so protecting the aircraft from winds which later rose to 70 knots. Lastly a fence of heavy steel wire mesh was built close in front of the plane on the south side. This was to reduce the direct force of the southerly winds without allowing the accumulation of drift to bury the plane. This fence was suspended two feet above the snow to allow the wind to scour the surface beneath. During the course of the winter, drifts were formed by both southerly and northerly winds but, aided by occasional laborious but judicious digging, the Otter remained clear until the following spring.

Protection for the Auster was not so difficult to devise since the size of the ailerons, elevators and rudder allowed them to be locked with wooden clamps and the entire plane was so light that it could easily be moved to face into wind. In practice this was seldom necessary and the Auster survived the winter with a minimum of attention.

A major task was the building of the vehicle workshop. This was a heavily constructed wooden hut to which Ralph Lenton added a small annex. From the apex of the main structure hung a small traveling hoist which could lift engines or even one end of a Weasel. On the benches and in the annex were electric drills, grinders, a press and a lathe, the power for which came from the generators in the main hut about two hundred yards away. The doors at the west end were large enough to admit a Sno-cat, and an inspection pit was dug in the floor to permit work beneath the vehicles.

Until this was finished our engineers had used the temporary shelter of an inflatable rubber garage. This folded into the shape of a large valise and weighed about 120 pounds. With a small electric blower it could be inflated in three or four minutes and then stood 30 feet long, 15 feet wide and 9 feet high, and could be picked up by four men quite easily. In conditions of changing temperature it had one curious and uncanny characteristic. When the sun was high its warmth heated the air within and the structure stood up firm and rigid, but as the sun sank it shrank and slowly collapsed, enveloping, as in a shroud, any vehicle it contained. Next morning in warmer conditions, it would again be found fully erect, ready for the engineers to continue their tasks. It served us well until really low temperatures occurred when the rubberized cloth became brittle and torn.

For several weeks we, in our warm hut, had watched the wind speed recorder showing 40, 50 or 60 mph, while the thermometer registered lower and lower temperatures, and we had visualized the dogs lying curled up on the snow above us with only their fur and blubber to protect them. As the wind continually swept the snow from the hard compacted surface they were even denied the usual protection of accumulating drift. Sometimes when we went to visit them they would rise reluctantly to greet us, but often their warmth had melted the snow they lay on, which then froze again tearing the hair from their bodies or tails as they struggled to their feet.

We had been digging new tunnels to alleviate their conditions, determined that there must be plenty of head room and space to saw up seal meat under shelter. Accordingly we made a trench 140 feet long by 8 feet deep and 4 feet wide, by sawing blocks of snow and placing them along the sides of the cut from which they were taken. In the walls we cut alcoves on alternate sides to prevent the dogs reaching each other at the end of their chains. Finally the whole trench system was roofed over with thin boarding and tarred paper to form tunnels. Thus we had plenty of space for the dogs and also room to stand up when walking about to feed them. Later the main power system provided electricity for about twelve hours each day so that not only did they have protection from the weather, but also light which they would not have had outside.

On March 29 the temperature had fallen to −33°F and the first dogs entered their winter quarters. We chose those which seemed to be suffering most from the deteriorating weather and it was a delight to watch their immediate response to the improved conditions. By the middle of April all the dogs were under cover and enjoying calm and relative warmth, for even with an outdoor temperature of −60°F the tunnels remained above zero.

Up at South Ice, Hal Lister, Ken Blaiklock and Jon Stephenson began setting up their equipment for the winter's work. A Dexion lattice mast was erected for the meteorological anemometer but it soon became festooned with other equipment, including anemometers and thermometers every few feet down to the surface. These were to provide Lister with a wind and temperature profile above the surface for his glaciological studies. At the top of this mast they fixed a small red light, which could be switched on from inside the hut, to call absorbed scientists in when lunch was ready.

They also began to dig a deep pit for the study of past precipitation and the work on ice crystals which was to be done by Stephenson, in the hope that the crystal orientation might reveal differential movement in the surface layers of the snowfield. From now on we maintained twice-daily radio schedules between Shackleton and South Ice which were only interrupted by bad conditions.

At Shackleton Allan Rogers had already been having some trouble with his "IMPS" (Integrating motor pneumotachographs) which he was using to study the energy of men, both at work and at rest. By the beginning of April, after several weeks of constant labor, he made these two complicated instruments work properly, and soon many members of the party could be seen cooking or sweeping, hauling sledges or building, while wearing a rubber mask and a curious pack on the back. This was not considered a popular pastime, but many submitted with a fair grace. The chief sufferer was Geoffrey Pratt who undertook to wear the IMP (except for meals) night and day for a whole week, while Allan remained constantly near him to change the cylinders and maintain a check on the instruments. Although Geoffrey was certainly uncomfortable, and even suffered frostbite of the face, Allan exhausted himself by always doing everything that his energetic patient did, besides staying awake at night to make sure that the mask remained in place while he slept. Both were glad when the ordeal was over.

As a doctor, Allan did not have many customers, for apart from cuts, bruises and strains, we were a healthy community; but, as always at a polar base, there was frequent dental trouble. Here his meticulous care was a great blessing and saved many teeth. We also found that his skill with small instruments could be put to other uses, so that all through the winter he was being persuaded to undertake tasks ranging from watch and clock repairs to the construction of new parts for meteorological instruments.

Before the sun was finally lost to us, Geoffrey Pratt fitted out a Sno-cat with his seismic equipment and began a series of experimental shots over a period of some three weeks. He and George Lowe or David Stratton would disappear for the day to lay out the geophones, bore holes in which to fire small explosive charges or, on occasion, to dig pits in which to bury the large charges of 25 pounds. As a result of this work the seismic gear was brought into proper working order, the speed of the shock waves passing through the ice was established, and we also learned that the floating ice sheet on which we lived was 1300 feet thick.

From time to time we found that certain boxes or pieces of equipment were missing. This was often due to the formation of snowdrifts and the loss of marker stakes. After prospective digging had failed, we would call for David Pratt to bring the mine detector, which was an invaluable piece of equipment, although not very discerning. Digging hole after hole at indicated places, only to find a box lid with a few nails in it or a piece of baling wire, caused considerable pungent comment. On occasion it even managed to find, and we shall never know how, a single board without any nails or metal attachments of any kind. This may have been fortuitous, but as a community we were thereafter disposed to view the instrument more as an infernal machine than a true aid in trouble.

On April 15 we made our first radio contact with the American South Pole Station which had been established by air and was operating under the charge of Dr. Paul A. Siple. Conditions remained good enough for us to have a long exchange of news about our two bases and the work in progress. It was of particular interest to us to establish this contact which we endeavored to keep going from time to time, because we should ultimately be traveling via the Pole to Scott Base and later, when the RAF party flew across the continent, they would be glad to have weather reports along the route.

Gradually our weekly list of radio contacts with other Antarctic stations increased, and Taffy Williams and Ralph Lenton also made many amateur radio friends all over the world. Our regular official schedules were twice daily with Port Stanley in the Falkland Islands and once weekly direct with the GPO in London, nearly 10,000 miles away. Considering the size of our transmitter — it was only 350 watts — it says much for the trouble taken by the Post Office operators that we never missed passing our traffic throughout the winter. Later, when arrangements were made for us to be able to telephone to our relatives and friends in England, it was seldom indeed that we were unsuccessful.

Our most important circuit was that with Scott Base which was first established on February 18. After that we endeavored to speak every week and had many useful exchanges of information, but conditions were not always good enough for voice; on these days we had to fall back on sending messages by key.

On April 16 the BBC started the season's series of programs entitled "Calling Antarctica," produced especially for the bases of the Falkland Islands Dependencies, the Royal Society Base at Halley Bay and for us. Every week three or four men from the different stations received personal broadcasts from their families, while the programs also included up-to-date information likely to be of particular interest. We looked forward eagerly to these programs, which were often recorded at base so that they could be played over again to those who might be away at the time of the broadcast.

After a period of bad weather, Good Friday came calm and cold, making it possible to complete much of the outside work which had been held up, and for the seismic party it was just in time to allow David Stratton to carry a line of levels from the sea to the top of the ice shelf at 150 feet, thence to Shackleton at 195 feet, and so to the area where they had been carrying out the refraction and reflection shooting, before the sun disappeared.

On April 23 the sun finally left us and although some hours of twilight continued for many days we decided to postpone some of the seismic work until the return of the moon a fortnight later. We were therefore astonished when we went outside three days afterwards and found the whole base bathed in sunlight! This was due to refraction, but our newborn sun only remained over the horizon for twenty minutes, and the next day the same phenomena again occurred.

The last day of the month was fine and calm. To the north the clouded sky was still faintly lit, but to the south it was a deep indigo blue, giving the impression of seeing into outer space or, as David Pratt said: "Like looking at someone else's night sky from a distance."

At the beginning of May, David Stratton began regular indoor-climate observations which involved the use of numerous thermometers, thermographs and hygrographs at various levels from floor to roof, together with other periodic readings which entailed clambering about the rafters at all hours of the night and day. The results of these measurements revealed a remarkable temperature gradient. At foot level it would perhaps be just above freezing, at chest height 50°F, while in the apex of the roof 70° or 80° could be expected.

Later on we used fans to give greater circulation, but even so the temperature at floor level remained lower than the rest of the hut. The results of David's labors will be used principally by the Building Research Section of the Department of Scientific and Industrial Research, but they will also be of interest to the Medical Research Council.

For some time we had been experiencing considerable difficulty with a number of doors which had apparently warped. Then we realized that the hut might be moving, and on leveling carefully, we found that it had sunk about three inches along the north side. It was a very heavy structure and although it had certainly been difficult for eight men to build, and had sometimes been criticized as overdesigned, it was now a relief to remember its enormous strength and to feel confident that it would survive any stresses during the period of our occupation. It seemed, too, that the raft of timber and expanded metal on which the foundations had been laid would stand us in good stead by helping the whole building to move as one. We never decided what was the cause of this movement, but it was probably due either to the greater load of snow on the north side of the roof or to the proximity of a hidden crevasse which we knew from air observation extended from the front of the ice shelf to a point south of the base. Later in the winter we found that this crevasse passed within thirty feet of the hut.

At the beginning of May, I heard that Roy Homard and David Pratt had made a large fish trap out of wire netting. This had been lowered through a hole cut in the sea ice, but as the water was 3000 feet deep there was no hope of bottom fishing. At 25 feet they had caught nothing but enormous quantities of beautiful platelike crystals which seemed to be swept along by the current beneath the surface of the ice. Later the trap had been left at 250 feet and when it was hauled up they found the two wires which held it twisted and coiled about one another in fantastic confusion. This, they thought, might have been caused by a seal becoming entangled while trying to breathe, and could explain why they still caught nothing.

One evening George Lowe and I went down to the sea ice with David and Roy to visit the trap. When we left Shackleton at 9:45 a brisk wind and heavy snow made it difficult to find our way along the two-mile route in the dark, but aided by the marker stakes and stretches of the old track not yet drifted over, we successfully reached the edge of the sea ice. The hole through which the trap had been let down was frozen over and when we broke through, countless clusters of ice crystals an inch or more in diameter floated to the surface. At last a patch of clear water was obtained and we could see by the light of our torches numerous pink shrimplike animals. These were Euphausia, or "krill," the main food of many species of whale. The trap proved to contain nothing but krill and ice crystals, but not intending to return empty-handed we collected as many as we could of these pink crustacea, thinking they would make a surprise dish for David Stratton's birthday next day. Suddenly there was a swirl of water and a seal surfaced to breathe, but he was as startled as we were and disappeared in an instant. A few moments later we heard a remarkable and continuous sound like a vibrant ringing purr which we thought might be the seal's protest or warning to others. At first it was to the east, then to the west, continually repeated. Was this one animal moving about or were several answering each other? It seemed that the sound came from beneath the ice and that the ice itself acted as a sounding board.

As we turned back towards the Shackleton beacon light shining through the driving snow, it occurred to me that people at home might think us slightly mad to go shrimping in a snowstorm, at dead of night in the Antarctic winter. To us it was a relaxation to leave base and do something unessential and different from the daily routine.

Our special dish of seafood was duly prepared in honor of David's birthday and certainly it looked most attractive. Manfully he tackled the delicate pink pile, only to find that each multi-legged corpse contained no more than a few drops of pink oil. Regretfully he pushed the bowl to one side, but this was only a temporary disappointment and the evening developed into one of our more enjoyable parties.

An outdoor task undertaken by David Pratt was the measurement of friction between different types of sledge runner materials in varying temperatures and on different snow surfaces. At first he used small manhauled sledges carrying a known load, the amount of effort required to "break out" the sledge or to keep it in movement being measured electrically by the use of strain gauges. For this work he impressed various people when he thought he could persuade them that they had nothing more important of their own to do. I know that I was lucky to do my stint of forty hauls in good conditions with the temperature at only $-19°F$. A few days later Allan Rogers found himself doing the same thing in $-60°F$. This gave Allan the idea that he could make use of the same activity for his IMP work, and in no time at all Taffy Williams found himself divorced from the warm radio room and wearing an IMP while man-hauling a sledge in the outer darkness. As he stumbled from one invisible snowdrift to another Allan and David each cried their own directions till the protesting Taffy was discharged from duty and another victim sought.

Because of the great depth of the sea it was not possible to use any normal method of measuring the tides, but since the ice shelf on which we were living was afloat, we reasoned that, despite its thickness, it must rise and fall. Geoffrey Pratt decided that his Worden gravimeter would be sensitive enough to measure this movement and he set about devising automatic equipment for this purpose. First he dug a pit twenty feet deep a few hundred yards from the base. In this he installed the main hut. Then he built a complicated piece of apparatus which switched itself on automatically for ten minutes every hour, during which time a series of photographs was taken of the gravimeter reading, while a light flashed on a pole above the surface to warn off vehicle drivers and heavy-footed pedestrians. Indoors, flashing lights also showed that the apparatus was working, but more remarkable still, if anything went wrong, the instrument called for help by regularly switching on and off the bunk light over Geoffrey's bed. The immediate comment was that this was useless because he was known to be a phenomenal sleeper who had literally to be rolled over and over or turned out onto the floor before he could be woken. On the only occasion when the gravimeter automatic alarm did work, it was 3 A.M. and I happened to be on night "met" duty. To my surprise Geoffrey was roused at the first attempt and was soon outside putting things right. As a result of his work we have many weeks' records of the tides at the head of the Weddell

Sea, an area where this information could not have been obtained in any other way.

By May 9 the temperature had fallen to −50°F, accompanied by a 40 mph wind which made outdoor work difficult and unpleasant. Next day the wind eased to 10 mph but the temperature was below −60°F. At this time I took the Muskeg tractor to bring seal meat to the dog tunnels where it could be sawed up more comfortably in a temperature of plus 3°F. Driving was curiously difficult because of the clouds of condensed exhaust blowing ahead of the vehicle, making it impossible to see even a few yards. Jinking from side to side so as to get an occasional view ahead, I found that my knees were being burned by the cold air where the windproofs were stretched taut against them in the driving position. I then remembered that I was only using short underwear, but as soon as I stood up and moved about, the "burn" disappeared, illustrating the efficiency of the windproof principle, that a body of air retained next to the skin is the primary requirement for warmth.

For some time we had been digging an extension tunnel from the bottom of the snow steps used to reach the surface from the hut beneath. This was because it was becoming increasingly difficult to keep the entrance free and we wished to have an alternative exit available in case of need. The new tunnel was 12 yards long and 6 feet 6 inches high. Along the sides were various niches and shelves for a variety of purposes, but the most important feature was the "gash" pit. For a long time we had endured the irksome task of carrying twelve-gallon buckets of kitchen-waste water up a flight of snow steps to the surface. There, more often than not, the wind would whip the contents over the unfortunate bearers as they staggered away across the snow. Now we made a deep waste pit by digging a small hole about 18 inches deep in the snow and pouring into it a pint of petrol. When this had soaked in and was ignited it burned slowly, melting a cavity. Each time the flames went out, gradually increasing quantities of petrol were poured into the deepening hole and set alight. In two hours, and with the use of four gallons, we had a pit 24 feet deep and about 2 feet in diameter which served us until Shackleton was closed in November.

After a few weeks we began to notice that when a bucket of water had been tipped into the waste pit there was a pause, followed by a distant rumbling gurgle which indicated a second chamber somewhere below. Later we found that a lighted mass of paper thrown down would burn like a blowtorch in the blast of air rising from the bottom. Clearly our constant buckets of warm water had melted a channel into a crevasse below.

Another laborsaving device was a hole cut in the floor thus allowing the bathwater to run away into the snow. This may sound an obvious and simple expedient, but when an Antarctic hut is built on rock it is an unwise procedure because the water freezes on the rock below and gradually builds up ice beneath the floor, very soon preventing its own escape. With this knowledge we had expected to bail the water from the bath and empty it outside. Now we reasoned that the great depth of snow beneath us would accept the bath waste, but there was a problem — our bath had no waste plug!

It was a mystery to us why any baths were supplied without waste holes, but David Stratton had learned that these were especially made for sale in Aden as Arabs did not require waste pipes. But why not? We pictured to ourselves a long camel caravan winding over the hot sands of Arabia, each camel bearing white enameled cast-iron baths, like panniers on either side of their swaying humps. But what did the Arabs do with the waste water when the baths were finally in use? Surely evaporation was no solution?

However that might be, our own solution was to make a hole in the normal place, no easy task without chipping the enamel or cracking the iron; but finally, after some experiment and dearly bought experience, the engineers succeeded and also devised a plug which did not suddenly cease to function, leaving one high, dry and soapy. After two weeks we plumbed the depth of the hole in the snow below and the sounding was 22 feet. Nine days later it was 10 feet deeper, but in another two weeks it had only increased by a few inches and thereafter remained constant at that depth.

To our surprise, the movement of the pack ice under the influence of the westerly current maintained constantly changing leads of open water. Occasionally a strong blow from the south would drive the pack out of sight, so that all through the winter there were periods when open water extended many miles to east and west of Shackleton. As soon as the wind dropped, the low temperatures caused the sea to freeze, then the pack, returning under the influence of currents and northerly winds, would crack, buckle, and over-raft the thin new ice until it formed a smaller area of rough and corrugated floes. These areas of open water in winter may therefore be regarded as the breeding grounds of pack ice which will move on in the endless mill of the Weddell Sea, perhaps to survive for many years. On several occasions when such open water occurred we threw a number of bottles into the lapping waves. Each contained a note prepared by Hannes La Grange giving the date and place, together with instructions to the finders. Perhaps after circulating for many years with the ice, some will be released into the Southern Ocean and finally be found on a distant beach, thereby giving an indication of the time taken for the journey from the head of the Weddell Sea.

Up at South Ice the weather was nearly always more severe than at Shackleton, for not only was the station farther south and away from the sea, but it stood at a much greater altitude. For May the party reported a mean temperature of $-38°F$ and a mean wind speed of 35 mph, while the lowest temperature was $-67°F$. As Shackleton could only boast a minimum temperature of $-60°F$ it became known as "The Banana Belt."

A curious event which often accompanied cold conditions at Shackleton was the reversal of the air flow in the radio-room chimney. This would happen if the small coal stove was shut down too low for the night. The column of cold air that formed in the upper part of the chimney would gradually overcome the upward draft and suddenly a cataract of air would rush down, fanning the fire into life, and blue flames, smoke and sparks would belch from the lower part of the stove. Soon the room would become full of smoke and fumes which gradually spread to the rest of the hut. At first we could not understand what had happened, but we soon discovered that the only cure was to cover the top of the chimney with a sack and use blowlamps to heat the metal stovepipe. When this was really hot the sack would be snatched away and the contained hot air would re-start the right cycle of events. Apart from the unpleasantness, it was distinctly unhealthy to allow this back-draft to occur, for on the first occasion it happened we found that there was sufficient carbon monoxide in the radio room to be dangerous to life in one hour. After that the night "met" man kept a careful eye on the stove in cold weather.

In early June, Ralph Lenton, assisted by many others, at last had time to paint the inside of the living room a pale cream with green doors and windows. This lightened it considerably and provided a much better setting for the decorations we were planning for our Midwinter celebrations. He also varnished the long windowseat which extended the full length of the room and made covered cushions with smart white piping.

By June 19 the spirit of Midwinter had arrived and most of our indoor activities were directed towards preparations for the great day. The Queen's portrait hung as a centerpiece over the only bit of polished furniture we had — a mahogany sideboard, on which stood an artistic arrangement of artificial flowers. Across the room hung paper chains, with clusters of colored balloons suspended from the beams above.

David Stratton was finishing the lettering on individual menu cards while George Lowe printed the photographs which would be inserted in them. Ralph Lenton and John Lewis were very busy in the kitchen, John producing our regular meals while Ralph turned out a succession of cakes, pastries, sausage rolls and innumerable cocktail snacks. David Pratt and Roy Homard were tidying up and decorating the engineering workshop where they had invited us to a special party on Midwinter morning, while Gordon Haslop had for some time been busy with secret preparations of his own which included digging several trenches and the assembly of various flares, bangers, Very pistols, and detonators.

From our meat store, a snow pit not far from the hut, we brought in a trussed turkey, a large joint of pork, half a side of bacon which had been saved for the occasion and several pounds of fresh potatoes. These had frozen so hard that they rattled in the sack like stones, and indeed looked and handled like pebbles from any beach. We had discovered that as long as they were kept frozen and then suddenly thawed by cooking, they remained in excellent condition.

The day before Midwinter we enjoyed a two-way radio conversation with our other half at Scott Base, 2000 miles across the continent. Greetings were exchanged and after hilarious confusion as to Zone Time, Local Time, Greenwich Mean Time and opening time, it was firmly established that they had stolen a march on us and were about to begin their pre-Midwinter Dinner cocktail party.

On June 21, Midwinter Day, we rose late and breakfasted at 9:30, then carried out the normal chores of sweeping, cleaning and bringing in ice and coal as a community effort, before dressing for the Pratt-Homard cocktail party. We set out for the workshop fully clothed in windproofs and gloves, expecting to stumble over the intervening drifts, but to our surprise and delight the snow reflected the flickering light of dozens of paraffin flares that marked the 200-yard route. At the door our hosts greeted us formally before thrusting a glass into each eager hand. Inside it was beautifully warm as the small coal fire in the annex was roaring and with the door open the whole building had been raised to plus 35°F. We were able to strip off our outdoor clothing and stand about in comfort admiring the new photographs and colored posters which covered the walls. When one thought of the many months we had all spent together in close proximity, it was remarkable to hear the steady buzz of animated conversation, only interrupted by the shouts of welcome that greeted each new arrival, while the general air of gaiety was enhanced by a background of Irish jigs from a record player. Suddenly someone thought of fixing a large meteorological balloon to the exhaust of a Weasel, and started the engine. Slowly at first, but with increasing speed, it grew to gigantic size before exploding amid cries of acclamation.

Soon we were crowding outside for the "Haslop Firework Display" which began with a series of detonations that spelt out "T A E" in Morse and continued with flares and rockets, the dark figure of Gordon silhouetted against the light, clearly clutching a beer mug in one hand while setting off fireworks with the other. It was a fine show.

Returning late to the hut to prepare for the midday feast we were just about to sit down when South Ice came through on the radio to exchange greetings and tell us about the roast beef lunch they had just finished and how they were already looking forward to chicken for dinner. At 3:30 P.M. we sat down to a splendid meal which included green turtle soup, roast turkey, plum pudding and ice cream. The table was decorated with cracker bonbons and presents and in due course paper hats and musical instruments enlivened the atmosphere. Later that evening, after a suitable pause for digestion and recovery, we enjoyed a buffet supper prepared by Ralph, including even mustard and cress sandwiches, the first fresh vegetable we had tasted since the departure of the *Magga Dan*.

Such was our Midwinter, and now we looked forward to the second half of the dark nights, for not until August 18 would the sun return to Shackleton.

Next day we were back to the regular routine of tending our instruments, looking after the dogs, working on the vehicles, digging out buried sledges and the thousand other things which made the time of preparation for spring all too short. At the beginning of July, I began planning a complicated program of field work which I knew would inevitably be altered by conditions at the time, for the weather was certainly unpredictable at the change of season. Nevertheless it presented a fair idea of the requirements and provided objectives toward which all could work.

The early part of the month was relatively warm, but by the first week temperatures had dropped to the minus forties, then to −53°F with a full gale on the 13th. The faint but ruddy glow of the sun over the northern sky was visible, but the wall of drift blotted out the horizon. Now we were working hard on our camping equipment, mending tents, binding tent poles with tape or balloon cord to strengthen them, checking and repacking ration boxes — laborious tasks that took many hours. Sledges, radio, indeed all equipment, had to be brought to perfection and very often modified. All the time the engineers worked at the vehicles one after the other, stripping down tracks, welding on recovery equipment, besides a score of other things in every field of their activity. Towards the end of the month the temperature again dropped to the minus fifties and on July 29 to −64°F with a wind of 30 mph.

At South Ice, where the altitude had now been accepted as 4430 feet, they had little wind but the temperature had at one time dropped to −71°F. Their winter had been extremely busy, for besides Blaiklock's regular meteorological observations, reported twice daily to Shackleton, their glaciological program had been ambitious. The pit for the study of snow strata had reached to 50 feet, at which point the snow temperature was −22°F. In the bottom they were beginning to bore a hole three inches in diameter for another 100 feet. Jon Stephenson had done this work from within the snow tunnels around the hut, but Hal Lister's microclimate and drift studies had to be carried out in the open, often in exposed positions high on the lattice mast, in low temperatures and high winds. Perhaps their greatest difficulty was to maintain their scientific work and at the same time continue the ordinary chores of cooking, bringing in fuel and ice, keeping radio schedules and looking after generators and other equipment.

From the beginning of August, at both bases the glow of the sun below the horizon became daily more colorful, the reflected light steadily increasing until it was possible to move about with the snow surface clearly visible. Then on the 14th Peter Weston rushed into the hut calling out that the sun was back. Some, less disbelieving than others, ran outside into −56°F and a 20 mph wind, only to see a red glow on the northern horizon. Then a fraction of the sun's disc appeared again, flickered and disappeared. For some time it came and went, the greatest elevation revealing about one tenth of the orb. Sometimes as it reappeared a red flash seemed to shoot out and pulsate along the horizon. This was an exciting moment, not only because the sun had come back to us, but because it had returned by refraction four days earlier than expected.

With the rapidly returning daylight, work outside could be accelerated and the tempo of our preparations for traveling quickened. September 1 had been set as the first possible date of departure and this, we decided, would mark the beginning of our spring.

X I

Winter at Scott Base

The positions of Shackleton and Scott Base were almost identical in latitude and each was situated at the head of a great sea extending toward the heart of the Antarctic continent. Being equally far south the same length of summer and winter was experienced at both, but in other matters there were great dissimilarities. Scott Base lay close to a high range of mountains extending for hundreds of miles to north and south, and in the summer the open sea reached close to the base itself, which was built on solid rock. In contrast, only low, snow-covered hills were visible from Shackleton, seven hundred miles of sea ice lay between it and the open water, while the base was built on a floating ice shelf. These factors could be expected to provide some climatic differences, but life at Scott Base was also influenced by the close proximity of the Americans at Hut Point only two miles distant. Now Sir Edmund Hillary again takes up the story to describe how the Ross Sea Party spent the winter.

By the beginning of May we were getting very little daylight, and the winter routine had now been adopted in earnest. Our work outside was usually confined to the essentials — collecting snow for our water supply, obtaining food and fuel from the supply dumps, and disposing of the rubbish. We tried to keep ample reserves in close proximity to the base so that we wouldn't run short in the event of a prolonged period of bad weather. But though we had experienced some unpleasant conditions, with strong winds and cold temperatures, we had not as yet had a really bad storm. On the evening of May 12, it started to blow strongly from the north, with clouds of drift, although in the sky above the stars could still be seen. During the night the wind reached 42 knots, and we wondered if our first storm was on its way. To our surprise, it was a good deal quieter by morning, although the day proved to be gusty and unsettled, and the temperatures had become ominously mild.

We were wakened the following night by the huts shaking under the force of the wind. A stiff southerly was now blowing and due to the prominent position of our base, and to the fact that our buildings were not drifted up with snow, we were receiving the full force of the wind as it screamed off the Ross Ice Shelf. By breakfast time it was gusting powerfully to 54 knots and by 10:30 A.M. to 67 knots. As this was the first real test to which our huts had been subjected, we kept a very close watch for any weaknesses. By noon, our anemometer was registering over 70 knots, and our lives had become dominated by the continuous roaring of the wind. The huts were lashed with drifting snow and small particles of ice. Going outside into the darkness was an unpleasant and hazardous business. Two hours later a fiercer gust reached 79 knots or 90 miles an hour.

We were watching our two generator huts with some concern. Under the terrific suction caused by the wind sweeping up the slope in front of the base, the roofs of these huts were flapping up and down with a maximum movement of several inches. Although we knew they had a certain amount of resilience, we found this somewhat disturbing, but there was nothing we could do about it until the storm ceased. Late in the afternoon the wind did ease a little and we swarmed outside with electric torches to assess the damage: to our relief everything seemed to be in good shape. For three more days the storm continued, the wind at times reaching over 70 knots again, and for one period of over three hours it averaged more than 55 knots. When it was all finished and the base was peaceful once more, we seemed none the worse for it all and our confidence was greatly increased. Just as a precaution we wired down the two offending roofs and strengthened the junctions in our covered way. Huge snowdrifts had built up on the lee sides of the buildings, and these remained a permanent feature for the rest of the winter.

The scientific activities of the base took on an increased importance as the field work ceased. Our group of scientists, in co-operation with hundreds of stations in all parts of the world, were carrying out an investigation into related phenomena of the upper atmosphere such as auroras, meteorology, magnetic disturbances and ionospheric variations. Although the International Geophysical Year did not actually commence until July 1, all our equipment was operating and a full series of observations were being recorded by April 1.

Apart from keeping a controlling interest in all of these activities, Dr. Hatherton had taken as his special task the auroral observations. This entailed his staying up all night, and when other members of the expedition were snug in bed Hatherton would be standing with his head out of an open hatch in the laboratory building recording with numbed fingers the phases of the display in progress. In addition to his visual observations, Hatherton operated the All Sky Camera which was mounted on top of the building and took a series of photographs of the complete sky. In fine weather the auroras were rarely absent, and after a succession of cloudless nights Hatherton could hardly be blamed for heaving a sigh of relief when cloud cover or a storm gave him a much-needed rest. The auroral observations during the daytime were split up amongst the other members of the scientific team. In general we were rather disappointed with the displays as they were rarely as vivid as we had come to expect from viewing Dr. Edward Wilson's beautiful paintings. However, on one occasion we did have one that was more intense than usual, when it flared into glorious greens and reds near the zenith, and for a period of half a minute gave a suggestion of a colored hanging curtain, as painted by Wilson. On another occasion the southern sky glowed molten red and was sufficiently vivid to produce a hasty inquiry from our neighboring American base as to whether Scott Base was burning down.

Gerard, who was carrying out the magnetic observations, was one of the few expedition members who had to go outside every day. The small Magnetic hut, constructed throughout of non-magnetic materials, was some distance from the laboratory and Gerard used to visit it each day to check up on his delicate instruments which were recording the vertical and horizontal components of the earth's magnetic field. The actual recording by the magnetic variometers was done continuously in the laboratory which was connected by cables with the Magnetic hut. In bad weather it would have been a simple matter for Gerard to have strayed unwittingly from the path when on his daily visit, so a lifeline was suspended along his route and by keeping his hand on this he could find his way in the worst conditions. Gerard carried out one useful task which was not in his original program — the locating by magnetic means of several drums of aviation gasoline which had been buried under some five feet of snow. Using a portable variometer, he took some careful observations around the suspected site and then recommended a point at which the airmen should dig. His forecast proved accurate and the drums were recovered.

Few of the scientific activities created more interest amongst the lay members of the expedition than the seismic recordings carried out by Orr. When we first established Scott Base on Ross Island, there was some concern as to whether a volcanic island of that nature would prove satisfactory for a seismic station. In practice the results were most successful. The seismometers were mounted on a solid block of concrete in the ground and a continuous recording of their readings was made on 35-mm film. The developing and interpretation of this film was a daily task and many interesting earth movements were recorded. These varied from major earthquakes in the Aleutian Islands to many local quakes in the vicinity of the Antarctic continent. Our seismic information was coded up and radioed out each day to swell the international pool of seismic observations.

The most impressive corner of the laboratory was that containing two very large pieces of equipment: the ionosonde and the pulse transmitter. The ionosonde was an extremely complex transmitter and receiver which at intervals carried out an investigation of the ionized layers above the earth's surface. The operation was wholly automatic and at the specified times the machine would suddenly spring into life with a flashing of lights and a whirring of mechanism, only to subside into silence once again when its short period was over. The pulse transmitter standing nearby also operated on a regular timetable and its purpose was to test the efficiency of various wave lengths over varying distances. A number of Antarctic and

other widely spaced stations had been supplied with automatic receivers which would keep a record of the strength with which the
different wave lengths were received. Sandford, who operated these
complicated machines, was also responsible for the two 84-foot vertical scientific masts. During a blizzard one of his aerial wires broke
and after the storm subsided he carried out the unenviable task of
climbing halfway up the mast to recover the broken end. The smooth
bole of the mast had holes at intervals into which steel rods could
be placed as a foothold, but even this, plus a safety belt, did not completely remove the hazard of carrying out such a job in complete
darkness at extremely low temperatures.

The fifth member of the scientific party was Macdonald. Apart
from the assistance he gave with the other operations in the laboratory, Macdonald's particular interests were solar radiation and measuring the Antarctic tides. His tide gauge was mounted in a hole cut
in the bay ice just below Scott Base, and its operation was constantly
threatened by the ice movement of the Ross Ice Shelf. However, the
major concern was the effect of the extreme cold on the clockwork
drive of the tide gauge and this was constantly freezing up. None of
the methods used to overcome this was wholly successful, and later
on in the winter the gauge was rendered completely inoperative
by the increasing depth of ice that formed on the surface of the
Sound.

Our neighboring American station at Hut Point was carrying out
extensive weather observations including the releasing of two radiosonde balloons each day to investigate the upper winds. Our weather
records were therefore on a more modest scale. Dr. Balham carried
out the usual six-hourly synoptic observations of temperature, pressure, humidity, wind speed and direction, and cloud over. Most of
this work could be done in his meteorological office or in close proximity to the base, but the temperature screens were mounted some
little distance away and reading the thermometers often became a
task of some magnitude when the weather was proving unkind. In
times of storm the weather office became a popular corner as amateur
observers gathered around the barometer and the wind speed indi-
cator and made learned forecasts on the probable extent and intensity of the disturbance.

All of these scientific activities had assumed a greater prominence in the life of the base, but there was still plenty to do during the winter for the members of the field parties. The dog sledging equipment was brought into the sledging hut and completely overhauled. The six sledges were stripped down to their component parts and then lashed together again — often with minor modifications to suit the particular driver's taste. Tents were carefully dried out and any holes and weak parts mended. New dog traces were spliced and lampwick dog harnesses sewn up. Most of us did not like the food contained in the field ration boxes, so these were now modified. Many tins were taken out, a greater variety of food introduced, and what we considered a much more palatable and equally nutritious diet obtained for the same overall weight. The electric sewing machine was rarely idle. A lot of our standard clothing met with criticism, and individuals spent a great deal of time in modifying it. In fact we thought that although the quality of materials and cloth had improved since the days of Captain Scott, the same could not be said in many cases to the design of garments. Quite often we found that the modifications we thought necessary were identical with similar ones illustrated in the books on Scott's and Shackleton's expeditions, and it appeared that much the old explorers had learned was not being used by later expeditions.

Whatever the weather, fine or stormy, the dogs still had to be fed. The sixty of them were tethered out on the snow in front of the base and probably the most unpopular chore in the camp was cutting up their seal meat. We had collected one hundred and sixty seals in the autumn, and as these were now frozen solid the only way to tackle them was with a saw. The carcass of the seal would be lifted onto a sawhorse by using the fork lift on a tractor and then cut into segments by two men wielding a great crosscut saw. These segments were then split up with an ax and a large chunk given to each dog. If the weather was too severe for this task, we fed the dogs on tinned dog food which they gulped down with considerable relish. When the moon came up each month, and it was possible to move around without a light, the dogs were harnessed up in their sledges and given a run. Racing over the rough sea ice was an exhilarating experience both for dogs and men, as it was impossible to pick out obstacles in the moonlight and the only thing to do was to hold onto the sledge and hope for the best. We ran our dogs right through the winter and they seemed able to pull a sledge at temperatures down to −40°F without any great discomfort.

The radio room was always a scene of activity. Our twice-daily radio telegraphy schedules with New Zealand carried a great deal of traffic, since scientific information, together with messages of a more personal nature, was transmitted every day. The most popular service was undoubtedly the radio telephone, and generally we were in contact with New Zealand both in the morning and the evening for telephone circuits. As we were only charged 1s. 6d. a minute to any part of New Zealand, it was often difficult to restrain the more garrulous members from speaking at some length to those at home. We were in contact with a number of other expedition bases in the Antarctic, the most important of these for us being, of course, Shackleton. Ironically enough, Shackleton proved to be our most unsatisfactory contact, and we rarely had conditions good enough for an easy and relaxed discussion with our opposite numbers on the other side of the continent.

While our base radio service was supplying us with better communications than our most sanguine forecast, the same could not be said for our field radio communications the previous summer. The small radio sets used in the field had arrived in New Zealand too late to be thoroughly tested before we left to go south, and in practice they proved to be an almost complete failure. We discovered that they had originally been designed for use in the desert, so this was perhaps not surprising. I regarded field communications as vitally important in an expedition such as ours, where there were a number of small parties moving around and being maintained by aircraft. A party which is camping under cold and windy conditions, or whose members are tired after a long day's run, has little inclination to operate a radio set which is unreliable or needs one of the men to sit outside the tent cranking furiously to build up power. I asked my radio men to use their experience and draw up specifications for a new field set and this they did. Our Radio Subcommittee in Wellington had the sets made for us and they were flown down by the Americans early in the spring. They proved an outstanding success. The sets were battery-operated, and to save power they could transmit only on Morse, although they could receive both on Morse and voice. This had the effect of reducing the chattiness which is inevitable on such a circuit, but it did mean that all the field party and the airmen had to be conversant with the Morse code. Classes were instituted and every morning the mess hut was filled with a band of beginners straining their ears and trying to receive the immaculate Morse of their instructor, Ted Gawn. The first few months were the worst, but after that everyone became reasonably proficient. By the end of the winter we could all send and receive Morse at between six and twelve words a minute, and had sufficient knowledge of radio procedure to handle traffic responsibly.

The other main instructional class was in navigation. Miller, Brooke and Carlyon were the expedition surveyors and would do the navigation for their respective parties, while I intended using my Air Force navigation experience to guide the tractor train. However, it was essential in case an emergency arose that each man should have a fundamental knowledge of polar navigation — sufficient at least to enable him to find his way home if something happened to his navigator. Miller conducted a series of classes and had an interested audience. He dealt with dead reckoning and astronomical navigation, and although at the end of it all it is doubtful if every man could work out his position from a series of sun shots, yet it did result in each party having a sufficient body of knowledge to carry on in the event of their navigator being incapacitated.

We also had a series of lectures by our geologists Gunn and Warren, designed to give the members of the field party sufficient knowledge to enable them to make an intelligent collection of rock specimens for later expert examination. A large number of specimens had already been acquired, particularly from the Skelton Glacier, and our geologists spent many hours on these, cutting slides with the diamond circular saw and examining them under the microscope. Our surveyors worked out all their field observations and plotted them and finally produced the first detailed map ever drawn of the hundreds of square miles of the Skelton Glacier system.

One of the busiest places in camp was the garage. Here a large-scale operation was under way preparing three Ferguson tractors

and one Weasel for the southern journey. A large number of modifications were incorporated and this took a long time. Over the driver's
seat of the Ferguson we welded a powerful crash bar to give the
driver some protection if the vehicle went down a crevasse or rolled
over. Around this a cab, or rather a windbreak, was constructed from
canvas to keep out a little of the Antarctic wind. The track system
was strengthened and modified and an enormous amount of work
was done on the tracks themselves in an attempt to improve their
gripping ability in soft snow. The motors were completely overhauled
and all worn parts replaced; the electrical wiring system was simpli-
fied; and any unnecessary parts of the body were cut away. Aes-
thetic considerations were unimportant, and everything possible was
done to ease the problems of maintenance in the field. A light, portable garage was constructed out of canvas with a collapsible framework of three-quarter inch piping, mainly for use in the event of
some major breakdown. A strong towbar was welded onto the front
of each vehicle and sixty-foot lengths of Terylene tow rope with an
eight tons' breaking strain were cut and spliced.

Sledges were one of our main worries, as they had received a great
deal of punishment in the onerous task of unloading the ships. We
carried out any necessary repairs and reinforced the turnups on any
damaged runners. From three of the Maudheim sledges we removed
the steel sole specially provided for unloading in rock areas and
glued and bolted into place strips of Tufnol — a plastic material
with a very low coefficient of friction for use on snow. We welded
extra width onto the steel runners of our articulated sledges to de-
crease their bearing pressure on the snow. It was difficult not to be
disheartened at times by the knowledge that our equipment was in
many cases already worn and had never been designed for the job
for which we now intended to use it. But I had a great deal of confidence in the resourcefulness and adaptability of my two amateur
mechanics, Bates and Ellis, and I felt sure that once we got on the
trail we would go a long way.

One lesson we had learned from our autumn trip to Cape Crozier
had been the need for some warmth and protection for the men in
the party who were not actually driving at the time. On the Crozier
trip these men rested on the sledge until they became too cold and

then ran alongside it until they were warm or their breath gave out. This was a miserable process and would not do for a long trip. We also needed some protected place for our radio transmitter. To this end we set to work to build a light but strong caravan on the back of one of the sledges. The "caboose," as we called it, had an internal framework of one and a quarter inch piping. Onto this we bolted plywood and then covered the lot with heavy canvas. The caboose was eleven feet long and only four feet wide, but we crammed a great deal into it. One end was fitted up with the radio transmitter, numerous cupboards, benches, and a stand for two Primus stoves. The other end was completely filled with two shelf bunks capable of sleeping (we hoped) four men. To keep the caboose warm while we were traveling, Bates had constructed a simple heater which extracted the heat from the tractor exhaust gases. Altogether it looked a very unusual structure, but it was strong and functional, and we were rather proud of it.

The Beaver aircraft had been put away once its flying operations were completed. This involved removing the wings and stowing them safely in a large crate. The fuselage was towed to an exposed position and carefully tied down; the motor inhibited and every door, window and crack sealed against the drift. But our flying didn't cease with the coming of darkness for we had decided to keep the Auster operational all winter, and it was left out on the airfield behind a windbreak of wire netting. Each month when the moon was up and the dogs were running, there would be signs of great activity on the airstrip — the twinkle of lights and the roar of hot-air blowers — and Wally Tarr would be in the process of getting the plane in flying condition. This involved removing the large quantities of snow that lodged in the wings and fuselage, and freeing up the frozen motor. A few lamps were spread down the runway and then the Auster would roar off into the moonlit sky. As the plane was not equipped for night flying, Tarr had mounted the large red rear light from a tractor on the fuselage, and this could clearly be seen from a considerable distance as the plane circled over McMurdo Sound. Useful work was carried out in keeping track of the progress of the freezing of the Sound, and a careful watch was maintained for the appearance of any seals or penguins. The main difficulty with aircraft opera-

The aluminum framework of the hut at South Ice.

The South Ice hut completed and drifted over, with the Otter bringing further stores.

Stores in one of the snow tunnels at South Ice.

Constructing underground winter quarters for the dogs at Shackleton.

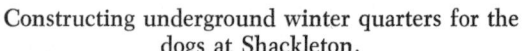

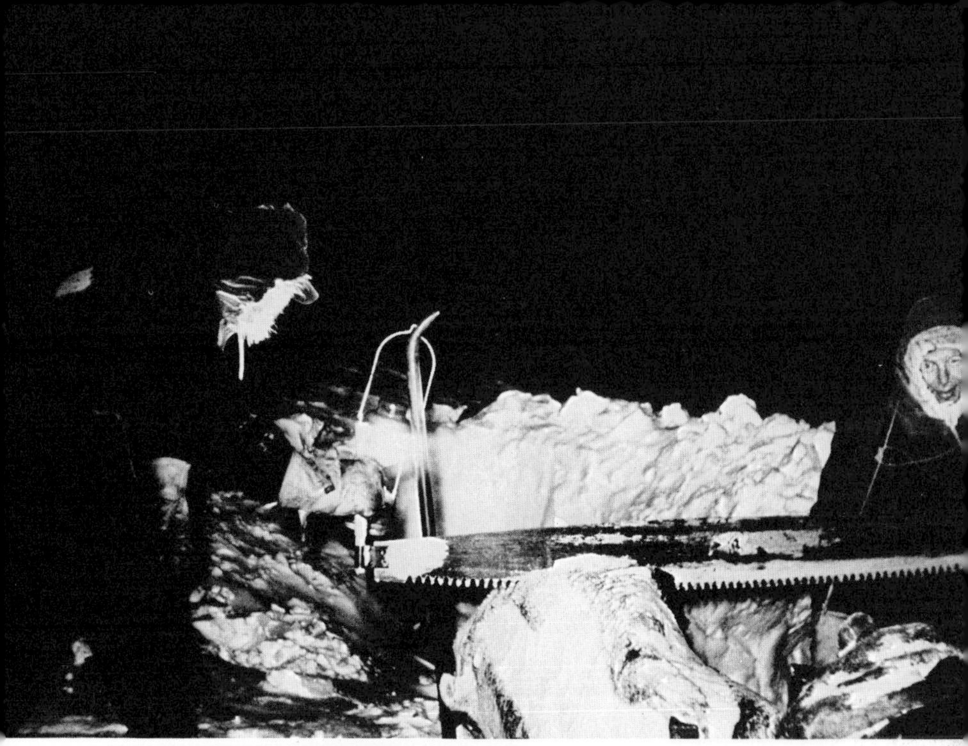

Sawing seal meat for the dogs during the winter.

Feeding time in the underground dog tunnels at Shackleton.
Electric light was provided during the day.

Windscoop at the eastern end of the base hut at Shackleton,
with the meteorological tower in the background.

Hannes La Grange attending to the wind-speed recorder
in the meteorological office at Shackleton.

Aurora over Shackleton during winter.

...ssing the siting of South Ice. Left to right: Dr. Vivian Fuchs, Allan Rogers, Ken Blaiklock, and Hal Lister.

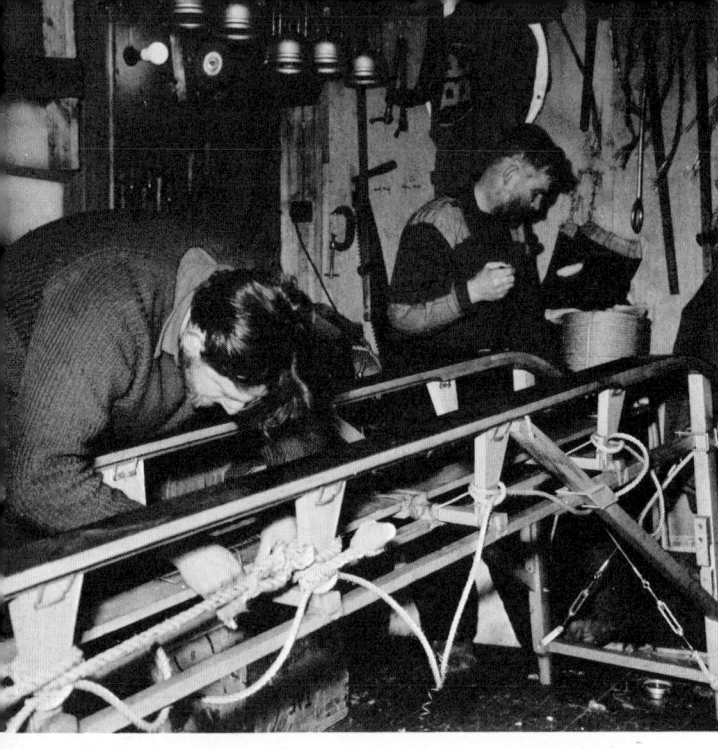

Sledge repairs in the carpenter's shop at Shackleton.

Gordon Haslop taking his turn in the galley.
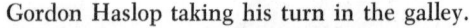

Geoffrey Pratt at work while wearing the IMP.

Roy Homard using the acetylene cutter in the vehicle
workshop at Shackleton.

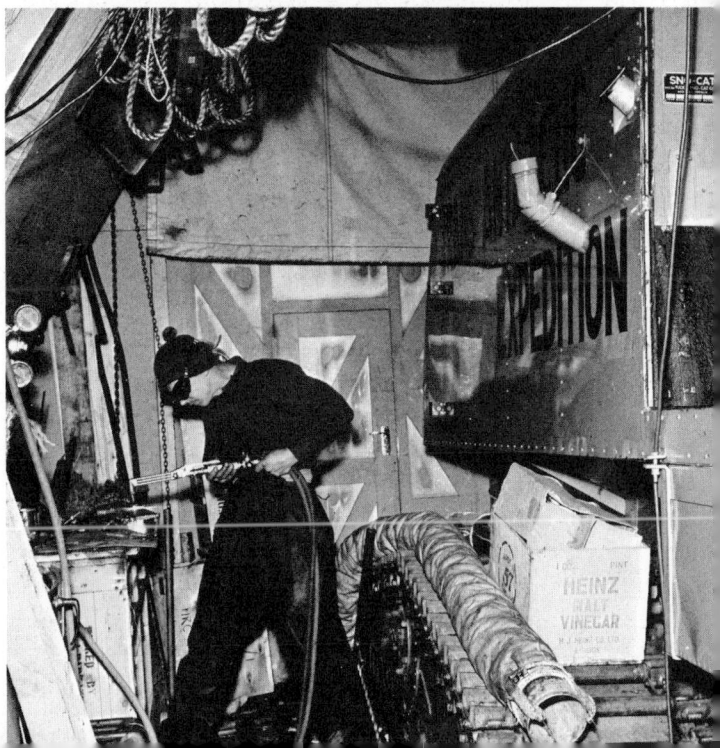

Typical view in the Theron Mountains, showing a frozen melt-water pool at the foot of the cliffs. Numerous coal seams were found in these rocks.

Surveying in the Shackleton Mountains.

tions was the enormous amount of drift snow that built up around the Auster during a storm. Indeed, after one severe storm, the Auster was completely engulfed with snow and its position could only be located by the few inches of orange tail that showed above the surface. Digging it out was a big job and the fuselage suffered many tears and dents in the process. Once the snow had been cleared away we raised the aircraft to the surface again, and Tarr gave it a thorough inspection. There was no serious damage, but it took a long while to fix it in the dark, cold conditions, and we lost a month's flying in consequence.

By Midwinter's Day, June 21, life at Scott Base had settled down into a very comfortable pattern. Breakfast was at 8:15 A.M., lunch at 1 P.M., and dinner at 6 P.M. All the expedition members took their turn at doing mess duties and two men would be on for a week at a time. Their tasks included keeping the mess hut and the ablution hut clean; digging tractor loads of snow and shoveling it into the snow melters for water; supplying the ten or twelve drums of fuel required each week for our heaters, stoves and generators; taking away all the rubbish; getting supplies from the food dump; washing up the pots and pans after each meal; and washing up all the eating utensils after dinner at night. On Sunday our cook had a complete rest, and the cooking that day was also one of the duties of the two mess stewards, and some magnificent meals resulted. But by Sunday night, the two men would be thoroughly exhausted after their week of activity, and it was always a relief when life reverted to its somewhat easier routine.

The evenings in the mess hut were characterized by much noise and hearty laughter. There was quite a large selection of records for our radiogram and it was rarely silent. Contract bridge, chess, and various games of chance were very popular, and our library was well patronized. If a man preferred a little more quietness, he could retire to the peace of the sleeping huts to write letters in his cubicle, or lie on his bed and read and doze. Saturday night was party night, and the hut rocked and shook under a hearty Scottish reel or shuddered under the impact of boisterous rugby scrums. Once a week we'd have a lecture by one of the party, and these covered a wide range of topics from "Bullfighting in Mexico" to "How to Make an

Eight-inch Reflecting Telescope." And on Sunday morning we had a service, usually conducted by Bob Miller, and although we lacked a piano the singing of hymns was both enthusiastic and vociferous. It was a pleasant and comfortable life and much of the sense of isolation experienced by earlier expeditions was lacking. The main hardship was the separation from one's family, and even this could be assuaged by frequent telephone calls. Even the winter weather at Scott Base was a pleasant surprise. We had a number of storm periods with high winds and vast quantities of drifting snow, but in general the outside conditions were not unpleasant. Moving around in the darkness soon became second nature to us as we learned the lie of the land, although we always took a torch or lantern with us outside. It could in fact be very refreshing to walk around even at temperatures below −40°F if there was little or no wind. It was only when something went wrong — a tractor broke down or became stuck in a snowdrift — that life became rather miserable, and if any sort of a wind was blowing a constant watch had to be kept for frostbite. Our highest gust of wind was 95 mph, and our lowest temperature −58.7°F.

I had decided to split the coming summer's activities into three main parts. The Northern Party, composed of Brooke, Gunn, Warren and Douglas, would head north along the coast of Victoria Land and explore and geologize in the numerous dry valleys we had sighted from the air. They would then force a route up one of the glaciers to the polar plateau and continue their survey and geology on the western side of the ranges. They would conclude their trip by traveling over the plateau past the head of the Ferrar Glacier to the Skelton névé, and complete the mapping of this extensive area. This party would be using two dog teams and would be supported from the air. Their trip was in many ways the most interesting one as it combined an enormous variety of country with certainly the finest opportunities for survey and geology.

The Southern Party of Miller, Marsh, Ayres and Carlyon, would operate four dog teams. They would be flown in to the Skelton Depot at the beginning of the season, would travel up the glacier to the Plateau Depot and would then continue on out over the polar plateau to establish Depots 480 and 700. They would be supported by the

Beaver aircraft and, as we still had no real knowledge as to how well our tractors would function, the Southern Party was still regarded as our main means of establishing the southern depots. It was hoped that once the depot establishing tasks were complete, the Southern Party would split into two teams and then carry out survey and exploration in the ranges between the Skelton and the Beardmore Glaciers.

The Tractor Party made up the third group. Ellis, Bates, Mulgrew and I were the solid core of the team and I intended dragging in any other drivers as they became available. We would use three Ferguson tractors and one Weasel and leave Scott Base with sufficient fuel to get as far as Depot 480. If we reached the Plateau Depot satisfactorily, the Beaver would fly in a great deal more petrol to us there, and we would continue on over the polar plateau with sufficient fuel on board, not only to get to Depot 700, but also to actually stock it for the Transpolar Party. This plan meant that the setting up of the southern depots would be more assured, as it was unlikely that both the aircraft and the tractors would come to grief. If all went well, I intended accumulating sufficient fuel at Depot 700 to enable me to push on south with several tractors — possibly as far as the Pole, although it seemed unlikely that there would be time to do this if Fuchs was able to keep to his schedule and arrive at the Pole by Christmas Day.

By the beginning of July there was a distinct lightening of the sky at midday and the tempo of our preparations increased a great deal. As the month lengthened the Western Mountains became visible again, delicately pink, and there was a rosy glow to the north — all signs of the returning sun. But it wasn't until August 23 that Cranfield in the Auster aircraft first saw the sun from high over McMurdo Sound, for bad weather during the previous few days had stopped us seeing it earlier. Scott Base was still cut off by the bulk of Observation Hill, but we could see the sunshine out on the sea ice, and all the dog drivers harnessed up their teams and raced out to revel in it. It was amazing what a lift it gave to our spirits and how the feeling of impatience was more evident than ever — the urge to get out into the field and on with the job. The next fortnight was one of great activity as we prepared for the spring journeys we intended carrying out as preliminaries to the main operations. The weather had been rather unsettled and the temperatures were still at times reaching below $-50\,°F$, but most of our journeying was to be in the vicinity of McMurdo Sound, so we considered it quite safe to start early in September.

XII

The Spring Journeys from Shackleton

IN PLANNING our spring activities I had decided to aim at starting
the field work on September 1. From the Advance Party's experiences we knew that the weather would still be cold, with the probability of blizzards, but on the principle that conditions may always
be better than one expects, and because there was so much to do,
this was accepted.

The original intention was to organize five field parties. On
September 1, six men and four vehicles were to leave with additional
fuel for the 50-mile depot that had been established by Blaiklock
and Goldsmith; at the same time the party would investigate the
structure of the great chasm south of Shackleton. We believed this to
be caused by the movement of the ice shelf past an area of higher
snow-covered ground that had been observed from the air many miles
to the west and south. On September 10, we planned to relieve South
Ice by air, and on the 13th two men and one dog team were to be
flown to the Theron Mountains for survey and geological work. On
the 27th four men, with two dog teams, were to fly to the western
end of the Shackleton Range where they would be set down on the
ice shelf close to the mountains. Their first task would be to find and
mark a route from the heavily crevassed ice shelf up the steep and
broken "ice wall"; this done they would make a survey of the mountains. On the 30th, four men and four vehicles would leave on the
all-important reconnaissance journey to South Ice. By October 22
it was intended to have everyone back at Shackleton preparing for
the start of the transcontinental journey on November 14. As will
be seen later, these plans had to be greatly modified.

In spite of the return of the sun, during August we experienced

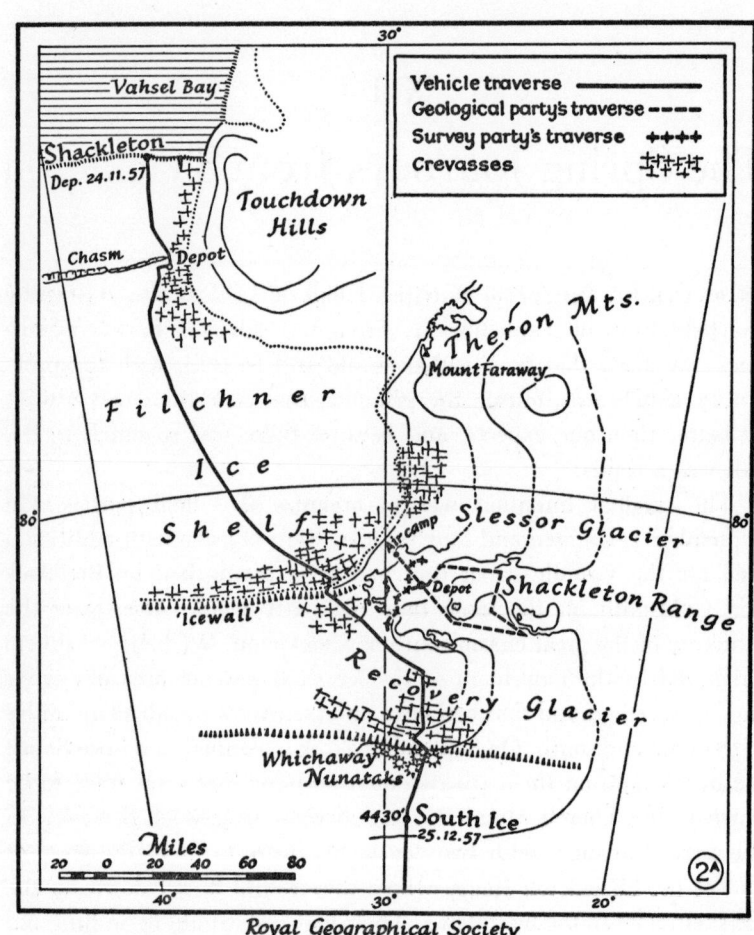

Shackleton to South Ice (Ground Party).

the most severe conditions. The mean temperature was −35°F and the mean wind speed 20 mph. Although the lowest temperature was −67°F and the highest wind 63 mph, the most testing time occurred when we experienced a combination of −60°F and a wind of 37 mph. Choosing the better weather periods, we began to dig away the large drifts which had formed around the Otter, and by the 28th it stood clear of snow, in a wide pit eight feet deep with the bottom shelving to the surface beyond the tail. After some experiment, and with considerable labor, it was hauled to the surface by a Sno-cat and then drawn to a level place near the aircraft workshop. Throughout this operation the temperature remained between −50°F and −53°F, which made shoveling snow a rather more attractive occupation than the manipulation of tow ropes and shackles.

On September 1 the temperature was again −60°F, which was unsuitable for the start of our first vehicle journey. By the 4th it had risen to −40°F, but the wind was then blowing at 45 mph, enveloping the area in driving drift. Already we were four days behind schedule and it was clear that the preliminary seven-day journey to the 50-mile depot would have to be abandoned. The weather also made it impossible for Peter Weston to work on the Otter, and it seemed more and more certain that the relief of South Ice could not take place until October.

To enable Peter to prepare the small Auster plane, over the engine we erected a tent in which he could work regardless of the weather conditions. Everyone else was busy digging out sledges which had been drifted over, making up steel wire and Terylene safety ropes for the vehicles, mending tents, making dog harnesses, digging up stores to last until our departure in November and, most important, training the dogs after their long period underground.

Then suddenly, on September 17, we received bad news. Joe McDowall, deputy leader at Halley Bay, told us by radio that Robin Smart, their leader and medical officer, had fallen and received internal injuries. At first he had attempted to treat himself and had refused to call for assistance, knowing that it might hinder our program. Now McDowall had taken it upon himself to ask Allan Rogers for advice. As Smart needed urgent medical attention, and the Auster was almost ready to fly, I decided to send Allan to Halley Bay at the first break in the weather. Two days later conditions had improved sufficiently for a test flight and on the 20th he took off with Gordon Haslop, in brilliant sunshine, to make the two and a half hour flight to the Royal Society Base.

Five hours later David Stratton and I returned from a dog training run to hear that the plane had not arrived at Halley Bay and was still in the air. John Lewis was talking to Gordon, who reported that it was getting dark and that he could not see the colored lights put out by the Royal Society Base. Believing he had overshot it, he had already turned back and had been flying south for some time. He had decided to land while there was still sufficient light, and we told him to come down on the ice shelf, as close to the edge as possible, so that if a search became necessary, we would only have to follow the coast to find him. As he went down he reported that he only had sufficient fuel for another hour's flying, and we next heard that he had landed safely on a good surface. Before he closed down to conserve his batteries he acknowledged our message telling him that we would keep radio watch every day from eight o'clock each morning.

Now work on the Otter had to begin in earnest. That evening we divided into day and night shifts, and at the same time I told Captain Ronne at Ellsworth what had happened. He and his chief pilot, Commander McCarthy, offered assistance as soon as their plane could be brought to readiness and test flown. From then onwards, day after day, either the wind blew or whiteout conditions prevailed; certainly no flying was possible.

We worked throughout the 24 hours, and by September 29 the Otter was ready — the drift inside the wings had been melted out, the engines had been run, and the rudder replaced. We only needed a short period of suitable flying weather.

That morning Gordon called us again, to say that he and Allan were well but "feeling short of food" (they were living on RAF survival rations of about 700 calories a day) and he wanted to know what the weather was like at Halley Bay. We had to tell him that visibility was too bad for flying, but added that we were standing by to look for them as soon as conditions improved. That evening the Otter was test flown, but low cloud limited its ceiling to 500 feet and its range to within two or three miles of the base.

On the 30th, the weather report from Halley Bay encouraged us to make an attempt. Just as the Otter was ready to leave, Captain Ronne arrived, having flown from Ellsworth in bad conditions and bringing a special drug for the treatment of the patient at the Royal Society Base. He and Commander McCarthy were still with us when John Lewis and David Stratton took off, heading into the dark and murky sky that still brooded over the ice to the northeast. Soon they flew into icing conditions and found it impossible to climb above the cloud, while visibility dropped to a few hundred yards. Forced down by icing, unable to see through the snow squalls, they were soon iceberg-hopping at 50 feet, with a maximum speed of 75 knots on full throttle, while startled penguins peered anxiously up at the plane. As these dangerous conditions developed, John turned back, sweeping west over the Weddell Sea to avoid further icing on the return journey. To his urgent query about weather conditions at base we could send a comforting reply, for our sky was cloudless, with the sun a golden orb such as we had not seen for many months.

That night we had a number of radio schedules with Halley Bay to ensure that we had a completely up-to-date weather situation for flying in the morning. At Shackleton it was overcast with whiteout and icing up to 2000 feet all along the route almost to Halley Bay. There conditions were expected to improve, so John and David set off once more with the intention of flying at 5000 feet — above the icing and below a higher cloud layer. Two hours and twenty minutes later they were circling over Halley Bay. Before landing they searched for 70 miles to the south, then went down to refuel before setting off north to the area where we had calculated the Auster had come down.

Beyond Halley Bay the aircraft was radio-controlled from the Royal Society Base, but we, too, could hear the exchanges. It seemed no time before John was reporting that he had picked up the Auster's SARAH beacon and, a few minutes later, that he could see a small black speck on the ice.

Soon he was safely down and the Auster was being refueled. Fifty minutes later both planes were airborne and on their way to Halley Bay, where they landed at a quarter to seven that evening. A few minutes later John and David were telling us at Shackleton that both

Gordon and Allan, though thinner, were "in good fighting trim." It was not until they all returned to Shackleton that we heard the full story.

They had been wearing thick down clothing and had with them single lightweight sleeping bags, RAF survival rations for three weeks and enough paraffin to have a "brew-up" first thing in the morning and last thing at night. This only allowed them a pint and a half of fluid a day so they became very thirsty, and living on meager rations precluded them from taking much exercise to keep warm. The first evening they dug a hole in the snow, as Gordon put it, "about the size of a two-man coffin," using a sheath knife and their hands. This took them nearly six hours, then the top was roofed with the engine cover from the aircraft and they settled down to a cramped and uncomfortable night, shivering a good deal and sleeping intermittently. As the days passed, their hole was gradually enlarged until they could stand up in comfort. By the end of the week there was a ledge down each side on which they slept, another across one end on which the Primus stood, and they had cut shelves and niches in the walls for their belongings. As the blizzards continued, the aircraft had constantly to be dug free of snowdrifts and kept facing into wind, and to assist a search party they marked out a runway with slabs of ice and fluorescent dye.

Meanwhile nature had worked a miraculous cure on Robin Smart, and when after twelve days the aircraft arrived safely at Halley Bay, he went down to the airstrip wondering if he would find himself with two patients to look after. As Allan got out there was some uncertainty as to who should treat whom, but the visitors, with impressive restraint, still had intact what their host described as "a bottle of a preparation calculated to hasten recovery." — and as they thawed out with the brandy the doctors agreed that they were both in the best of spirits.

The weather prevented the planes from returning to Shackleton until October 4, but now we were again able to turn our eyes to the south and began final preparations for the departure of the South Ice reconnaissance party, which was to consist of David Pratt, Geoffrey Pratt, Roy Homard and myself, with three Weasels and one Sno-cat.

Owing to the continually bad weather conditions and the time spent by all members of the base in making ready the Otter, we were now even more behind with our preparations, particularly for the main journey in November, but Robin Smart very kindly agreed that two of his men should come down to Shackleton for a few weeks to provide additional manpower. Accordingly, on October 5, John Lewis and Ralph Lenton flew to Halley Bay, collected Ivor Beney and Fred Morris, returning the same day. Geoffrey Pratt took this opportunity to send the Worden gravimeter with them to be checked for "drift" at the point where he had established a gravity value in early January.

At last, on October 8, the Otter flew to relieve South Ice, the first personal contact we had had with them since March 25. On that flight Allan Rogers and Fred Morris replaced Ken Blaiklock and Jon Stephenson, leaving Hal Lister for a few days longer to hand over the station before he himself flew to Shackleton.

Late on the same day the vehicle party finally left on the reconnaissance journey to South Ice. The vicissitudes of our long journey are described in a later chapter, but while we were slowly feeling our way over the ice shelf, other work was taking place. Only two days after our departure a first attempt to fly the dog teams to the Shackleton Range was defeated by whiteout conditions near the mountains, and they had to turn back. David Stratton, Ken Blaiklock, Jon Stephenson and George Lowe, together with two teams, the "Black and Tans" and the "Number Twos," made up the party.

The object of this journey was threefold. First they were to find a route up the "ice wall" which extended from the western extremity of the Shackleton Range and blocked the line of advance of the vehicle party which was already moving across the crevassed ice shelf from the north. Secondly, a survey party, with one dog team, would work along the range to its eastern extremity, which had been seen during an Otter flight in the autumn, and, if possible, return on the opposite side of the mountains. Lastly, Stephenson would determine the most profitable area for geology and concentrate his work there.

Those taking part in this spring dog journey were both excited and expectant, as the trip could well prove to be the only occasion on which the surveyors and geologist could have the satisfaction of working in a hitherto unexamined region of alpine topography. We expected that if the polar plateau inland from South Ice did reveal mountains during the crossing of the continent, they would probably be vestigial, in the form of nunataks, with comparatively easy snow and ice slopes between rocky hills. It was true that on the far side of the continent our proposed route would take us to the Victoria Land mountains, but there Hillary's field parties would have already covered the area in much greater detail than we could attempt in the time available.

February 1957 had seen two Otter flights across the Shackleton Range at the time when our primary concern was to find a safe inland route onto the polar plateau. From these reconnaissance trips and the many flights made to establish South Ice, we had some general knowledge of the form and extent of the range. The mountains reached roughly 100 miles in an east-west direction at a point 200 miles inland from Shackleton. They were noticeably grouped around two central massifs at the western and eastern extremities. A number of small valley glaciers flowed down from these two central uplands which were connected by a snow pass estimated from the aircraft to lie between 4000 and 6000 feet. A rocky escarpment formed the greater part of the northern side of the mountains, with some outlying nunataks standing between it and the Slessor Glacier. On the southern side, which received less warmth from the sun, the mountains were more heavily glaciated and bounded by the wide Recovery Glacier. The highest peaks were thought to lie about 1000 to 2000 feet above the high snow pass between the two massifs, while the foot of the western extension fringed the Filchner Ice Shelf at a height of about 500 feet.

The decision to airlift the two teams and men stemmed from the need to save time and to spare the dogs many unproductive miles before the working area was reached. Indeed, even if the dogs had moved into the range over the ground, they would have required an airlift to supply them before they could begin working in the mountains. From previous experience we knew that the husky's efficiency and endurance were impaired over long journeys if he was expected to pull more than 120 pounds, and for this reason the comfortable endurance of a two-team four-man party was about thirty days.

The abortive flight on October 10 at least gave some practice at loading the aircraft with the twelve-foot Nansen sledge, ten dogs and the food and equipment for two men for thirty days. They were happy to find that the dogs readily took to air travel, and if at least inveterate enemies were parted by a box or two, they were fairly certain that peace would reign in the big cabin of the Otter. However, dog drivers have seen too many fights to be anything but disillusioned, so to make assurance trebly sure one "steward" was perched on top of the sledge, neck doubled up against the cabin roof, surrounded by his passengers. Then the cabin heater was turned full on to ensure that they were at least as somnolent as possible. These precautions were successful, and once John Lewis had accepted the fact that the lead dog, Nanok, intended to breathe encouragingly down the back of his neck throughout the flight, all was quiet.

October 11 turned out to be a perfect cloudless spring day with little wind and the temperature at −9°F. At eleven o'clock the Otter took off with George Lowe, David Stratton and the Black and Tans. Some thirty miles south of Shackleton they flew over the vehicle party which had left base on the 8th, and Stratton admits to some feelings of superiority on the part of the dog drivers in the plane, although this was tinged with sympathy for the predicament of those below, where one Weasel sledge could be seen jammed in a crevasse. The flight was uneventful and on arrival at the "Ice Wall" the Otter circled over this formidable obstacle, then flew across to the western rock outcrops of the Shackleton Range to see once more if a better surface route might exist close under the cliffs.

The plane then flew nine miles to the northeast, toward a likely landing place below a rocky 3000-foot pyramid-shaped peak which made a convenient landmark for any future flights. There Lewis brought the Otter down on a frozen melt-water lake below the peak, which provided a safe but bumpy landing place.

The dogs came to life at once, and after an undignified scuffle over the honor of disembarking first, they were safely picketed on a rope span. In the process poor George was nipped and, having had only two runs with the dogs, when he had already been bitten once, was feeling rather disenchanted with huskies. With better luck two bites would normally be reckoned about two years' ration for most dog drivers, for accidents of this nature seldom occur save from time to time when breaking up a dog fight. After an hour on the ground the plane had been unloaded and took off at once for Shackleton. If possible the second flight, with the remaining dog team and two more men, was to be made on the same day, since at this latitude aircraft could operate all night by the light of the midnight sun.

A suitable site for the camp was found 800 yards from the frozen lake and some 300 feet higher up on a small level expanse of snow. From then on this was known as the Air Camp. When the dogs had been fed, the humans were free to walk across to the moraines below the rocky peak and to enjoy the thrill of being on solid rock for the first time since leaving the subantarctic island of South Georgia the previous December. By midnight the sky had become overcast and cloud obscured the tops of the higher peaks: clearly the second flight must have been canceled. These overcast conditions prevailed throughout the next day, and it was not until the afternoon of the 13th that the Otter landed with Gordon Haslop "up," carrying Ken Blaiklock and Jon Stephenson with the Number Twos. The four men at the Air Camp were now in the happy position of being self-contained with supplies for forty days.

On the following day the party split, with the intention that Blaiklock and Stratton should proceed to the "ice wall" to reconnoiter a route to the top, while Stephenson and Lowe did some local geology until their return. Ten miles out the survey party ran into an area of cone-shaped ice hummocks with associated crevasses, but they experienced no difficulty in crossing them and by camping time had run sixteen miles to a position just below the "ice wall," where, for the first time, there appeared to be a possible route between two areas of incipient icefall.

The next day was overcast with whiteout conditions, but they were able to travel up a gully to the top of the "ice wall" some 700 feet above the ice shelf. Stratton's diary states:

> . . . ran towards the "ice wall" and soon started to climb in virtually no visibility, having stumbled on a gulley up the front. Terrain rather similar to the ice front at base, but rather more well-bridged crevasses . . . depoted the dog pemmican at the summit and re-

turned to camp, a run of 9½ miles. We have proved the route an easy one for dogs, but need some visibility now to flag the best line for the vehicles; I believe with care they can make it quite comfortably.

On October 16 whiteout made travel impossible, and the only activity was a rammsonde measurement. During the night periodic creaks and rumbles beneath their tent denoted the movement of the ice. When, on the 17th, the sky cleared, a better route was found and marked with red and black trail pennants up the "ice wall," and the more treacherous-looking crevasses were marked with red and white checkered flags, with certain frivolous and possibly encouraging messages attached to them: "If you throw a six you can jump this one."

The surface was hard and fast, conditions which unfortunately did not obtain when the vehicles finally arrived, owing to a recent snowfall. The larger crevasses had sunken bridges, but they appeared to be immensely thick and the men became convinced that this was the best route in the area. From the summit they followed a course of 125°M toward the rock wall of the Shackleton Range, because air reconnaissance had shown that an impassable area lay immediately to the south. The next four miles were unpleasant as the track ran generally parallel to the long line of crevasses which followed the trend of the "ice wall," but from that point the crevasses became fewer and some nineteen miles from the foot of the "ice wall" they were able to terminate the marked route with a large snow cairn surmounted by a flag.

The party returned to the Air Camp having checked and rejected the possibility of a safer route close to the rock cliffs where they collected some geological specimens. At the camp, where much work remained to be done, Taffy Williams had been flown in to replace George Lowe so that the latter could proceed with his photographic program elsewhere. It was decided that all four men should move in company to the head of the glacier extending eastward from the camp into the western massif of the Shackleton Range. Somewhere on the névé of this glacier a depot would be laid, and both parties would rendezvous there at a given date to await the arrival of the Otter to take them to South Ice. To guard against the possibility of an accident to the aircraft, the depot was sited on the direct overland route, via the Recovery Glacier and the Whichaway Nunataks, and from this point, if necessary, the dog teams would have sufficient endurance to do the journey unaided.

By the end of the day they had moved 10 miles and climbed 1200 feet up the glacier, with the dogs pulling well to move a total payload of one ton on two sledges. On the evening of October 19 the depot was laid, 25 miles up the glacier in the center of the névé, with two miles of perfect landing surface in all directions. This was to be the rendezvous with the aircraft at noon on October 30. The plan really depended on the ability of the dog parties to communicate with base, the Otter and the vehicle party. Owing to the failure of the short-wave hand-cranking transceivers, communications broke down and base was reduced to transmitting "blind" to the dog sledge parties, in the hope that their messages would be picked up on small battery receivers normally used to obtain time signals. This hope was fulfilled and it was possible to recall the survey party sooner than had been originally expected.

At the depot, which lay at 2800 feet, the two parties split once more as Stephenson was eager to study the rock walls containing the glacier, while the surveyors, Blaiklock and Stratton, wished to map as many of the mountains as possible during the time available. On the 20th the survey party's route lay up a steep, apparently crevasse-free, snow slope between a nunatak at the head of the glacier and an ice fall on the southern side. The passage was made without incident, with dogs and drivers pulling and pushing well. When the time came for a welcome pint of cocoa and four biscuits with butter and marmite, the sledge was on the snow dome which dominated the head of the glacier at some 4500 feet.

This was the first place at which they had enjoyed an unobstructed all-round view since being landed at the Air Camp. On all sides the wonderful alpine scene was almost overwhelming after so many months of the flat featureless ice shelf at Shackleton. The sun, still less than 30° above the horizon, picked out veins and crags of brighter colors in the otherwise dark walls and buttresses of rock far below, while between them the swells and troughs of the glacier were thrown into relief by the long shadows. To the northeast a new glacier lay open to view, its center a broad, white, uncreased ribbon of snow but its edges puckered and crinkled by crevasses where the ribbon had been deflected and held back by the restraining walls of rock. Sixty miles to the north the snowy peak of Mount Faraway was gleaming in the afternoon sunlight, while closer in, on the Slessor Glacier, they could see every feature of the echelon crevasses and pressure ridges. To the east, in the direction of the proposed track, the rock and ice topography appeared higher and wilder, promising to be the most interesting part of the range, while to the south the corrugated central portion of the Recovery Glacier boded ill for the vehicle party. Beyond the Recovery Glacier, the Whichaway Nunataks pointed the way to South Ice; through binoculars the blue ice between the small, rocky peaks reflected the sunlight, and on either side of the nunataks a precipitous snow-clad wall extended as far as the eye could see to east and west — yet another problem for the tractors.

Between October 20 and 22, the survey party traveled some 60 miles along the southern side of the Shackleton Range. At first they moved over an undulating plain on the middle slopes of the range, about 1000 feet above the Recovery Glacier, then the area became more interesting, with re-entrants running up into the mountains. Occasionally they were forced down onto the Glacier to pass rocky ridges, while sometimes it was possible to make short cuts over the snow passes which lay behind them. To the delight of the dogs, some of these short cuts led to descents steeper and more rapid than had been expected, for the dogs have the very human trait of getting at least some sort of pleasure out of a really good crisis, and enjoyed the tangled confusion which resulted.

The weather was perfect for survey: clear skies, little wind, and the temperature between $-5°F$ and $-15°F$; they also had the chance to make collections from some of the rock walls. By this time both dogs and men were very fit, and it was difficult to tell who was enjoying themselves the most as they ran or skied over the hard, fast surfaces. The only two irritants were the constant failure to contact either base or the vehicle party by radio, and the foreboding that there might be too little time to do justice to the mountains.

Early on October 22 they ran past several miles of a sheer rock wall which terminated to the east in a prominent point to which they gave the descriptive name of "Ram Bow Bluff," then on below a snow col between the eastern and western parts of the Shackleton Range. Ahead lay a wonderfully impressive mountain mass of some complexity, and incomparably more dominating than the western massif. The camp that night was a busy one as they measured a 1000-foot base line and observed from both ends of it to secure as much detail as possible of the distant mountains.

Working conditions were slow because the temperature had dropped to −40°F with a fresh breeze, and observing into the wind meant frostbitten cheeks and fingers. On returning to the tent they made one more abortive radio schedule, and, rather unusually, on this occasion they were not even able to hear base on their battery receiver. That night there was an almost total eclipse of the sun, the glacier and slopes of the mountains being bathed in a spectral blue light, but, strangely, the dogs were quite unconcerned by the sudden and unexpected onset of darkness.

The following morning, at my request, Shackleton broadcast a general recall to the dog parties telling them to go to the Air Camp, for the vehicle party had been so badly held up by crevasses on the Filchner Ice Shelf that every available man was required at base to prepare the remaining tractors and equipment for the main journey.

At three o'clock, after completing a sun-sight and a rammsonde measurement, the survey party turned away from the eastern mountains to reach the summit of the pass between the two massifs at 4750 feet. They planned to make the best speed possible along the northern slopes back to the Air Camp, and at the same time do as much survey and geology as the terrain permitted.

Next day a new panorama of mountains lay before them as they descended from the pass. Fortunately, only one sudden detour was required to avoid a very steep and heavily crevassed slope, so that their main concern lay with the leading dogs, which were reluctant to proceed on a straight course, or, sometimes, to proceed at all. This hesitation was due to a frequent and peculiar booming noise as they moved down the slopes and the upper layers of snow subsided with the vibration of the sledge's approach. This is a well-known phenomenon in certain snow structures and temperature conditions, but it was impossible to reassure the dogs with a scientific explanation. On this occasion Nanok, with many a reproachful backward look, refused to obey most of the driving orders.

The camp site that night was beside a nunatak about 1500 feet below the pass, and from its summit a rough line could be chosen for the intended traverse of the next two days. They decided to follow the line of the rock and ice wall of the range to the west, until they found the glacier which had been seen extending toward the northeast during the lunch halt on the 20th. It had then appeared to be unbroken along its median line and would lead them back to the depot where the two parties had separated.

Another day saw them 17 miles farther on, having sometimes gained height, sometimes lost it, as they dodged the many outlying nunataks and more dangerous-looking crevassed slopes. Their camp on the 25th lay beneath the southwest ridge of a distinctive table mountain, which had always been referred to as "Flat Top" during the aircraft flights. The mountain lay foursquare at the confluence of three glaciers, with its steep rocky cliffs rising 1000 to 2000 feet out of the valley. It was a two-hour climb from the tent, with a short pitch of step-cutting, before they reached the summit, which they found to be a gently undulating plain of frost-shattered boulders. Resisting the temptation to fill their pockets with rocks, they made their descent down a steep *couloir* in ten minutes — to the detriment of their windproof trousers.

During the following two days they found the glacier leading back to the depot, which they collected, leaving only five days' rations to cover any emergency need of the geological party. At the Air Camp they found Gordon Haslop and George Lowe whom I had called forward with the Auster in close support of the vehicle party. These two were full of news and local gossip, the latter always of great interest to sledge parties as in the field one's thoughts tend to become parochial and focused on the work in hand.

From them the survey party heard that the day before Jon Stephenson had mysteriously appeared out of the mountains on skis. The geological party's receiver had failed, and they had heard no word of the general recall to base, nor of the arrival of the Auster.

Then, while working near the summit of a peak some ten miles from the Air Camp, they were amazed to see the plane taking off farther down the glacier. At once they decided to investigate. Having gleaned all the news, Jon had been flown back to Taffy Williams and the dog team in the mountains. As none of them knew where the survey party was and thought they might also have had complete radio failure, Jon and Taffy started for the rendezvous depot at the head of the glacier intending to leave a message there.

The surveyors also heard of the "pond weed" which had been discovered in the frozen lake below the camp. It appeared to be a large leaf like algal growth, frozen into the ice and an attempt was made to preserve some of this strange plant which they thought had not been previously recorded in the Antarctic.

The morning of October 28 was overcast with low cloud, but by midday the cloud base lifted to just below the higher summits, so David Stratton decided to fly up the glacier and turn back the geological party who were still laboriously working their way to the depot at 2800 feet. Gordon made a difficult take-off from the landing strip, which had been transformed by the sun of the last fortnight, the smooth snow surface on the frozen lake having melted to leave a succession of shallow ice ridges. A quarter of an hour later the plane appeared over Jon and Taffy, much to their discomforture, for, while their attention was distracted, they, together with dogs and sledge, plunged over a steep snow bank about 200 feet high extending from a nearby nunatak. A confusion of dogs, men and sledge rolled down the slope to within a few yards of the bottom. At the same moment the Auster landed close by, and David Stratton was in time to run across and help right the sledge. Both the occupants of the plane felt that this was surely the acme of "gamesmanship."

But the dog party were to have the last laugh. Five minutes later, after telling Jon and Taffy about the general recall, Gordon taxied away to begin his take-off toward the nunataks. In this way he had the advantage of a horizon and avoided the whiteout conditions in the center of the glacier. Taffy Williams was also stationed as a marker 50 yards ahead. With an upward slope and two men on board, all was not well and the account in David Stratton's diary reads:

. . . it was soon obvious that we were not going to be able to gain sufficient height to clear the snow and ice ridge by the side of the nunatak, and sure enough we gave the crest a number of good heavy glancing blows, then fluttered down into the hollow which presented itself on the other side. Unfortunately this was neither deep nor long enough to allow us to gain flying speed and full control, and it became apparent that we were bumping and boring into the wind-scoop by the side of the nunatak, with a 200-foot ice wall at the head of it. At this point Gordon took the only possible course — cut his engine, and we bumped and slithered along a surface of bare ice, luckily on not too steep a slope, but on the side of the wind-scoop, running parallel to the rock wall. It seemed to take an interminable time to reduce speed, and as we did so a boulder appeared right ahead. Hard-a-port meant descent onto the rocky scree ten yards to our left, and hard-a-starboard meant ascending the side of the windscoop. Gordon chose the latter, and as we made a violent lurch up the hill, the tail ski jammed in a small meltwater crack and was torn off, bringing us to an abrupt halt. . . .

Fortunately the occupants were safe enough, but over the ridge behind them Jon Stephenson and Taffy Williams were having a very anxious time, for they had seen the plane hit the ridge, then disappear without any further sight or sound. Racing to the top of the slope, they were relieved to see it safely, but precariously, perched like a fly on the steep wall of the windscoop.

Happily radio conditions were good, and using the Auster's set, Gordon was able to talk direct to base and arrange for the Otter to fly Peter Weston up with spares. Before all four started off with the dogs for the Air Camp, they picketed the Auster safely and marked out a runway for the Otter. The visibility was soon reduced to a few hundred yards as the weather deteriorated, but in three hours they reached the camp and were able to reassure Ken Blaiklock and George Lowe, who had had no means of knowing what had happened.

Next day, October 29, Ken Blaiklock and David Stratton left with the Black and Tans to intercept our vehicle party at the "Ice Wall" in order to discuss the future program. Ken drove back with Roy Homard, leaving David with us.

When the Auster had been repaired, the Air Camp was closed, but first the Otter carried Jon and Ken, with both dog teams, to South

Ice. Then returning with Allan Rogers and Fred Morris, it picked up the Air Camp stores and a considerable weight of rock specimens to be taken back to Shackleton. When the results are finally assessed, the geology and survey accomplished will show this to have been a successful combined operation between air and ground parties.

X I I I

The Route to South Ice

WHILE THE DOG TEAMS were working among the mountains of the Shackleton Range, the vehicle party had been moving steadily, if slowly, southward on what was to prove the worst part of our entire journey across the continent. I had always expected to find difficulty in climbing from Shackleton to the inland ice sheet, but the actual problems we had to overcome were far greater than we could possibly have envisaged.

Leaving Shackleton in the evening of October 8, we traveled only six miles before camping, but at least we were away from base and no more last-minute requirements would delay the start next morning. Our hopes of a rapid advance were doomed to disappointment — only a mile and a half after leaving camp the first mechanical trouble hit us. A track top guide roller on Roy Homard's Weasel broke away and jammed between track and sprocket, bending the axle. By eleven o'clock that night we had almost finished removing and replacing the track, but it could only be a temporary repair, and by noon the next day a very disappointed Roy was on his way back to base. He even talked of straightening the axle and then catching us up.

On the third day, as we continued over the undulating waves of the ice shelf, I found myself driving on an unusually rough, upward slope, and began to suspect the existence of crevasses. Near the crest it was quite apparent that I was climbing over a succession of them, but I could only continue steadily and hope to reach firm ground beside two crossed flags which had come into sight over the top of the ridge. These had been put down by Ken Blaiklock and Rhino Goldsmith to mark the first group of wide filled chasms, and we examined the open marginal cracks of each crevasse before deciding it was safe enough to bring the other vehicles across.

163

None of us then had any idea how thick a snow-bridge should be to bear a Weasel, Sno-cat or sledge. We were to learn by degrees in the coming weeks, and if at first we were a little foolhardy, we later made up for it by infinite patience and sensitive assessment, based on earlier mistakes.

As we approached the dog party's "Corner Flag Camp," where they had turned south, we had already entered a wide area of small crevasses hidden beneath the snow. Only four miles to the east lay the wide belt of fractures along the foot of the southern Touchdown Hills. Remembering what I had seen from the air on our many flights, I thought we were fortunate indeed to be crossing this area with so little trouble, for it was virtually a complex of bridge crevasses and open holes, covered with a carpet of snow.

As we made good speed of about 8 mph, the Weasels bucking over the rough surface, narrow holes appeared every few yards where the tracks broke the small crevasse bridges. Periodically we examined these and always found them narrow and harmless, but our rising feeling of confidence was soon curbed. The surface visibility had been deteriorating and I was telling myself that I really ought to stop; then, suddenly, a small dark hole appeared about thirty yards ahead and to the right. As I gazed at this, and tried to determine whether there was any connection between it and the white ridge a little way ahead, my Weasel gave an uncomfortable sinking lurch, went on for a moment, then stopped abruptly with the 2½-ton sledge tilted sideways through the broken bridge of a crevasse.

Until a few moments before the others had been following close behind, and I climbed out thinking they would be there to help, but soon saw that they, too, were in trouble a quarter of a mile back. Returning on skis I found that a bridge which I had safely crossed had collapsed under David Pratt's Weasel. Luckily his speed had carried both Weasel and sledge across, leaving a gaping hole five feet wide. After some discussion, Geoffrey Pratt drove his Sno-cat containing all his seismic equipment over, and both vehicles then followed me toward my own Weasel. Keeping a radio schedule with base one evening, Geoffrey had identified himself as "Hallo, Shackleton — this is Haywire calling." From that moment the seismic Sno-cat, which he drove right across the continent, was always known as "Haywire."

Here and there small holes had broken open along the line of my tracks and while I was examining each as I came to it David's Weasel slewed sideways and fell with one track into a crevasse that I had not even seen. One of the greatest troubles was our inability to recognize a crevasse on the surface because the usual warning depressions were covered by a windcrust which gave a smooth comfortable look to the whole area.

Faced with our first recovery problem, we were lucky that Roy Homard, remembering his experiences in Greenland, had fixed metal brackets onto the sides of each Weasel. We passed a rope from the Sno-cat over the top of the Weasel and shackled it to these brackets and then hauled the Weasel into an upright position, with the fallen track still hanging over the abyss. Finally, using my vehicle (which had already been recovered from its lesser predicament), the front was towed slightly to one side until David could drive clear on the one track still resting on firm snow. By one o'clock in the morning we had also managed to extract my sunken sledge and had radioed to John Lewis at Shackleton asking for the Auster next day. Clearly, with three near-catastrophes in 300 yards, it was time to extricate ourselves from the area, and to do so safely required air reconnaissance. To strengthen our party I had also asked Roy to rejoin us.

Next day while awaiting the plane's arrival I skied ahead along the line of our course and found a continuous series of large and small crevasses, the most dangerous being those of characteristic oval shape which were almost all completely, but thinly, covered. Inspection of one open hole revealed a huge chasm formed by the conjunction of a number of crevasses running in different directions. Although none of them had marginal cracks, careful examination of the surface revealed countless shallow basins which proved to be the lids over the wider parts.

During the morning John Lewis and Roy Homard arrived, the Auster homing onto our SARAH beacon and coming down on a flagged strip 100 yards long. We had had difficulty finding a safe stretch and even in that distance the landing was made at right angles across eight crevasses.

Flying over the area with John, I could see that we were heading into a really bad patch and that our only course was to withdraw to the 50-mile depot, then strike west for about four miles through the narrowest part of the crevassed area, before turning south once more.

At our camp we could hear incessant noise due to movement of the ice below. In one crevasse the staccato metallic sound of breaking ice made us liken it to two men building a metal shed in the dark depths beneath. Another, about five feet from our tents, was even louder, sounding as though boilermakers were at work. We noticed that while at night there were a few sudden cracks, the hammering increased rapidly with the rising sun, to reach a crescendo in the middle of the day, then gradually to lessen and cease by the later afternoon.

We had now only to strike camp, turn the sledges round, rope the vehicles together, using Terylene safety lines with a breaking strain of 15 tons, and retire to the depot. Being encompassed on all sides by crevasses made this a long and laborious task, involving endless probing of the surface to establish safe areas where the vehicles had sufficient room to maneuver. At last all was safely accomplished and we began our first attempt at driving the vehicles roped together like climbers on a mountain. From the rear of each Weasel a double steel wire rope passed under the sledge behind, to be attached to 65 feet of 3-inch Terylene rope linked with the front of the next vehicle. This served as a safety rope for any tractor falling into a crevasse, and also allowed the leading vehicle to aid the one behind it if the power of the latter was insufficient to pull out of a difficult place.

Driving roped together presents its own problems, for the rope must not be so taut as to restrict the rapid acceleration of the man in front, nor must it be loose on the surface to be run over and snapped by the tracks of the following vehicle — it is even possible for a rope to break a track. Later we were to acquire very considerable skill in "roped driving" but on this occasion our maximum speed was 3½ mph. Finally we arrived back at the depot without further mishap and the nightly refueling was carried out at −35°F. Needless to say we were glad to climb into our sleeping bags when it was done.

Because of high drift it was not possible to start off on our new course next day, but on October 15, although there was a complete whiteout, the drift had ceased. Knowing that time was short, but yet unwilling because conditions were still unsuitable, we set off on a course of 300°M which would take us across the general trend of the crevasses at a reasonable angle. It also ensured that we would clear by a considerable margin an immense open hole which I had seen from the air. After two miles I judged we were beyond it and turned to 270°M for four miles before directing our course to the south once more. By then I was sure that we were clear of the disturbed area; it was not until the main journey, late in November, that I was to realize how lucky we had been in avoiding more trouble.

By the evening, in spite of poor conditions and a stop to repair a fractured oil pipe on David's Weasel, we had traveled 25 miles. The following day there was again no visible horizon but we ploughed on, on a slightly more westerly course (150°M) to make sure of avoiding any disturbance of the ice shelf caused by the great Slessor Glacier moving into it from the east. After ten miles a slight tick that had been apparent in my Weasel engine was noticeably increasing and proved to be a "run" big-end on No. 2 piston. This was rather disastrous, for we could not reasonably turn back now and even in a workshop the repair might take three days, for such a job requires the removal of the entire engine. After much cogitation and discussion we decided to short-circuit the plug and drive on for as long as the engine lasted. If it went completely, we would then consider flying out a spare from Shackleton. My load was lightened by filling all tanks and half-empty barrels on the other sledges and we abandoned three fuel drums to act as a depot for our next run. At this time our position by the compass traverse was 79°00'S, 37°40'W.

Setting off again with the damaged Weasel limping ahead, we traveled another 30 miles, making a total of 40 miles for the day, over a surface that had become gradually rougher and more undulating. Another 37 miles next day began to give a more encouraging average, but still there was no visibility and it was only on the third evening that at last we saw sunlit mountains of the Shackleton Range in the distance.

All day the Weasels had been laboring through soft snow that hid hard sastrugi running across our course. These made the vehicles and sledges heave and plunge like small ships at sea, their tracks churning out a spray of snow. In contrast, the Sno-cat sailed majestically, like a battleship over the snowy waves, its four independently articulated tracks accommodating the rough ridges below the snow.

During the day Gordon Haslop had flown over in the Otter on his way first to South Ice, and then to the dog teams in the Shackleton Range where he picked up George Lowe and flew over to us, bringing thicker oil for my engine and a toothbrush and diary for Roy Homard.

As two U bolts on David's Weasel had broken, we had determined to spend the next day in repair and maintenance. Typically contrary, the weather became fine and clear, but David and Roy found work on the springs uncomfortable in a temperature of $-28°F$. During the day Geoffrey and I laid out the seismic equipment and fired four separate shots to determine the thickness of the ice shelf.

It was also on the morning that we spoke to David Stratton and Ken Blaiklock. They had completed the route reconnaissance of the "ice wall," and were able to give us precise instructions as to course and distances along the track they had flagged. As a result we now had a better idea of where to direct our course in relation to the mountains. We knew that we should soon enter a complex area of crevasses, but although they had been seen from the air their relative position and that of the mountains was only approximately known from our flights, while our own position at the end of a long traverse by dead reckoning could not be more than approximate. We were therefore uncertain when we should encounter the first crevasses.

Suddenly, after traveling 35 miles on the 19th, the vehicles began to break numerous small holes in the surface. David Pratt again found the largest and bounced across to stop with his Weasel on one side and his sledge on the other. This made it a simple matter of disconnecting the sledge, towing it away from the crevasse and hitching up again.

For nine miles we had been descending gently over a gradually improving surface to what seemed a wide area of smooth snow extending to the "ice wall," barring our path some 15 miles to the south. Unfortunately, instead of bringing better conditions, it was the change of surface that marked the advent of the crevasses. Having learned from our previous experience, we withdrew 5 miles along our tracks and turned west for another five, before moving south again in an attempt to avoid the crevassed zone.

This time, as soon as the first crevasse appeared we roped up the vehicles and continued cautiously at 3 mph. Whenever I felt a snow bridge sag beneath my Weasel, I waved to David behind, and he in turn to Geoffrey, each of them moving slightly to one side to cross at a fresh point.

I had decided to halt at 8:15 but, with a minute to go, there was a sudden backward lurch as the Weasel tilted steeply upward, and jerked to a stop. To leave it in gear and turn off the master switch was now automatic; then peering out I found myself suspended over a dark abyss that widened downward in all directions. The Weasel was resting against the edge of the crevasse on its rear flotation tank and was held in that position by the sledge towbar. Only the first bogey and very front of the tracks were lodged on the far side, but I climbed out safely enough after the others had taken the photographs they wanted.

The next move was to probe the whole area and find the shape and extent of the cavern I had revealed. It quickly transpired that although the surface was riddled with small crevasses it was possible to cross the big one fifteen yards to the left. Geoffrey then drove *Haywire* over, together with two sledges, unhitched, and, using a wire rope, hauled the Weasel forward while I lay over the back and held the sledge towbar clear of the towing hook. This left the front of the sledge overhanging the brink of the crevasse, so I drove back, pulled it clear, maneuvered to hitch on again, and rejoined Geoffrey and Roy on the far side. By the time David joined us with his Weasel it was ten o'clock and we decided that we had had enough for one day. Quickly we prodded the snow surface to find secure places for our tents, and settled down for the night.

Very often the recovery of a vehicle was not the time-consuming factor, it was the examination of the surrounding area to give us room to maneuver which took so long. This was particularly the case when all the vehicles and sledges had to be turned round in places where the crevassing was so close that tracks inevitably had to run along the length of a crevasse, instead of at right angles to it. The time taken to turn three vehicles and their sledges round would be perhaps three or four hours, while the actual recovery of the one in trouble would be under half an hour.

Since the previous day we had been having difficult radio conditions and could not convey to Shackleton our urgent need for air reconnaissance. It was possible to continue probing the crevasse belt at intervals of a few miles, but it would only be by chance that we should find a way in the time available. The only alternative was to take severe risks with the crevasses, and, in all probability, lose one or more vehicles.

Reluctant to commit ourselves to what might prove to be an impossible route, without air support, I spent October 21 probing the snow every yard of the way for a mile and a half ahead, marking a possible track around the worst places for a move next day if the plane did not arrive. This was our first attempt to prove a route by probing, the method which was later highly developed and ultimately brought us safely to South Ice.

The 22nd was a beautiful, sunny day with clear sky, visibility 40 miles and temperature −26°F. Unhappily radio communication was at its worst and we made no contact with base. I therefore decided to continue, but little success attended our efforts. In spite of careful probing my leading Weasel broke through within twenty yards, but hauled itself out on the far side. Then, as David pulled to one side to avoid the hole, I went deep into another.

More probing was now necessary before the Sno-cat could pull ahead to tow me out. Everywhere there were endless cracks, all hidden by surface sastrugi, and though the plunging of our poles gave a drumlike sound where there were crevasses, the same noise was made in many places by solid windcrust layers buried beneath the surface. Still inexperienced in our judgment of such conditions, it seemed a hopeless task to force a route for many miles over such country. Great was our relief, therefore, when we made contact with Shackleton early in the afternoon and heard that the weather was good enough for the Auster to fly out to us immediately.

When my Weasel had been recovered, the vehicles and sledges were left where they were until I could decide from the forthcoming flight whether or not we had to turn back. That afternoon John Lewis, having flown the 200 miles from Shackleton, arrived rather cold from sitting in the unheated cockpit, for the outside temperature was −25°F. After stamping around for a few moments to restore circulation, he announced himself ready to go.

Circling over the vehicles, it was immediately apparent that a really bad area lay ahead of us and that the only solution would be to make another attempt elsewhere. Flying east we picked up the end of our previous track and continued to the southeast where a potentially clear route could be seen for a few miles. Then a great belt of crevasses extended in a sweeping curve from the "ice wall" to the heavily broken ridge of ice which formed the northern margin of the Slessor Glacier that pushed out into the ice shelf.

As we flew we could see that the narrowest part of this crevasse belt was ten to eleven miles wide, and that evening I wrote: "If we can break through that belt we have a chance of good going beyond. It will certainly be a tough job and a dangerous one, but if we are to have a trans-Antarctic journey it has to be attempted, and somehow we must be successful."

Flying back to the vehicles, I told John that we should need to set up a close-support Air Camp and that a suitable point seemed to be the site at the foot of the Shackleton Range where the dog parties had been put down. This would be only about 20 miles away from us, and also near enough to assist the dog parties if necessary. With the plane so close, it would be working with us in our weather conditions, instead of relying on the more variable coastal weather 200 miles away.

We refueled the plane and John Lewis left for base with feet colder than ever, while we set about extricating our vehicles and sledges from their existing predicament. This was finished by nine o'clock, when the temperature was −40°F, and we were all glad to pitch our tents in almost the same place as the previous night. That morning we had moved 50 yards forward — in the evening 100 yards back!

Next morning, when we started our return trek with all three vehicles roped together for the first six miles, the temperature was up to −30°F. I am not sure whether it is more pleasant to rumble back over the gaping holes one has previously left behind, or to break new ground, wondering when the next sickening lurch will herald a new discovery. It was David Pratt who said that it reminded him of driving a tank over a mine field, except that in this case you were waiting for something to go down!

Apart from a few small break-throughs, we made easy progress back to the junction with our old track to the south. There, turning onto a course of 110°M, we continued unroped, for the previous day's flight had shown safe going for several miles.

After five miles there was an indefinable change of surface, and two miles farther on a gray streak appeared across our path in the lowering sun. Stopping a few yards short, I went forward to probe the surface, and found an apparently well-filled crevasse. But it was impossible to estimate the thickness of its bridge, and hearing from base that the proposed Air Camp would be established that evening, I determined not to commit us to possible trouble ahead until a flight had confirmed that this was the best place for our passage. In my journal I wrote: "In my opinion the next ten miles are going to make or break the expedition, for we may well lose vehicles over the ground close ahead. With crash helmets, safety straps and roped vehicles we have taken all the precautions we can."

Before pitching the tents, we inspected the ground and in one place David Pratt dug a large hole through the lid of a shallow crevasse and rather unwisely lowered himself down inside, leaving his scarlet crash helmet on the snow. No one was with him at the time for we were speaking on the radio. Turning round and seeing the helmet, I exclaimed, "Good heavens — where's David?" "Oh!" said Roy, "I saw his helmet by that hole a little while ago and wondered where he was — I meant to remark on it, but forgot!"

It may seem that we were getting a little casual about crevasses, but in our vehicles we were only too aware of their presence. To my relief, as we hurried over to the hole David peered up at us waving some beautiful ice crystals he had found on the walls below. Some of these were of unusual size, each side of the hexagonal plates up to 2½ inches long.

In our tent that night David and I listened in to a four-way radio conversation between the two aircraft flying in to establish the Air

Geological camp in the Shackleton Range.

Taffy Williams with dog team in the Shackleton Range.

Evening in the Shackleton Range.

Northwest end of the Shackleton Range. The Air Camp was near the moraine in the middle distance.

Moraine near the Air Camp at the northwest end of the Shackleton Range.

Vehicles passing the western end of the Shackleton Range towards Recovery Glacier.

Sno-cat Rock 'n Roll's first crevasse.

Junction of Mill and Beardmore Glaciers, seen during the transpolar flight.

Camp, Shackleton, and Geoffrey Pratt, who was operating our own transmitter from his Sno-cat. In the morning Gordon Haslop and George Lowe arrived in the Auster, and I went up for a low-level reconnaissance of the surrounding area and then flew on to look at the route up the "ice wall" selected by the survey dog party. The surface ahead looked forbidding, for great, open trenchlike crevasses curved toward one another from the "ice wall" and the Slessor Glacier, while the intervening level stretch over which we hoped to pass was broken by countless thousands of hidden crevasses, revealed only by the basin-shaped depressions we had come to know so well.

Flying over eight or nine miles of smooth snow, we reached the snow cairn which marked the beginning of the route flagged by Stratton and Blaiklock. From a height of over 2000 feet, I was appalled to see that while the track led straight up a relatively gentle slope of the "ice wall" it crossed a complex of filled crevasses of great size. From a lower altitude conditions looked less alarming and, after a close examination of the only alternative route nearer to the mountains, I decided that we must follow our fortunes along the line of little red and black flags that fluttered below.

Clearly the next ten miles would be difficult and we decided to probe the surface every yard to ensure that we found and investigated each hidden crack. In my journal I find: "It has been a very slow task, but some of the monstrous caverns which we have discovered beneath the innocent surface have certainly justified the work. Some of them would have accepted a double-decker bus, and there is no doubt that we should have lost at least one Weasel if we had not spent so much time on the ground. . . . As vehicles rumble over the booming caverns below, it is with a sense of some considerable relief that each driver reaches the far side."

At first the weather was excellent and each day the Auster flew one or other of us low over the area immediately ahead, while George Lowe, accompanying Gordon Haslop from the Air Camp, joined the ground party in their endless probing.

On October 27 there was a whiteout and no flying was possible, nor could we guide our slow advance by the mountains, which were now obscured by cloud. We therefore lined up stakes with a compass and worked toward each other in pairs. Each pair worked side by side, separated by a distance slightly greater than the width of the vehicle tracks. Shuffling forward, each man plunged his wooden or aluminum pole to a depth of five feet every yard, a distance sometimes reduced from a yard to six inches if there was reason to suspect the area. When a crevasse was found the cracks along its edges were opened up at one or more points, so that the nature of the filling could be observed. If it appeared unsafe to cross, a diversion would be made to avoid the dangerous part and to return to the original line of march. Fortunately, the curious wide but short nature of the crevasses made this fairly easy; even so, it was often necessary to probe routes in three or four directions before a safe passage could be found.

Diversions were marked by arrows drawn in the snow some way before the turnoff was reached; or some stakes, flags or ski sticks would draw attention to particular points. Rules of the road were developed, and drivers were always to leave the arrows on flags on their left — all vehicles were left-hand drive — and travel with their tracks within a foot of the markers.

The latest date for our arrival at South Ice was to have been October 28, yet we were then still among the crevasses on the ice shelf, at least 150 miles away. That day we covered 2¼ miles and felt that we were almost clear of the bad area. There was an enormous temptation to get into the vehicles and drive on hoping for the best, but after all the care we had taken in getting ourselves over an area which we believed to be worse than any previously attempted with vehicles, it would have been a pity to make an error in the last stages.

That night we heard from base that there had been an accident to the Auster in the Shackleton Range and we knew that for a time we would have no further air support. Fortunately this was to prove unnecessary, for the very next day we cleared the last of the crevasses and motored steadily for 12 miles over a smooth surface toward the snow cairn marking the beginning of the ascent of the "ice wall."

Intercepting the track half a mile to the west of the cairn, we began to follow the flags over the undulations at the foot of the steep main slope. Before attempting the major climb, we skied upward for about 600 feet to assess the strength of the bridges in the light of our recent experiences. Apart from some soft patches, the route seemed remarkably good, and we returned to the vehicles, already roped up for the climb.

At first all went well, then my Weasel sank in the soft snow until the underneath of the body was resting on the surface and the tracks could get no grip. After much digging and a number of useless attempts to get clear, Geoffrey had to bring forward the Sno-cat to pull me out. Immediately afterwards the same thing happened to David's Weasel. The slope was proving hard on my damaged engine, which had been making more and more ominous noises; so, hitching my sledge as a third behind the Sno-cat, I moved unroped, and crossed a wide crevasse which seemed to mark the top of the "ice wall," there to wait for the others to arrive.

When we first skied up the slope we had noticed a thin white line gradually extending toward us from the east, and could make out a tiny black dot at the head of it, giving the appearance of a plane and its vapor trail far below us. We realized this must be a dog team coming over from the Air Camp 19 miles away.

Waiting at the top of the "ice wall," and keeping a radio schedule with base, I heard dogs out of sight below and knew that they had caught us up. Soon the whole convoy, Weasel, Sno-cat and dogs, appeared over the brow and we decided to camp where we were. That night David Stratton and Ken Blaiklock told us the full story of the Auster's mishap and about their journey of 230 miles in the mountains.

I was becoming concerned about the amount of work which remained to be done at base, where Ralph Lenton and the others were busy preparing stores and material for the main journey, planned to start on November 14. Particularly important was the work on the rest of the vehicles, and it was essential that one of the engineers should return for that purpose. The next day Roy Homard and Ken Blaiklock left with the dog team, to return to the Air Camp from where Roy would fly back to base. David Stratton remained with the vehicles to guide us over the rest of the selected route, to maintain our manpower, and to gain experience of vehicle travel in the field.

Two events made October 30 a bad day. After half a mile my poor Weasel finally stopped with a broken camshaft drive. This meant leaving it behind, together with a sledge and some unwanted

175

material, which involved reloading and relashing our sledges after selecting the essential items we could not abandon. When we moved on, our route led eastward along the line of some very large, heavily bridged crevasses. One of these, about 40 feet wide, was marked with a red and white checkered flag, indicating that it had appeared dangerous to the dog party. But after examination we decided to cross. David's Weasel, now in the lead, sank in the soft snow, so Geoffrey drove across, unhitched his sledges, and returned to pull out the Weasel and its load. My journal tells the sequence:

> While this was being done David S. was standing on the far side, I on the near side of the crevasse, while Geoffrey and David P. were driving. As they moved across I heard a tremendous rumble and the snow beneath me quaked, making me want to move rapidly to some other place, but as I had no idea where the noise originated, I stood where I was. As the vehicle continued to move slowly, I saw a cloud of snow rising in the air from an immense crater which had appeared only six feet to the left of the Weasel. It was about 20 feet across and 40 feet deep, with dark and deep caverns descending to unknown depths. For a long time clouds of snow dust rose from it and drifted away, the whole thing appearing as though a bomb had fallen. The hole was large enough to have swallowed Sno-cat, Weasel, sledge and all, but with amazing good fortune the bridge broke to the left of the vehicles and not under them! After taking photographs we proceeded chastened on our way. . . .

That night the temperature was still low at −32°F, but our evening meal was enhanced when the Otter flew over on its way to South Ice, and dropped four cooked steaks, a welcome variant on the interminable pemmican. John made an excellent shot, the package with its red streamers landing about 10 yards from the Sno-cat.

In the morning we cleared the last of the crevassed zone at the top of the "ice wall," and came to the end of the flagged trail marked by another snow cairn. By this time we were only four miles from the nearest rocks. The mountains were a fine sight — smooth snow slopes, broken by rock ridges, and here and there a face too nearly vertical for the winter snow to remain clinging to it.

Directing our course toward the southwestern corner of the range, we continued unroped for a few miles, then suddenly found that we were crossing a number of very wide and pronounced crevasses.

Looking to the west, we could see that we were far too near to a heavily broken area of the great Recovery Glacier, where it swung round to the north. To the east was another warning — a huge open hole in one of the crevasses that we had already crossed. Very cautiously we moved closer to the mountains, our obvious course of action despite our uncertainty as to the crevassed nature of the ground ahead.

Soon we were traveling within half a mile of the rocky spurs, while all the time the surface rose steeply southward and the vehicles ground along in low gear. As we approached the corner where the rocks turned away to the east, the climb became steeper and we encountered huge sastrugi that rose four or five feet above the general level of the surface. By the evening we had rounded the corner of the range and were ploughing along the south side at an altitude approaching 3000 feet with a temperature of −35°F.

Next day was a maintenance day, largely spent in tightening the Weasel tracks, in greasing and in changing all oils — a cold task in the 10-knot wind. It was not until about five o'clock that we were ready to start. After heading southeast for a few miles we turned south directly across the glacier toward the Whichaway Nunataks, which we hoped every moment would appear over the horizon. On and on we went, topping one rise after another, but always it was a false horizon. Somewhere ahead we knew from air reconnaissance that a great belt of crevasses extended along the length of the glacier, but I had observed that there were one or two places where these appeared to be covered with snow, and it was toward one of these gaps that we were now feeling our way.

On November 2 we continued south for four miles until, 25 miles out on the glacier, we were stopped by a maze of hummocks through which it was clearly going to be very difficult to find a way — or indeed to make any headway at all. Skiing ahead, searching for a route, we found ourselves surrounded by a veritable forest of hummocks up to 15 feet high, while between them a mosaic of crevasses seemed to run in every direction. The whole had a queer "lost world" effect, as though one had suddenly begun to wander in some region of the moon.

Knowing that the Otter was likely to be flying to South Ice, I called Shackleton and asked John to make a reconnaissance of the area and suggest which way we should turn to find the "break" which I had seen from the air the year before. I also suggested that this might be the occasion for the long-distance southern flight which we had planned to investigate the region beyond South Ice as far as 84°S. We then pitched our tents temporarily and awaited the plane. It duly arrived about half past six that evening, and before flying away to South Ice John had advised us to move five miles to the east where there seemed to be a possible route. Later they said that the weather was sufficiently good for them to make the southern flight and that they would be back over us at about one o'clock in the morning, when we could expect another short reconnaissance if we needed it.

Quickly striking the tents, we moved over to the area they had indicated and began a careful examination on skis, only to find that there, too, the ground was heavily crevassed and not at all suitable to our attempt. Deciding to await the return of the aircraft before making any further move, we pitched camp. David Stratton and I were still refueling the vehicles when the Otter flew over at ten minutes past one. As they circled the area, Ken Blaiklock, who was with John Lewis and George Lowe in the plane, said that they could see a much better point still five miles farther to the east. Shortly afterwards John landed and we all had a quick discussion, while Ken handed over the sketch he had made of the crevasse areas we were likely to encounter. As the temperature was below −40°F they were as glad to climb back into the warm aircraft as we were to scramble into our tents at last.

When we arrived at the suggested area the following morning, it seemed far better than the previous places, and we quickly skied forward to investigate the situation. Here the ridge, bearing the chaotic mass of ice hummocks like some gigantic ploughed field, was replaced for a few miles by an elongated basin about 2½ miles wide. At first sight the smooth surface looked easy enough, but soon I was dismayed to find the well-known "basins," or tadpole-shaped depressions, occurring in profusion over the whole area. This threatened much work; and so it proved, for it took five days to force a passage across this narrow belt.

Now that we only had two vehicles left we had to take even greater care, for the loss of one would place us in a very dangerous position, and although the Sno-cat could recover the Weasel, there was little hope of the Weasel helping the "cat" out of a hole.

On the second day we moved forward another half-mile, but the Weasel broke through twice in 100 yards and the second time we very nearly lost it altogether, for it hung precariously lengthwise along a crevasse bridge which had already broken along one side. It was only possible to pull it out along the length of the bridge, and so certain were we that it was going down that every useful item was carefully unloaded before the attempt was made. When at last we were successful, it was a great sight to see David Pratt's beaming face, for it was his Weasel and he had been quite convinced that it would not be recovered.

So slow was our progress at this time that the date of our arrival at South Ice was becoming more and more uncertain. Owing to the treacherous surface it was now impossible for the plane to land anywhere in our area but I asked for more food to be dropped to us on the next flight. On the evening of November 5 the Otter circled our camp three times, on each occasion dropping two bundles of rations, which gave us an ample reserve. The temperature at our altitude was now consistently low, and when we finished work each night it was −35°F to −40°F. Sometimes there would be a brisk breeze, making conditions particularly uncomfortable as we prodded our way slowly onward. When we came to undress in the evenings, stockings, outer leg duffels, three pairs of foot duffels and the thick felt and plastic insoles would be frozen to the inside of the moccasins in one solid mass of rime and ice.

Each long and tiring day of prodding took us forward but half a mile. We used thin aluminum tubes six feet long to probe through the layers of snow and ice, and assumed the area safe if resistance was still encountered at the full depth of the thrust. The ice chisels mounted on solid wooden poles were used differently. When the butt end of the pole was plunged in, a crevasse bridge would reverberate loudly, and these we came to call "boomers." Then, using the chisel end, a hole would be cut and enlarged until it was possible to thrust one's head, and sometimes shoulders, far enough through the lid to

179

see the width and direction of the crevasse. Hanging head down over a bottomless pit with sloping blue-white sides disappearing into the depths gave the impression of gazing into deep water; but it can also be somewhat alarming when you know that very soon you will be driving a 2- or 3-ton vehicle, together with heavy sledges, over the precarious snow-bridge above the dark abyss. Yes, one certainly takes a keen interest in one's own, and other people's, probing!

By the end of the day on November 6 we had prepared another half-mile of the route, and were bringing forward the vehicles in what seemed to be a relatively trouble-free area, when we were surrounded by a rumbling noise like underground thunder; at the same time a shuddering of the surface and a gentle collapse of the whole snow surface made those skiing ahead of the vehicles wish to be elsewhere. Then, before our eyes, two enormous holes, 30 to 40 feet long and 12 feet wide, appeared on either side of the track just ahead of the vehicles. They stopped! Their vibration had caused the bridge of a crevasse just ahead to fall in; but along the probed route it had stood firm. After further examination, David Pratt cautiously led on with his Weasel, followed by the Sno-cat, but 50 yards farther he suddenly plunged through a snow-bridge six feet thick, and remained precariously suspended by the very front of the vehicle and by a short length of track at the rear. Had the crevasse been six inches wider he would certainly have fallen headlong down, to hang suspended by the safety-rope attached to the Sno-cat behind. By midnight when the cat had pulled him out backwards there was a semi-whiteout and we were very tired, so we camped where we were, surrounded by the gaping holes for which our passage had been responsible.

Next day we finally cleared this unpleasant area, but by the afternoon of the 8th, after ploughing across fields of high sastrugi, suddenly found ourselves crossing a series of wide chasms. Although some of them were as much as 100 feet across, they all seemed very well filled with snow and we had crossed several before we realized they were there. Here we camped to examine the ground ahead. In the distance we could see a curious line of snow hills, which we knew from air reconnaissance to be gigantic snowdrifts associated with a fracture belt known to us as the "echelon crevasses." In the morning

David Stratton and I went forward on skis to find the best approach, leaving David Pratt and Geoffrey Pratt to find a clear route across the remaining crevasses by the camp.

After three and a half miles we reached a most impressive series of snow hills rising to 80 feet above the surrounding surface. To our surprise, the few visible crevasses were easy to cross and by climbing over one of the hills we discovered a route to the far side. Between each of the hills lay enormous, and apparently bottomless, pits. Many were 20 to 30 yards across, and indicated the size of the crevasses which were otherwise hidden by the large drifts.

Quickly we skied back to the vehicles — a round trip of eight miles — and set off, roped for the first quarter of a mile, to cross the remaining crevasses by the camp. Then running free, we followed our ski tracks through the rift and hillock zone, before roping up again to cross some filled chasms about 50 feet wide.

Once we had passed these hazards we had a clear run of four miles before reaching the first crevasses of the heavily broken zone lying beneath the Whichaway Nunataks. For days we had been seeing these rocks first loom over the horizon, then become individual entities, till now they commanded our attention as they barred the route to the south. We camped with the rocks only two miles distant, but a fearsome-looking mass of crevasses and hummocks lay between us and the steep glacier slopes up which we had yet to find a way.

The only reasonable gradient appeared to lie between the two most easterly nunataks, and it was toward this glacier that we began to seek a route. Setting off on skis in a cold gusty wind, David Stratton and I started toward the most easterly nunatak, while David Pratt and Geoffrey went farther to the west. At first it seemed that the way would be easier than we expected, for the hummocks appeared to be disposed in lines and the crevasses between them were old and well filled. Unhappily this situation did not continue, and, leaving our skis behind, we found ourselves wandering among a fantastic maze of hummocks, largely of bare, blue ice, while all the possible vehicle routes ended in confused ridges and crevasses. Clearly we had to look down on the area to judge where it would be best to go.

Intending to climb the nearest nunatak, we made directly toward it but before reaching the moraines at its foot found that we had to descend a precipitous 100 feet of blue ice, over which it was obviously impossible for any vehicle to move. On foot it was easy enough, and while I examined the moraines and rocks, David climbed to the top to study our crevasse problem from above. As he returned with the news that there seemed to be a gap some miles to the west, the two Pratts appeared saying that they too had had no luck in finding a way. Together we scrambled across the scree slopes, then over the glacier between the nunataks on our way to the "gap." We saw that, though this was a possible route, it would certainly not be easy and we should have to move the vehicles five miles to the west and make our approach from that direction.

That night we camped among the first crevasses at the entrance to the gap, but in the morning a wind gusting to 45 mph enveloped the area in high drift, made any route reconnaissance quite impossible and confined us to our tents for the day. The following morning we resumed the well-known process of prodding until, by half past three that afternoon, we had established a reasonable route to the foot of the glacier leading up between the nunataks. Although we considered that some of the places were distinctly "dicey," there was no alternative. Fortunately the whole area was composed of very hard ice which clearly revealed the majority of the crevasses at the surface, and, more important still, the soft crevasse walls to which we had become accustomed, were replaced by really solid ice.

As the roped vehicles moved off, I skied 20 yards ahead of David's Weasel to make sure that he was correctly aligned to cross the bad places at right angles, while David Stratton moved forward some 30 yards in front of me, picking out our arrows and other marks made in the snow to indicate the chosen course. As we moved forward at 2 mph we were happy to find that our route proved a safe one, and after a mile and a half we arrived safely at an upstanding mass of ice which we had called the "Obelisk."

From that point onward there remained only a few hundred yards to the foot of the glacier that rose toward the nunataks, but even this area, and the first half-mile of the glacier itself, was riddled with crevasses. Then, as though reluctant to let us get away, the lid of the last crevasse on the Recovery Glacier collapsed, and for the first time the Sno-cat was caught with one track pontoon hanging over the hole.

With the two Davids standing on the pontoon to swing it into position, Geoffrey was able to inch forward until he was once more on firm snow. Half an hour later we had cleared the last of the crevasses and were moving steadily over the solid surface between the nunataks above. What a sense of relief it was to be traveling over firm ground once more, and to feel sure that we had a clear route to South Ice 30 miles away.

Our camp that night at 4000 feet was less than a mile from the nearest rocks, but we had no time to visit them. Despite the sastrugi up to 2 feet 6 inches high that lay across our path and kept our speed down to between 2 and 4 mph, we intended to complete the journey by next day, November 13.

As we approached South Ice, we spoke to them by radio and Hal Lister set out on skis to meet us. Presently we saw a black dot on the horizon which came and went as we dipped into the hollows or rose to the tops of the ridges. Then suddenly there he was, quite close over the top of the ridge! But this splendid moment of meeting was somewhat spoilt by David's Weasel running out of fuel, and Hal collapsing in a flailing heap as his skis caught under the sastrugi! When everyone had been straightened out, we rumbled on the last three and a half miles to South Ice, where Hannes La Grange, the only other occupant, came hastening out to meet us amid the excited yelping of the two dog teams tethered not far from the buried station.

It had taken us thirty-seven days and 400 miles to reach South Ice: we flew back to Shackleton in 2½ hours. Nine days later we started all over again!

XIV

Spring and Summer Journeys
from Scott Base

While we at Shackleton were prevented from traveling by bad weather throughout September, finally starting on the reconnaissance journey to South Ice and the exploration of the Shackleton Range in October and November, the Ross Sea Party was able to begin sledging in September and started on the longer summer journeys in October. Sir Edmund Hillary gives the following account of their activities.

OUR SPRING JOURNEYING started early in September and the first to get away were Marsh and Warren with one dog team: their destination was Cape Royde where Warren wanted to do some geology. On September 9 they left Scott Base and completed their 25-mile run over the sea ice in the same day. This was a most encouraging effort and showed how well the dogs had come through the winter. The next day I left base with a tractor train — three Fergusons towing the new caboose and four other sledges laden with food and fuel, making a total load of six and a half tons. This was to be a full-scale test of our winter's work on the vehicles.

We crossed the sea ice of McMurdo Sound and camped the first night at the foot of the Dailey Islands. We tramped over the largest of the islands and were interested to note a flat beach on its northern shore, probably wide enough to build a hut or two. It was possible to drive a tractor over smooth ice to within a few yards of this beach. Under these early-season conditions, the Dailey Islands appeared to have distinct possibilities as a base site, and we had in fact been recommended to use them. But it was also quite apparent that the warm summer sun reflecting from all this black rock would produce the same impassable quagmire that our observers had reported the previous year. After a crowded and uncomfortable night in the caboose we were glad to move off next morning, although it was raw and bitter. We had difficulty in keeping warm as we drove past the great ice cliffs of the Blue Glacier and along the sea ice below the Bowers Piedmont Glacier finally to reach Butter Point. We examined the depot we had left there the previous autumn, found it intact and almost free of snow, and added to it a further ton and a half of supplies off our sledges; then we camped on the smooth sea ice. The weather, which had been partly cloudy with night temperatures in the minus thirties, now took a turn for the better and we had bright sunny days.

I was anxious to make a further visit to the Ferrar Glacier to see if the decision made to abandon it as a route, when the glacier had been subjected to a winter's snow, was still correct. I was prepared to change my plans for the southern trip and use the shorter Ferrar route if it now proved feasible. We drove from Butter Point across easy stretches of ice which were broken by half a dozen tide cracks and reached the terminal face of the glacier without any difficulty. Establishing a camp and leaving the tractors there, we went ahead on foot to examine the approaches to the glacier and found them rather formidable from every angle. After a six-mile walk up the glacier, which was still bare and icy without any accumulation of snow, we were quite convinced that it was still an impracticable route for our purpose. We were joined at the Ferrar by Miller, Marsh, Carlyon and Warren with their dog teams, and they made an independent investigation of its possibilities as a dog route. They too decided it was unsatisfactory. We agreed that the route could not be regarded as impossible either for dogs or a rugged vehicle, but that the time involved and the damage done to equipment would make it a costly and useless venture. Certainly when the summer sun had made itself apparent and the glacier was covered with thaw pools and surface streams it would be virtually impassable.

The tractors and dog teams moved north along the coast in separate groups. At Gneiss Point the tractor party established a substantial depot of dog pemmican and man-rations for the later use of the

Northern Party. We then turned back, and as we were lightly laden, collected some seals for dog food, finally arriving at Scott Base after a trip of 150 miles. Miller's dog teams skirted the coast and carried on beyond Gneiss Point. They were caught out in a severe blizzard, but weathered the storm quite comfortably in their tents and then returned to base, finishing off with a fine day's run of 32 miles in seven hours.

Two other journeys were also carried out at this time. Brooke and Gunn had always been anxious to visit the unexplored area at the head of the Blue Glacier. Using a tough Greenland sledge, they took their dog team over some very rough ice on the lower Blue Glacier and forced a route into the upper reaches. Bad weather hampered their efforts, but they were able to carry out some useful mapping and geologizing and filled in very satisfactorily another small blank in the map. Our biologist, Dr. Balham, had his interests in another direction. He wished to visit the emperor penguin rookery at Cape Crozier to investigate the progress of the colony since Dr. Wilson's visit in 1911. Ayres and Douglas, with their two dog teams and accompanied by Sandford, one of the I.G.Y. scientists, took Balham over the Ross Ice Shelf to Cape Crozier. They were dogged by bad weather and fierce winds but ultimately reached their destination. From their last camp they went on foot, and by following a dangerous route underneath the rock cliffs they were able to cross the pressure ice to reach the rookery. They found it in a thriving condition and far larger than it had been forty-six years before. During all these operations the field parties maintained close radio communication with Scott Base and were supported by our aircraft which landed whenever it was feasible.

By the last week in September all our field parties had returned to base. The experience gained had been invaluable and much useful work had been accomplished. The dog teams and their drivers were now in the peak of condition for their main journeys. We had learned a great deal, too, about the operation of our tractors with their new modifications and had decided to make substantial changes in the layout and insulation of the caboose. Probably most important of all was that we had developed a technique of travel which reduced to a minimum the time wasted starting in the morning and stopping at night, and this could well save us valuable days in our long southern journey.

The last days of September and the early days of October were hectic ones as we made our final preparations. On October 1, our isolation from the outside world was broken when three American ski planes completed the long flight down from New Zealand and we reveled in our first mail for many months. Brooke did a long flight with Claydon in the Auster along the coast of Victoria Land to examine the possibilities of getting up to the polar plateau by one of the northern glaciers. He reported that both the Mawson Glacier and the Fry Glacier appeared too badly crevassed to give hope of a satisfactory passage, but the Mackay Glacier gave promise of a devious but possible route. We planned therefore on the basis of the Northern Party using the Mackay Glacier.

Friday, October 4, was rather a miserable day with a strong wind and a temperature of $-22°F$ — unpleasant conditions for dog driving, and a party could well be excused for not starting. But Brooke's Northern Party were anxious to be on their way and at eleven o'clock that morning they hitched up their dogs to the laden sledges, said good-by and headed off into the murk. They were fortunate to be away from base, for we entered a period of last-minute frustrations and worries, of emergencies and unexpected difficulties of the type that harass any party just before its departure. At one period it appeared we would have to delay for several weeks as the vehicles weren't ready; the sledges weren't loaded; and anyway there was no one available to drive the last tractor for us. But everything fell into line at the last moment, except personnel. Bates would have to remain behind for a few days and keep the generators going at base, and Balham would come along in his place. At half-past four in the afternoon of October 14, Ellis, Mulgrew, Balham and I started up our four vehicles, hitched on our heavily laden sledges, waved good-by to our companions and slowly drove away from Scott Base. We well knew that we carried with us the good wishes of all our companions, but that there was in actual fact little confidence in our onward progress, for it was widely held both at Scott and by our American neighbors that we wouldn't get more than fifty miles out onto the Ross Ice Shelf. Certainly our Ferguson tractors in their modified and battered condition did not inspire confidence in the casual observer, but we still felt that their reliability and ease of maintenance would counteract to some extent their inability to perform in soft snow like a Sno-cat or a Weasel.

Our start was not auspicious. We made our laborious way across the area of pressure ridges formed where the Ross Ice Shelf flowed into the bay ice and then onto the flat going of the shelf itself. But with our gross load of over ten and a half tons we were having trouble in progressing through the soft snow. Barely five miles from base my tractor was pulled up with a jerk and I looked behind to see that one of the sledges had broken into a crevasse and was tilted over at an alarming angle. This was an unpleasant surprise, since we had not expected any crevasses at this early stage. It was impossible to move the sledge as it was, and we had to unload each of the twelve drums separately, at the same time retaining the strain on the sledge with a tractor to prevent its falling further. It was several hours before we were ready to move on again. We camped the first night only six and a half miles in a direct line from Scott Base.

The next morning was fine and mild with a temperature of only −12°F. We started off, hoping for a good day's travel, but immediately struck trouble as first one tractor and then another bogged down in the deep soft snow. In the first two hours we covered only one mile. It was time for drastic action as we couldn't afford to be too long delayed at this early stage of the game. We pushed eight drums of fuel off our sledges and left them lying in the snow. This reduction of one and a half tons in our load made just that difference which enabled us to keep moving, and by the end of a difficult day's travel we had done 23 miles. Our main concern was the extensive crevassing which spread out from the tips of White Island and Minna Bluff. Both of these areas had been notorious in Scott's day and had always caused us a good deal of trouble. Our first reconnaissance by dogs had become unpleasantly involved in these crevasses, and even Miller and Carlyon on their trip to the Skelton Depot had crossed several areas, though they had swung wide in an attempt to dodge them. I decided to swing out farther still with the tractors, always keeping in mind that we must not go too far and stray into the long lines of crevasses running out from Cape Crozier.

For the next few days the temperature remained in the minus thirties, but calm and sunny conditions made for very pleasant traveling. The surface had improved and, despite a good deal of mechanical trouble with the Weasel, we were able to do more than 30 miles each day. The two leading tractors were roped together as a precaution against crevasses, and we kept a very careful watch for them as we swung south and then west in a long sweep. We entered areas of high sastrugi off Minna Bluff, but the surface of the snow was fairly firm, the Fergusons reveled in the improved traction while the Weasel had to work very hard to keep up. We cleared Minna Bluff with some relief, for it meant that we had dodged all the crevasse areas successfully and we could relax for a short time at least.

The Weasel was proving very troublesome and obviously needed some major repairs. We were regretting that time had not permitted us to overhaul the motor during the winter. Being now about 50 miles from the Skelton Depot, we decided to try and make a dash for it with the idea of carrying out the repairs there. For thirteen hours we drove steadily onward toward the great peaks of the Western Mountains and the mouth of the Skelton Glacier. We were traveling through the night, and the midnight sun, which was just above the horizon now, sculptured the waves of sastrugi in light and shadow. Our ears became attuned to the monotonous drone of the engines and the cold crept through our warm down clothing as we huddled over the controls in our unheated cabs. At the end of each three hours we'd feel too miserable to continue and would quickly brew up a hot cup of cocoa and a sustaining meal in the warmth of the caboose. And then we'd push on again. We were keeping a wary eye out for the two groups of large crevasses that guarded either side of the entrance to the Skelton Glacier and we did a big dogleg to ensure that we came directly in between them.

At six o'clock in the morning, on October 20, we were bumping over a hard rough surface under the cliffs of Teale Island, which stands on the south side of the glacier. Ahead of us we picked up a tiny black dot on the expanse of white. Miller, Marsh and Bates had been flown in with their two dog teams the previous day, and we knew this must be their camp. We rattled over the last few miles at top speed and could soon hear the howling of the dogs as they sensed our approach. At seven o'clock we drove into the Skelton Depot with the satisfaction of knowing we had the first 180 miles behind us. It was a happy moment when we greeted our companions and warmed ourselves with the hot cups of tea they thrust into our hands.

For two days Bates and Ellis labored over the Weasel. They had discovered that the drive shaft for the distributor had fractured and it seemed a miracle that we had been able to do the last 50 miles. We erected a rough bipod over the vehicle with balks of wood brought for possible crevasse rescue operations. From this we swung a pulley and chain, and when the motor had been disconnected we lifted it out of its bed so that the broken part could be reached. When the broken shaft was removed, Bates mended it and the motor was then replaced. We were particularly fortunate in having relatively mild conditions for this major operation, otherwise it would have been a miserable business. A test run with the Weasel showed that the motor was now operating satisfactorily but several other minor troubles had been located, including a broken spring, so further delay was necessary.

On the morning of October 22, Miller and Marsh loaded their sledges, hitched up their dogs and departed up the glacier. Our repairs were completed by late afternoon and at about five o'clock we too set off. Ahead of us the glacier rose very gradually in a broad sweep, and although we knew there was continuous crevassing at the foot of the great rock bluffs that lined either side of the valley, we were relying on the report of our autumn party that for the first 25 miles at least the center of the glacier was crevasse-free. The surface proved to be very hard and extremely rough. Vehicles and sledges were wracked and twisted, but the Fergusons were in their element here and we covered the 18 miles to the dog camp in four and a half hours. Miller and Marsh had experienced a torrid day of spills and tossouts on the slippery surface and were tired travelers by the time they crawled into their sleeping bags. The weather closed in as we camped beside them, and a violent wind and drifting snow blanketed out the scenery.

October 24 was a day of rest, for mist and snow and sudden fierce squalls of up to 50 knots made any traveling impossible. There was a complete whiteout and walking around the camp was a hazardous business and resulted in a few tumbles over invisible sastrugi. The following morning was a little better, but the wind still persisted. However, by midday it had improved considerably, so we decided to break camp and move on. The dog teams were away at one o'clock and soon disappeared into a cloud of returning drift. The tractors moved off half an hour later and we, too, had barely traveled a hundred yards before being enveloped in a blinding sheet of snow. The surface was extremely rough and we could see little of where we were going, but by determined driving we covered five miles in the first hour. This brought us out onto the clear ice of the middle portion of the Skelton Glacier and here we received the full force of the wind. It was impossible to stand on the slippery surface unless you had a firm grip on a tractor or sledge, but it had the redeeming feature that the drift was much less severe and we could catch periodical glimpses of the peaks round about.

We had seen nothing of Miller and Marsh and I was rather concerned about their welfare. I drove back a short way to look for them, but soon realized that my chances of finding them were negligible. I decided they must have stopped and camped somewhere behind us. As the wind was sweeping directly down the glacier, our route took us straight into it — the only way it would have been possible to travel on this icy surface. My companions were willing to persist under these decidedly unpleasant conditions, so we continued on. For two hours we battled into the gale, seeing enough of the peaks around to steer by. A slight moderation of the wind happily coincided with our arrival in an area of crevasses. They were clearly defined on the hard surface and were rarely more than two or three feet wide. It was impossible to dodge them so we kept going, winding our way along and crossing them where they were narrowest. Sometimes the bridges held under the weight of the tractors, but usually there was a violent lurch and we'd pass safely over, but leave a gaping hole behind. Although we knew the crevasses were not capable of engulfing a tractor, yet it was rather a trying business and we were not sorry when we cleared them after several miles and started climbing steadily upward. We camped at eight o'clock on firm snow, having covered 19½ miles. The wind had by now reduced to a fresh breeze and we could appreciate the magnificent mountain scenery around us.

Ahead of us stretched the steepest part of the glacier. The main body of ice tumbled down in a huge icefall to our left, but by following a devious route to the right it was possible to climb on much more reasonable gradients. The glacier rose in two great sweeps, called by us the Lower and Upper Staircase, with a flattish area in the middle which we called the Landing. If the snow was very soft on these steep areas we knew it would delay us considerably, although we were determined if necessary to winch our way to the top. Our departure was delayed in the morning by the same strong wind and heavy drift, but we moved off at 1:30 P.M. and began to climb laboriously upward. To our delight the surface was not too soft and gave adequate traction to our vehicles. Dodging crevasse areas, we made steady height and it was only on the steepest slopes that relaying of loads proved necessary. Bright sunlight, clear skies, only a light wind, and superb scenery made a happy combination, and despite the tension that is an inescapable part of vehicle travel through crevasse country, we were really enjoying ourselves. By the end of the day we had crossed the Lower Staircase and we pitched our camp on the Landing at a height of 2680 feet. We had covered twelve miles.

I was still feeling somewhat concerned about Miller and Marsh and their dog teams as we were carrying the greater part of their rations for them. I therefore decided to wait on the Landing until they caught up. It was an excellent opportunity to carry out the innumerable small jobs that were always waiting to be done, both on tractors and sledges, and we occupied our time very profitably. However, it was a great relief during the afternoon to hear the hearty shouts of the dog drivers as they came toiling into camp. As we had suspected, they had been forced to camp soon after we had parted in the storm. Most aggravatingly, our tractors had passed within thirty feet of them without our noticing, and we had then disappeared off into the drift. The two men had experienced difficulty in pitching their tent in the howling blizzard and it was some hours before they were comfortably sheltered against the storm. Once the weather had lifted, they had made very good time to join us.

Our eagerness to push on suffered a further setback. A rapid rise in temperature to 0°F was accompanied by a day of snowfall and clammy mist. I set the alarm for an early start on October 28, but at 4:45 A.M. it was still very thick outside. During the next hour it improved a little, so we commenced our preparations for moving on. The conditions were almost impossible — a complete cloud cover and a particularly bad whiteout. Also the area ahead was our most crucial one and would require delicate maneuvering to dodge frequent and extensive crevasse areas. But we had already been delayed and I considered that with our dog teams traveling ahead and all of us taking considerable care we should be safe enough.

The dogs were away at eight o'clock and the tractors followed an hour later. It was a day of fumbling over invisible surfaces, of rock bluffs appearing and disappearing and of constant tension and worry. Miller and Marsh did a magnificent job with their dogs; we soon lost sight of them, but we followed their tracks for many miles, although it was often necessary in the whiteout to get out of the tractor and peer closely at the snow to pick them out. We lost their tracks around Stepaside Spur and forged ahead on our own. We could see crevasse areas on either side of us in the mist, but felt our way along. Visibility decreased still further and we had almost decided to camp when we picked out a flag left by the dog men. We continued on, relaying over the steeper stretches, and finally emerged from the Upper Staircase onto the slopes running onto the Skelton névé. Ahead of us we could see a black dot and an hour later we had stopped beside the dog drivers' tent at 5000 feet. It had been a difficult day, but now the worst was behind us and it was some satisfaction to know that the route was proving so suitable for tractors.

During the night the wind freshened once more and it was bitterly cold. In the morning conditions were impossible for dog travel, but I decided to move off with the tractors as we considered ourselves free of crevasses for some time. Driving into the teeth of the wind and with heavy drift blanketing out the visibility was an unpleasant business, especially with temperatures in the minus thirties. In three hours we had climbed the last of the steep slopes and were making good time over the easy gradient of the névé. The wind had eased considerably and the sun was shining once again. At 2:30 P.M.

there was a roar overhead and Claydon passed over us in the Beaver. Next moment a small bag fluttered down and we rushed to collect our mail. Claydon reported that he had just landed Ayres and Carlyon near the Plateau Depot and that they had set up camp there with some of their dogs. The rest of their dogs and gear would be flown in as weather permitted. This was excellent news. Claydon roared off back to Scott Base and we drove on toward the névé rim.

For two more days we had our fill of strong winds, heavy drift, and cold temperatures as we dragged our loads up over the hard rough slope leading from the Skelton névé to the polar plateau. On October 30, in temperatures of −33°F and winds gusting to 50 knots, we only did two and a half miles and had to fight every inch of the way. But on the morning of the 31st it was fine and sunny and the thermometer had risen to −20°F. We had a difficult job getting our vehicles going after a bad night of wind and drift, but were away by eleven o'clock. I had taken advantage of the clearing to fix our position accurately from the surrounding peaks and the sun. It was a good thing I had done so, for to our disgust after a short run we entered the wind and mist again, but were able to keep going over the rough sastrugi. Steering an accurate course was difficult, but we knew we must be fast approaching the camp of Ayres and Carlyon. It was a satisfying moment when the mist cleared and we saw the black triangle of their tent several miles ahead of us. Before long we were pitching our camp beside them with the first major stage of our journey completed. We were 290 miles from Scott Base; we were on the polar plateau at a height of 8200 feet, and all our vehicles were intact. Our tractors had fulfilled all our hopes and had more than repaid the labors of the winter. I have rarely felt a greater sense of achievement.

Although we had covered nearly 300 miles with our vehicles, we were still, due to our westerly trend, only ten miles nearer to the South Pole than was Scott Base. However, we had arrived at the Plateau Depot with eighteen drums of petrol and sufficient food and paraffin oil to cover the whole summer's operations. The vehicles had run so satisfactorily that I had no hesitation in deciding to take them farther south and we were now in a strong position, for if any accident happened to the Beaver we already had sufficient fuel aboard to travel at least as far as Depot 480 and establish it with its requirements.

I determined to leave the Plateau Depot with full loads behind the tractors, so Claydon and Cranfield commenced flying in load after load of supplies — petrol, oil, man-rations, and dog food for Fuchs's party and ourselves. Bad weather was constantly interfering with flying operations, and much heavy cloud created a major hazard, for every flight had to pass through the 13,000-foot Western Mountains. My tractor party sustained a severe setback when two of the members suffered minor accidents — Mulgrew broke some ribs and Ellis strained his back. I had to evacuate them out to base and Balham also had to return to carry on his biological studies. Gawn and Wright came in as replacements but this still only gave us the weak minimum of four men to drive the four vehicles.

On November 8, the four dog teams driven by Miller, Marsh, Ayres and Carlyon pulled out of depot. They were very heavily laden — too heavily, it proved. In order to make progress in the soft snow at this altitude they were forced to dump a large share of their loads and leave it for the tractors to pick up. Each day they reported their progress on the radio and it was slow and laborious. They found the deep soft snow very difficult to cope with despite their light loads, and wind and temperatures into the minus forties proved an added burden. On the evening of the fifth day they camped only 47 miles out — an average of less than ten miles a day. This same evening we set off with the tractors. We were pulling a total load of eleven tons and we could barely move with it. We crept along for four and a half miles and then completely bogged down as the slope steepened. There was nothing to do but relay. By November 15 we had only done 35 miles and had consumed large quantities of petrol in getting that far. The soft snow, plus the loss of power due to the altitude, was proving almost too much for the Fergusons, while the Weasel was now bearing a greater share of the burden. At one stage the Weasel was pulling five tons while the three Fergusons were roped together and pulling a total load of only six tons. Our petrol consumption was so high and our progress so slow that at one period it appeared that our southern journey must come to an ignominious end. But to our relief, when we swung onto a southwesterly heading, the surface surprisingly improved and the tractors gained a new lease of life.

We now appeared to be traveling along the rim of a great basin which fell away very gradually to the east toward the Ross Ice Shelf. Following the advice of the dog men, we had swung a little to the west of their route and were successful in dodging some bad areas of crevasses. The surface was mostly hard and wind-blown with knobbly sastrugi and we were continually harassed by a strong westerly wind and heavy ground drift. As the temperatures were always below minus twenty, we found traveling in our poorly protected tractors an unpleasant business. The hard surfaces were suiting us and we started to do 30 miles a day, but the roughness played havoc with our heavily laden sledges and two runners were badly damaged.

On November 19 we passed some miles to the west of the dog teams who had been retarded even more than we had by the bad weather, and we pushed on ahead. We fumbled our way along for several days in miserable conditions and over extremely rough going, traveling blind most of the time, but greatly encouraged by the fact that we had been successful in avoiding all major crevasse areas. However it was too much to hope that we would dodge them altogether, and early on the morning of Sunday the 24th two of our tractors broke through the bridges over some enormous crevasses and we were only saved from disaster by extraordinary good luck. We discovered we were in the center of a most unpleasant area and retreated with a great deal of care and no further incidents occurred, apart from our uncovering a number of less spectacular crevasses. We struck west in an attempt to find a safe way around, but the lighting was very flat and we ended up in another group of crevasses with two vehicles on one side of a ten-foot crevasse and two on the other, with a very shaky bridge between. As we were all rather tired and a little nervous after these episodes, we camped where we were. Next morning the visibility was much improved and in our refreshed condition we had no difficulty in flagging a route through a wide band of crevasses. When we brought the vehicles over this route we experienced some uncomfortable lurches as we punched holes in some of the bridges, but nothing of great consequence, and we were soon traveling over an excellent surface and fast approaching our estimated position for Depot 480. At 6:30 P.M. on November 25 we reached an area suitable for aircraft landings and decided this would do. We were 210 miles from the Plateau Depot and our position was 79°51'S, 148°00'E.

Our time at Depot 480 was profitably spent. The tractors were given a thorough check and the broken sledges repaired. Unfavorable weather over the first few days prevented the Beaver from flying in to us, although loads were flown to an intermediate depot established on the Ross Ice Shelf at the foot of Darwin Glacier. On November 28, the four dog teams arrived. They were going much better now and had averaged 16 miles a day for the previous eight days. They were followed the next afternoon by Claydon in the Beaver, who found us without difficulty by homing on our small D/F radio transmitter. Our RNZAF unit was having a period of extreme activity. Not only was it supplying the southern depots at a considerable distance from Scott Base, but it was also flying a good deal of food to the Northern Party. Brooke's party had carried out a highly successful survey and geological program in the valleys along the sea coast of Victoria Land as far north as Mawson Glacier, and had then tackled the problem of finding a new way to the polar plateau. With their two dog teams they ascended the Debenham Glacier, crossed into the Miller Glacier and finally struggled up the Mackay Glacier to the plateau. Much of the traveling had been difficult, but they had arrived in excellent condition. They were now waiting to be supplied by the Beaver with more food so they could carry on with the second half of their program and explore the ranges from the west.

On December 1, Miller and Marsh left Depot 480 with light loads and began to reconnoiter the way to Depot 700. It was obvious now that the tractors were taking the burden of the southern journey so it was possible to split off two of the dog teams for more survey work. Ayres and Carlyon struck east into the mountains around Darwin Glacier. Claydon flew a subsidiary depot in for them, and their plan was to map the large area between the Mulock and Barne Glaciers. They would complete their task by making the first descent of the Darwin Glacier itself, and then be picked up by air from the Ross Ice Shelf. The tractors remained at Depot 480 to act as receiving group for the aerial lift. Eleven 44-gallon drums of petrol were finally depoted there for Fuchs, together with large quantities of food and paraffin oil. Ellis and Mulgrew had now recovered from their ills and rejoined my party, while Gawn returned to base. The addition of another summer party man, in McKenzie, gave me a total strength of six — the best number to date, and I anticipated a great easing of the burden of driving.

On December 6, the Beaver flew in the last load to complete the depot and the same evening we headed south with the tractors. In a determined effort to try to increase our daily mileages, we drove for long hours and succeeded in covering 93 miles in the first two days. But the efforts proved too much for the Weasel, and unpleasant grating noises in the clutch and differential made us expect the worst. By putting hours of effort into the vehicle, Bates and Ellis managed to keep it going, but it was obvious that the end was in sight, as we had no spare parts. In an effort to relieve our loads I had decided to put in an intermediate depot, and in a hummocky area at 81°30'S we established Midway Depot with six drums of fuel. We were 130 miles from Depot 480. Reducing the load behind the Weasel to only the caboose, we pushed on again. For ten miles we clattered through hard icy hummocks and ridges and the farther we went the more convinced we became that we were in a crevasse area. Despite these suspicions it was the usual disconcerting surprise when the leading tractor lurched through the first snow-bridge and clawed its way out the other side, leaving a gaping hole dropping away into bottomless depths. It proved to be an unpleasant area, and although few of the crevasses were much over four feet in width, they were wide enough to cause us considerable discomfort and concern as we crossed them. I roped up with several of my companions and went ahead on foot to flag a route, and we had to follow a tortuous path in order to dodge the wider parts of the crevasses. Then we returned and brought our vehicles through and, despite our care in selecting bridges, there was a succession of open holes behind us by the time the last vehicle had crossed. It took us eight and a half hours to travel over this three-mile area, and when we struck a line of immense crevasses a few miles farther on we called it a day and camped.

Bates and Ellis made one last effort to reclaim the Weasel. The thrust bearing in the differential had disintegrated and we had no spare. Bates constructed a temporary bearing out of brass welding rod, but despite a number of ingenious ideas for keeping it cool, it rapidly heated and proved unsatisfactory. There was nothing more we could do, so we abandoned the Weasel and put all the loads behind the three Fergusons. We left the Weasel with some reluctance, for though it had caused us considerable mechanical trouble, it had proved invaluable in areas of soft snow.

The next 90 miles were a trying experience. In the floor of every wide basin was deep soft snow and we were forced laboriously to relay across them and bitterly regretted the lack of the Weasel. The hard surfaces of the ridges were all too frequently split by crevasses and we had many uneasy moments. Seven miles short of Depot 700, we almost lost a tractor down a crevasse, but the crash bar over the driver jammed against the wall and just held the vehicle up. On the afternoon of December 15 we covered the last few miles to reach Depot 700 and rejoined Miller and Marsh. It was a considerable relief to rest again and not to have to think about soft snow and crevasses.

We were now beyond the Beaver's effective range from Scott Base. In order to supply us, therefore, the airmen put in a subsidiary depot at the foot of Shackleton Inlet and relayed through to us from there. The work our air contingent was carrying out with a small single-engined plane was quite prodigious, and much of their flying was over mountain and glacier regions where the likelihood of rescue in the event of disaster was extremely remote. But as regularly as weather permitted, the Beaver would appear over the eastern horizon and touch down on our rough airstrip and unload all the necessities for the depot. Late on the afternoon of December 20, the last load arrived and the depot was completed. We had fulfilled our obligations and behind us stretched a series of fully stocked depots all the way to Scott Base.

Now that our major task was concluded, we didn't plan to waste any of our time in inactivity. Miller and Marsh had already departed with their dogs to carry out a spectacular survey of the mountains and glaciers to the east of the Beardmore Glacier. A decision had to be made on the future role of the tractors. I had managed to accumulate twenty drums of fuel and we were only 500 miles from the Pole; our tractors were operating reasonably well and by this time we were very experienced travelers. We were still amongst crevasse areas and to drop our task here would be leaving it half done. I resolved to strike southwest in an attempt to clear all the crevasses and then, if fuel and the vehicles permitted and the Transpolar Party required no more assistance, we would go to the Pole, or meet Fuchs as near to it as time allowed. He had advised me on November 20, four days before he left Shackleton, that he still hoped to be at the Pole before New Year, and although it was difficult to see how this could be accomplished, it would mean that we would probably meet him within a hundred miles or so on our side of the Pole.

At 8:30 P.M. on December 20, Ellis, Bates, Mulgrew, Wright and I left Depot 700 behind. We had reduced our loads to the bare minimum and were towing only six tons behind our three tractors. We knew that from now on we were very much on our own, and that we could not afford to lose any more vehicles. Our southwesterly route gave us quite reasonable traveling for 27 miles, and we were just congratulating ourselves on having bypassed all the crevasses when the lead tractor broke through one and just managed to scratch its way across. It took us some hours to find a safe route through this area and we marked all the bridges with snow cairns for the use of Fuchs's party. Another 30 miles of good traveling raised our hopes again, only to have them dashed once more when we entered an area of enormous crevasses. These were well bridged, but we had several unpleasant incidents and nearly lost the caboose when a wide bridge gave way. This proved to be our last group of crevasses, and once we were clear of them we struck south. For the next six days we drove for long hours and averaged over 40 miles per day. We climbed steadily to a height of over 10,000 feet and found the power output of our tractors was dropping off to an alarming extent. But as long as the surface remained reasonably firm we were able to cope with it.

By December 30 we were less than 200 miles from the South Pole. Our progress became more difficult as we entered another area of deep, soft snow. The most alarming feature was our greatly increased consumption of our meager remaining stores of petrol. At times we had difficulty in moving, though our loads were now extremely light, and in one period of six hours we covered a total distance of six miles. Somewhat desperate measures were required, so we threw off the sledges everything we could possibly spare: food, paraffin, tractor spares, and even spare sledges were depoted and we continued on without reserves of any sort. On January 2 we were still more than 70 miles from the Pole and we had exactly 180 gallons of fuel left for our three tractors. It was just enough to get us there if no time was wasted in finding the Pole. And I wasn't entirely free of doubts on the score of navigation! My somewhat primitive bubble sextant was hardly a precision instrument and had been proving a little temperamental.

We decided to make a strong push for the Pole. For the next twenty hours we drove steadily on, rarely doing more than three miles an hour. Every six hours I shot the sun with my sextant and plotted a position line. By eight o'clock on January 3, we had covered 60 miles and were straining our eyes for some glimpse of human occupation. We were just stopping to refuel when I suddenly noticed a blackish dot ahead. I swerved toward it and then realized it was a marker flag. In considerable relief I waved to the others to stop and then switched off my motor. We were very tired and needed a sleep before pushing on.

Just after midday, on January 4, we drove through the last few miles of soft snow into the American South Pole Station. It was very pleasant to be greeted by friendly faces and welcoming voices and to feel we could relax again. Our tractors had performed quite remarkably when one considered their limitations, but we weren't sorry to clamber out of their cold seats for the last time and to know that our 1250-mile trip was over.

X V

Two Survey Journeys
from Scott Base

AMONG THE SLEDGE JOURNEYS made for survey and geological purposes from Scott Base were two of remarkable length. Both parties traveled with dog teams, and this chapter is compiled from material provided by Lieutenant Commander Richard Brooke, who led the Northern Party, and Dr. George Marsh, who accompanied Bob Miller beyond Depot 700, when Hillary left for the South Pole with the tractors.

On October 4 Richard Brooke's Northern Party set off with two dog teams. He was to drive one, Murray Douglas the other, and they would be accompanied by two geologists, Bernie Gunn and Guy Warren. Their object was to carry out survey and geological work over as wide an area as possible, and the original plan had been to travel north along the plateau edge from Plateau Depot. During the winter this had been changed, as it was felt that far more could be achieved if the party traveled north along the coast, penetrating the valleys en route, working their way up a suitable glacier to the plateau, and then running south along the plateau edge to the Skelton Depot. There were several glaciers to choose from, and after a reconnaissance flight in the autumn of 1956 the Fry Glacier was selected as the likely approach route.

When on September 10 John Claydon flew him up the glacier in the Auster, Richard Brooke soon realized that his previous glimpse of it from the air had been misleading. The lower part was barred by a huge icefall, and a possible route on the extreme north side

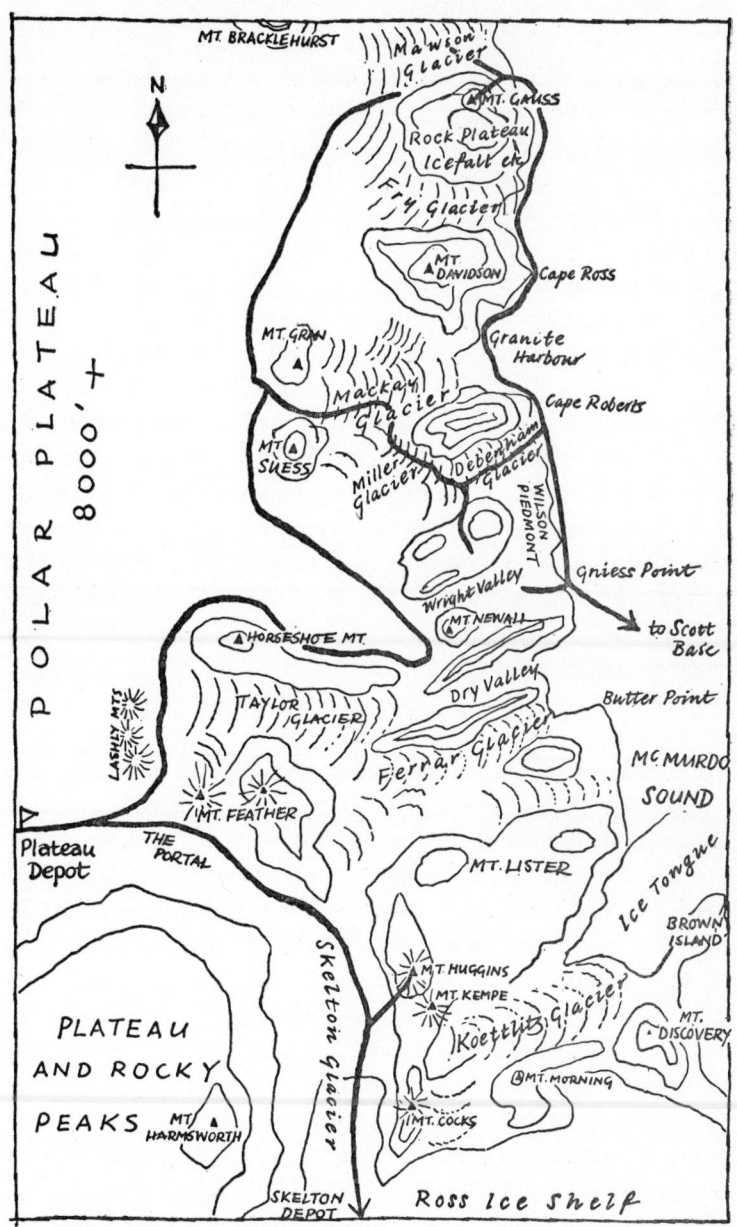

Track of Northern Parties from a sledge journal sketch map.

looked very steep and icy, with an unpleasant maze of crevasses over the lip. The Auster flew on to the Mackay Glacier. The upper part seemed practicable, and although Wright and Debenham had failed to ascend the lower part with dog teams in 1911, Brooke realized that this difficulty could be avoided by going up the Debenham Glacier and along the Miller Glacier, which lay in a deep-cut valley joining the Debenham to the Mackay.

One glacier still required air reconnaissance — the Mawson. Again John Claydon flew Brooke out in the Auster. Though visibility was poor, the surface was seen to be heavily crevassed and it was obvious that loads would have to be relayed over the frequent patches of moraine and broken ice. With light sledges, the Mawson Glacier might have been worth an attempt, but the Northern Party would have to carry enough food to enable them to reach the plateau, carry out their surveying and then, if the aircraft could not resupply them, make an emergency dash for the Plateau Depot. Too much time would be wasted relaying heavy loads up the Mawson or Fry Glaciers, so Brooke plumped for the Mackay.

The party was due to leave next day, October 4, and some hurried reorganization had to be done that night. The detailed plan was to establish a survey station on Mount Newall, south of Wright Valley, and then to reach Cape Roberts by October 15 to receive stores from the aircraft. The next fortnight would be spent surveying, both northward along the coast and during the return journey to Cape Roberts. In November they would be working their way up the Mackay Glacier via the Debenham, visiting the Dry Valley area en route, to reach the plateau by the end of the month and receive a supply of thirty days' food. This would leave the party independent of aircraft for the rest of the journey. During December they would work as far north as they could, getting back to the Plateau Depot by the end of the year, and in January they hoped to complete the survey of the Skelton Glacier. At the beginning of February they planned either to fly out from the Skelton Depot or possibly to sledge out.

Various methods can be used for surveying comparatively featureless areas like the Antarctic. One of the simplest and quickest, though not the most accurate, is to make compass traverses using a

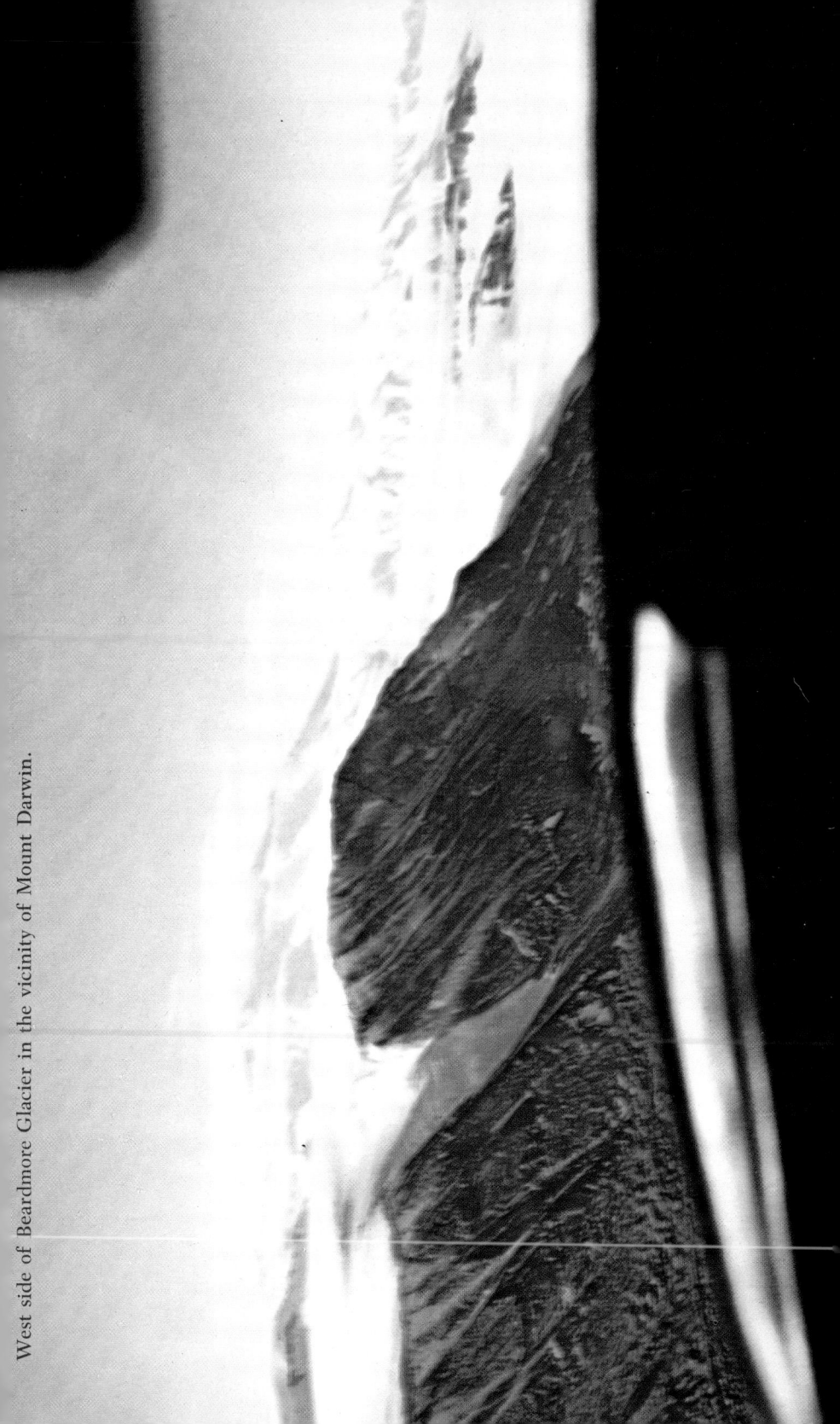

West side of Beardmore Glacier in the vicinity of Mount Darwin.

Solar halo frequently seen before reaching the Pole.

Gamle and Joe, approaching the South Pole.

Waves in the Ross Ice Shelf near Scott Base. White Island in the left distance.

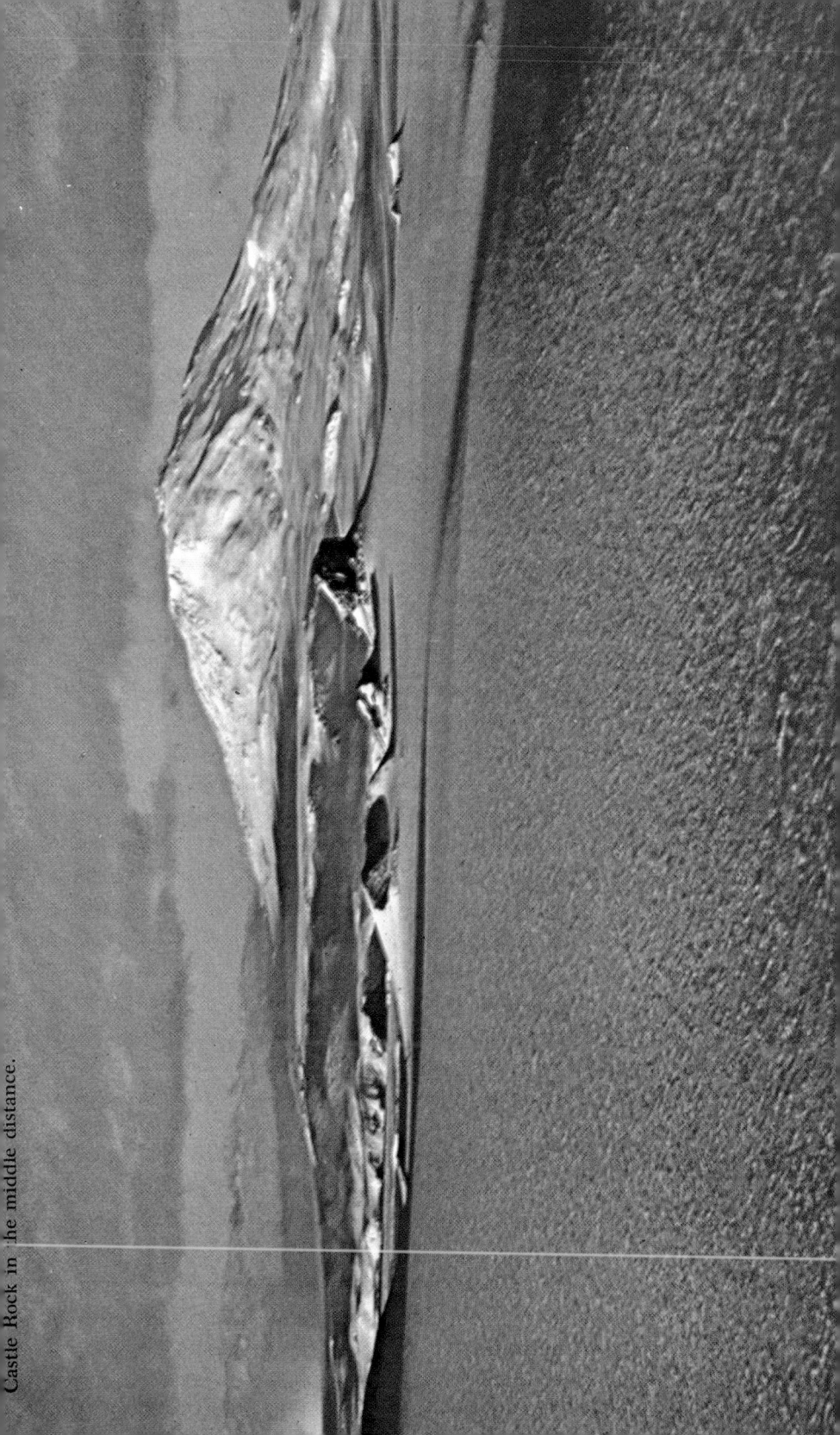

Castle Rock in the middle distance.

Camp for welding repairs to the Sno-cats.
Altitude 8000 feet, temperature −38°F.

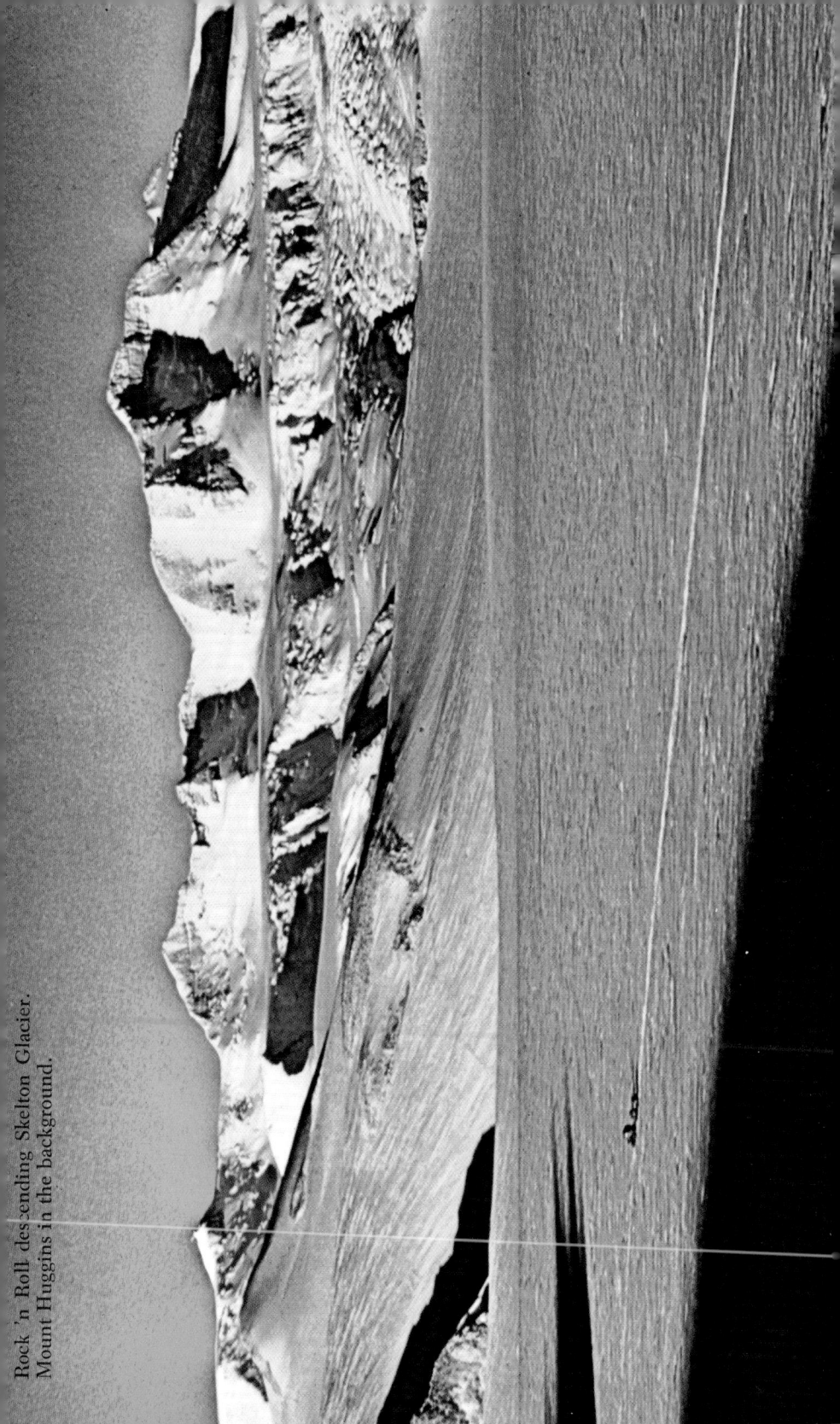

Rock 'n Roll descending Skelton Glacier. Mount Huggins in the background.

Mount Huggins (12,100 feet), from upper Skelton Glacier.

sledge wheel to measure distance, and correcting the whole with periodic astronomical fixes. A sledge wheel is no more than a bicycle wheel and mileometer trailed by the sledge. The slowest, and most accurate, method is triangulation, which depends on working outward from a precisely known base, taking theodolite bearings on prominent objects, and plotting their exact location on the ground. More stations are then established at some of these fixed points and the survey carried forward from them. The Northern Party's method fell somewhere between these two extremes. Brooke decided to use a theodolite with a calibrated camera mounted above to record the detail. He rejected the use of a running traverse, partly, as he ruefully admitted in his notes, because he was "adept at breaking sledge wheels on rough going," partly because they would be working in country where they had to follow the lie of the land and not a compass course, and partly because much of the coastal territory from the Skelton to the Mawson was made up of narrow valleys with steep, rocky dividing ridges. From sledge level in the valleys little could be seen, and so the surveying would have to be done from the peaks. There was yet another factor to be considered. The two major areas on the edge of the plateau, one of them the notorious Dry Valley between the Taylor and the Mackay, were mainly bare rock and impassable for sledges, so that until the plateau was reached the party's work would be more akin to mountain than to polar surveying.

Leaving Scott Base on October 4, the party reached Gneiss Point two days later, where a tractor team had laid a depot for them. For the next few days they carried out survey and geological work on Mount Newall, and made the remarkable find of a dead seal high up on a glacier and far from the sea. On October 14 they reached Cape Roberts where, a couple of days later, the Auster from Scott Base flew in their depot, to be sited 800 feet up on the snow piedmont above the Cape. For a week they explored the northwest corner of Granite Harbour, and managed to locate a glacier which Brooke had previously seen from the air. This involved a long day's climbing, when Guy Warren and Brooke reached a height of 6000 feet and occupied two survey stations.

During the last few days of October the party split up. Warren and Brooke continued geological and survey work in the lower Fry

Glacier area and at Cape Ross and Gregory Island. Gunn and Douglas went north to the Mawson, climbed Mount Gauss, and took photographs and prismatic angles. The two couples joined up again on November 1 at Gregory Island, and sledged back to Cape Roberts. After a rest day they moved up to the depot, and spent over a week relaying loads onto the Debenham Glacier and working their way to its head. Brooke and Warren penetrated the glacier valley to the south of the Debenham, and managed to do a round of angles looking into the Dry Valley area.

Meanwhile Gunn and Douglas had found a route onto the Miller Glacier, although it was barred by very rough pinnacle ice three feet high. The route was picked out in detail and the pinnacles hacked down with ice axes. By now the afternoons were becoming comparatively warm, so while the dogs dozed in the heat the humans relayed two loads, each of 300 pounds, on both the sledges down to the moraine under Killer Ridge. It was a somewhat chancy journey over very rough going, and as Brooke said afterwards, "I was lucky only to break my brake."

On November 12, while Warren repaired the sledge, Brooke and Gunn surveyed from Killer Ridge in the morning, and in the afternoon took the last loads down the moraine. All these loads had to be manhandled across ten yards of rocks, and then half of them were sledged six miles down the Miller Glacier to a point close to Queen Mountain. Brooke and Gunn climbed back up the glacier with their sledges and shifted the rest of the loads down the glacier, with the frowning cliffs of Killer Ridge on the east of it and a steep, broken hillside on the west. They camped about midnight, and got to bed at 3 A.M. after a very long and hard day.

During the rest of November the party relayed the loads up the Mackay Glacier, keeping hard against the south side until they were above the main icefalls. In this period they also surveyed Mount Suess, and the geologists continued their collecting, which up to date had been somewhat dull, consisting mainly of granite. But now fossils occurred, as reported by Debenham, but unfortunately none of them were *in situ*.

A likely spot for an airstrip had been noted on the watershed between the Mackay and Mawson Glaciers, and Bill Cranfield flew in supplies on December 1 and 2. Brooke and Gunn grabbed the chance of a short reconnaissance flight to the north. They noticed, with some dismay, that the plateau edge was lined with ice bulges which would complicate their journeys, and Gunn also sighted an area which seemed to be promising for detailed geological work. Next day he and his colleague Warren set off with Brooke's team to investigate, and found fairly extensive horizons of low-grade coal, besides numerous fossils.

For the next ten days the party moved north and east, traveling one day and stopping for surveys the next, along the south side of the Mawson Glacier, where Brooke obtained some excellent fixes of features on the north side. It was also discovered that the upper part of the Fry Glacier is really an overflow of the Mawson. By Christmas Eve they had sledged to the high peak near the head of Wright Valley, after making a wide sweep around the Mackay névé to avoid heavy crevassing. Once they reached an area of giant sastrugi, in Brooke's words, "four feet high and shaped like torpedoes on pedestals." These formed an impassable barrier, and so the party was forced far off its route by having to sledge "with the grain."

For the last week of December surveying went on along the edge of Taylor Glacier near Horseshoe Mountain and some miles to the east overlooking Wright Valley. They crossed the head of the Taylor Glacier, and later dropped down into the glacier between Lashly Mountains and Mount Feather, where the geologists were left while Brooke and Douglas sledged back with both teams to the Plateau Depot, picked up loads and returned to meet the geologists on New Year's Day.

So the work went on, to the south of the Lashly Mountains on the southern edge of the Skelton névé, and, by the middle of January, to the east of Mount Feather and the south arm of the Ferrar Glacier. On January 20 the party broke up when Warren and Douglas, who were to return to New Zealand in the American ship *Greenville Victory*, were flown back to Scott Base. The most interesting geological area had been left behind and there were too few instruments to keep four men occupied with the surveying.

Next day Brooke and Gunn planned to begin an assault on Mount Huggins, which had watched so many parties from Scott Base struggling up the Skelton Glacier. It offered a tempting target for climbers — and a useful one too, for photographs taken from its summit would be the only way of recording the elusive Koettlitz/Skelton watershed between Mounts Kempe and Cocks. By January 24 the two men had examined the mountain from Stepaside Spur, and then established a camp at the foot of the Trench Glacier on the north side. They carried a light camp to the head of the glacier, and on January 27 climbed to the top of Mount Huggins, taking eight hours on the final ascent, and thirteen on the return journey to camp.

Snow began to fall heavily, and the reduced party was running short of food. On the evening of January 29 they pushed on down the glacier valley, the foot of snow which had fallen on the already soft surface making the going slow and arduous for the dogs, so that one or other of the men had to go ahead breaking a trail. On the way down the Skelton Glacier to Teale Island, they found a small depot left by Brooke the previous season. After digging it out and noting a year's accumulation of five feet of snow, they pushed on to Teale Island. There they made a final survey station before reaching the Skelton Depot in the evening. Looking at the uninteresting Ross Ice Shelf, they felt it a waste of time to sledge back 180 miles over the flat surface, so decided to fly back to base. The aircraft picked them up on February 6.

It is still too soon to evaluate the scientific results from this long journey but some facts stand out. The party was away from base for 126 days and sledged over 1000 miles. Twenty-nine mountaintop survey stations were occupied, as well as sixteen camp survey stations. Almost the whole area between the Mulock and the Mawson Glaciers was covered and two peaks were climbed — Huggins (12,870 feet) and a lower peak at the south end of the Skelton névé. Several large and important pieces had been fitted into the incomplete jigsaw of Antarctica.

Bob Miller and George Marsh, with two dog teams, had been flown in from Scott Base to the Skelton Depot on October 19, and had then accompanied Ed Hillary's tractor party establishing the depots along our route. On December 15 they arrived, thirty miles ahead of the tractors, at the point chosen for Depot 700. It was a dull overcast day and they found it difficult to pick a suitable site for the aircraft to land. In the evening they called base and reported that they were ready to receive supplies.

The distance from Scott Base to this depot was greater than the Beaver's range, so while the ground party had been traveling, John Claydon had flown stores to a staging depot established in Shackleton Inlet. It was arranged that he would bring them forward to Depot 700 as soon as weather conditions allowed.

At noon on December 17 there was nothing in sight, but all the dogs suddenly began looking excitedly to the north, and sure enough, three quarters of an hour later the tractors appeared over the crest of a rise, and half an hour later they were camping at the depot site. The party now numbered eight, but for two days the weather was bad and the aircraft could not fly. At eight o'clock in the evening of the 19th, John Claydon brought in the first load, and the fuel drums and ration boxes were quickly heaved out. To assist the dog drivers, John then took them for an hour's reconnaissance flight over the route they proposed to follow to the southeast, then flew back to Scott Base, refueling en route at the depot established for the aircraft at Shackleton Inlet.

The tractor party remained to build the depot, but next morning Bob Miller and George Marsh left with two dog teams, steering 130°T to avoid some crevasses which they had seen on their flight the previous evening. Their start was duly filmed, the dogs showing considerable interest in the cameras.

It was a miserable day, with high drift, but it had been arranged that Bill Cranfield would fly in a depot for them during the evening of the next day, and to avoid carrying the heavy loads for longer than necessary they were anxious to cover as much distance as possible in the time available. The first evening they camped after completing 18½ miles, and on December 19 they got away early, traveling 17½ miles before having to pitch camp at half past three in order to keep a radio schedule with Depot 700 at four o'clock. They heard that the plane would be coming in at six o'clock, and as the surface was very bumpy, they busied themselves marking out the most suitable landing strip. Bill Cranfield arrived with twenty-five days' fuel and rations for men and dogs, two tins of pork, one of

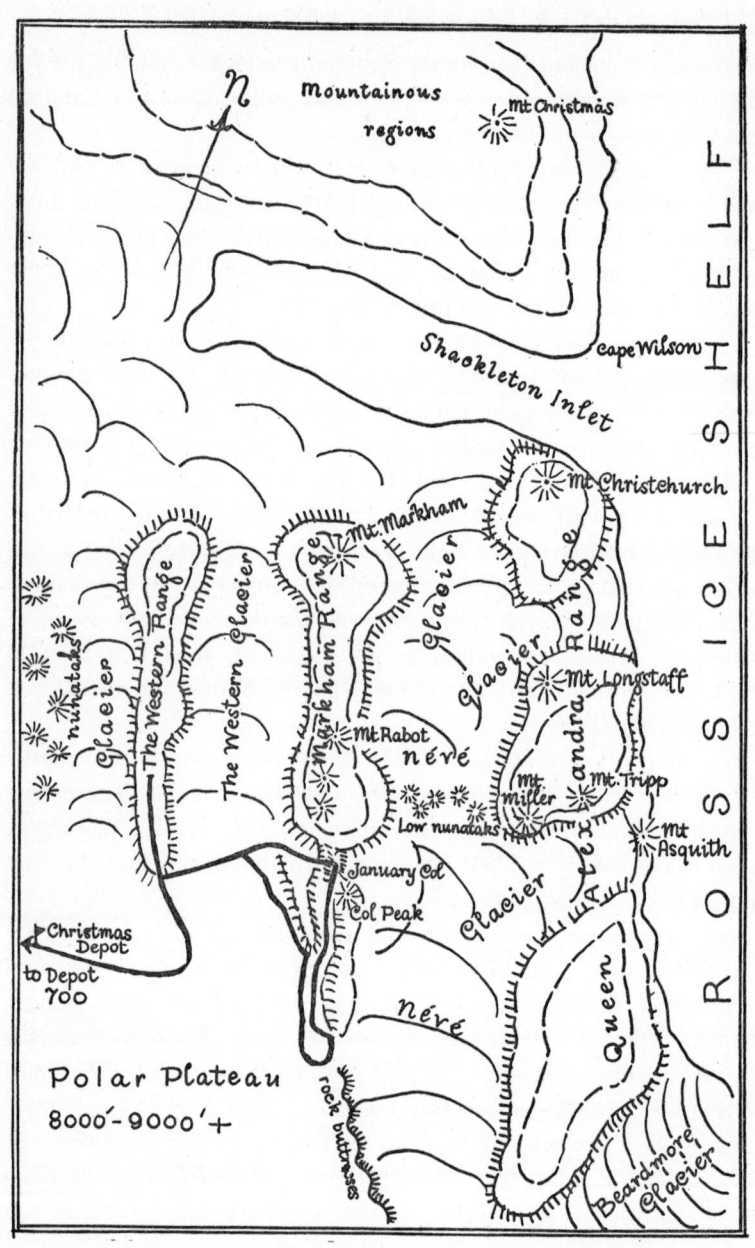

Track of Southern Party from a sledge journal sketch map.

frankfurter sausages, and two pounds of tobacco for George. This set Bob's mind at rest, for suspecting what George might be like if divorced from his pipe, he had threatened to return to base immediately if the aircraft failed to keep up the tobacco supplies. Within half an hour the plane had been unloaded, the pilot had shared a cup of tea with them, and was on his way back to base.

That evening they loaded their sledges ready for an early start. Each team led for three days at a time, and, it being Bob's turn, they loaded 750 pounds onto his sledge, George's team hauling the remaining 1150 pounds. By now they knew their dogs and could judge almost exactly what proportion of the load should go onto each sledge to ensure that the teams stayed the same distance apart when traveling. While they worked, a skua gull flew round the camp for half an hour before disappearing to the northwest. These skuas have been seen far inland by explorers in the past, and they thought that the birds must follow the campsites picking up the debris.

The next two days the weather was bad and prevented them from traveling, but both had developed gastroenteritis, possibly from the tinned pork which they had enjoyed the previous evening, and were therefore glad of the enforced rest. In the evening of the second day George went out to feed the dogs, and with the weather clearing, he saw Mount Markham (15,000 feet), the highest known peak in the Antarctic.

On December 23 they were able to move again, and for three days they made good progress despite patches of huge sastrugi five to six feet high. At half past five, on a beautiful, sunny Christmas evening, they camped 90 miles from Depot 700. The dogs seemed to know by instinct when work was finished for the day and, as the leading sledge halted, the following team would automatically turn away from the tracks and draw up alongside, ready to be picketed some twenty yards distant.

Expectant eyes would be turned on the men as they unlashed the sledges, and the appearance of the ration box was the signal for pandemonium to break out. The drivers had to move quickly, for the

---

The sketch map illustrating the Southern Journey includes the following names of convenience which are not officially recognized: Mount Markham Range, Western Range, Western Glacier, January Col, Col Peak.

dogs in their eagerness often pulled the pickets from the snow, and then there were scenes of complete chaos while the teams were sorted out and separated. Each dog was given between a pound and a pound and a half of pemmican a day.

Then, following the usual camping procedure, they pitched their tent and unloaded sleeping bags, the current man-ration box, the pots and pans box and the Primus, while the paraffin can was placed between the two layers of their double-skinned pyramid tent. The "inside man" then disappeared to lay the ground sheet, while the "outside man" shoveled snow blocks onto the tent skirt. As soon as the inside man called out that he was ready, the sleeping bags and other gear were all passed in to him and he would light the Primus to make a hot drink. His companion was meanwhile securing and marking the whereabouts of everything outside in case a storm blew and they became drifted up. He then handed in the maps on which they would later plot the day's run, and brought in the Thermos and lunch bag for the next day's meal. By this time a welcome hot drink would be ready.

On every alternate day Bob would set up the theodolite in order to obtain a sun fix of their position, while George recorded the findings. Twice a week they kept radio schedules with Scott Base, receiving them in voice but transmitting in rather labored Morse. Once every two weeks they mixed vitamin capsules in a hoosh of dog pemmican and took this outside to feed two spoonfuls to each husky.

At the Christmas camp they proposed to leave two tins of dog pemmican, half a man-ration box and two gallons of paraffin, sufficient for their return journey to Depot 700, so before supper they were out again building the cairn to mark what inevitably became known as "Christmas Depot." Supper was enhanced by the frankfurter sausages and a small tot of brandy which they had taken for the occasion, and it was after midnight before they were in bed.

Now their course veered due east toward what they took to be a chain of mountains with nunataks to the north. On Boxing Day they stopped at lunchtime and established their first survey station, taking a round of angles and a series of photographs. After two hours they ran on until they had covered 18½ miles for the day. By the 27th they were in trouble with crevasses. Bob Miller's sledge broke through a concealed snow-bridge and tipped over. Securing it with ice axes and a climbing rope, it had to be completely unloaded before they were able to haul it out. They decided on a detour northeast toward the nunataks, which would enable them to cross the crevassed area much more safely at right angles. For their lunchtime halt the area between crevasses was so small that both teams had to be picketed alongside each other to prevent them straying onto dangerous ground. After four miles they cleared the crevasses and ran down a gentle slope, only to find that the nunataks were in fact a continuous chain of mountains.

That night they camped on a glacier and, one of the fillings having come out of George Marsh's tooth, Bob tried his hand at dentistry. It was a beautiful evening, and after supper they climbed 1000 feet to the top of the most southern peak of the new mountain chain which they had found. From the top they could see the whole range extending north toward Shackleton Inlet. To the east lay the Mount Markham range, and in between flowed a large glacier which they judged to be thirty miles across. Beyond the Mount Markham range they saw high peaks which they realized must be the Queen Alexandra Range proper. Establishing a survey station at the peak on which they stood, they called their discovery the "Western Range" and decided to make another survey station somewhere along it.

For the next two days the weather was bad and constant drift confined them to their tent, but on the third day they filled their lunch bags, and, leaving the dogs at the camp, set out to walk along the range. It took them eighteen hours to reach the position they had chosen, establish the station, take the angles, and return to camp. As they descended the final snow slope George said he must sit down for a minute, but Bob decided he was too tired to risk it. On arrival at their camp they were so dehydrated that with their hot meal each man drank over a gallon of fluid.

They now planned to cross the glacier they were on, and attempt to reach a snow col on the Mount Markham range which, they hoped, would give them a view of the area immediately west and northwest of the Beardmore Glacier. On New Year's Day they had a splendid run covering 23 miles, and camped in a position whence they could see what appeared to be a good route leading up to the snow col.

On January 2 they started climbing the snow slopes of the Mount Markham range, and on the 3rd they reached their snow col. Unfortunately, although their camp site was some 2000 feet above the glacier, the visibility was now only 100 yards and they could see nothing to the east but a bank of cloud.

Next day visibility was still restricted, but they were able to do some survey in spite of the weather being unsuitable for traveling. Then on January 5 they succeeded in establishing a station on the top of a peak to the south of the col, and from there they had a truly magnificent view. To the west of the Mount Markham range three large glaciers flowed down to the Ross Barrier, one entering Shackleton Inlet, while the other two lay between the inlet and the Beardmore Glacier. With hardly a cloud in the sky they could look down from 10,500 feet onto the Barrier, while to the east and southeast huge ice walls rose up toward the peaks of the Queen Alexandra Range which Scott and Shackleton had seen from the other side during their ascent of the Beardmore. Mount Markham dominated the northern horizon, with the glacier flowing toward it 4000 feet below them. To the east Mount Miller stood nearly 8000 feet above the glacier, while to the south they could see Mount Kirkpatrick.

Their plan now was to sledge south along the snowfields of the Mount Markham range in the hope of determining its southern extremity, and two days later they had covered 37½ miles in this direction. From their camp they were again able to observe the mountains which bound the west side of the Beardmore. From here they looked down over a steep ice wall interspersed with rock buttresses on the vast névé of the glacier they had previously seen flowing toward Mount Asquith, while to the south lay the peaks of the Marshall Mountains. To reach this point they had found themselves sledging down a very steep slope, and, in addition to the normal foot brake, had found it necessary to fit rope brakes under the runners.

The area was covered with windcrust and quite suddenly there would be sharp sounds like pistol shots and several hundred square yards would subside a few inches. This had a terrifying effect on the dogs, and on one occasion George Marsh's team turned round through 180° and bolted along their old tracks. Simultaneously George fell over and lost control. After some confusion the miscreants were chased for a mile with the second team and eventually caught, and started all over again in the right direction.

That night, January 7, they kept their radio schedule with base and learned that the tractor party had successfully reached the Pole and had been flown back; that the RAF contingent had crossed from South Ice to Scott Base; and that we were still 250 miles from the Pole. By then I had asked Ed Hillary to boost the fuel supplies at Depot 700, and he was recalling Bob Miller and George Marsh to the depot to operate a SARAH beacon on which the aircraft could home, and to accept the additional supplies. As they turned back, they gave their estimated time of arrival as January 16.

On January 8 the weather again kept them tent-bound, but on the 9th they traveled to higher ground and established their last survey station. They had done 25 miles and were once more camped on the western glacier, having traveled 800 miles since leaving Skelton Depot. At four o'clock the next afternoon they found Christmas Depot, picked up the supplies and pressed on, camping at six o'clock after 22½ miles. This was their fifth consecutive day of wind and low drift, making traveling most uncomfortable. Talking to base that evening, they heard that the Northern Party had now covered 900 miles after being in the field for 100 days.

The last week back to Depot 700 was uneventful. At times they followed their outward tracks, but the surface was constantly very rough and the tips of the skis got broken over sastrugi. Finally they were down to one pair between them, which they shared for an hour at a time, while the man without trotted along beside the team. Later the aircraft brought them new pairs.

On the evening of January 15 they pitched their camp twenty yards away from Depot 700, having covered 30 miles that day, and called up base to say they were in position and ready to receive supplies. A further radio schedule was arranged for the next morning to give the pilot a weather report. That night the dogs enjoyed a feed of seal meat from the depot.

The following afternoon both the Otter and the Beaver flew in to the depot. In the Otter, John Lewis had a *Times* photographer as passenger, and it seemed hard to realize that the pictures he took would be radioed to London and appear in newspapers the following night. After the aircraft had left, they reloaded their sledges from the depot, ready to start home next morning.

On the return journey the dogs were very fit and going well — they never ran less than 20 miles each day. In four days they had reached Midway Depot, where they loaded their sledges with three tins of dog pemmican and one man-ration box. From January 23 to 26 they were held up by high winds and drifting snow, and by then we were already 80 miles past the Pole when I received a message from them saying, "Can you catch us up?" We sent back, "It looks like a long chase and a stern one."

Then the wind, which had been their foe, became their ally. It blew behind them up to a strength of 18 to 20 knots and helped the sledges along famously. By the 30th they had traveled 612 miles in the month, and reached Depot 480 just after midday. Now they could have a blowout, and while they stocked up with seal meat and pemmican for the dogs they treated themselves to an exotic lunch of anchovies and tinned peaches. Afternoon tea consisted of tinned cake and coffee, and the *pièce de résistance* at supper was a couple of tins of smoked blue cod followed by a tin of pineapple.

On February 8 when they arrived at the Plateau Depot we were already at Depot 700. That evening we had our first direct radio schedule, and as we were able to transmit by voice, many members of the party spoke to them. The replies came back in Morse, slowly and deliberately, and they were chagrined to hear David Stratton commenting, "That must be George — sending with his left foot."

They had now been on the plateau for 101 days at an altitude of never less than 7000 feet: it was time to begin the long downhill run to base. As they dropped in height the temperature rose rapidly. At eight o'clock on the morning of February 10 it was −22°F, at three in the afternoon it was +4°F. Two hours later it was +7°F, and even at nine o'clock that night it was still +4°F, and they were uncomfortably warm.

February 11 was a sad day. Hemp, one of the dogs in George's team, had been suffering for some while with a complaint they could not diagnose. He had become potbellied, sluggish and lame, and evidently suffered a great deal. There was no chance to stop and doctor him, even if the strange malady had been diagnosed. George Marsh had to take the difficult decision to put down a companion that had pulled his sledge for so many miles. He died at once, but his death cast a gloom over the pleasure of home-coming.

On February 14 the two teams reached the Skelton Depot at noon, and eighteen minutes later Bill Cranfield flew in to give them more supplies and a batch of mail.

On the morning of the 21st they were only 60 miles from Scott Base, and the familiar landmark of Mount Erebus came ever closer. During the lunch halt they unexpectedly heard the drone of aircraft, and there was John Lewis in the Otter, bringing out a newspaper reporter and Major Jim Adams, a physiologist from the Medical Research Council, who was working in McMurdo Sound, and who now wanted to travel the last few miles with them making his own examinations.

That night they camped 30 miles from base. Next day they were expected at Scott, and at seven o'clock in the evening all the New Zealanders walked out through the pressure ridges to greet them and escort them home. After the dogs were fed and picketed, they were given a special dinner, and then introduced to a bevy of newspaper reporters who had appeared from the American base wishing to hear about their journey. That night they greatly enjoyed their first bath for 4½ months.

As with the Northern Party, it has only been possible to give the barest outline of the very long journey of 1670 miles made by the Southern Party. The whole expedition is justly proud of their endurance, the distance they traveled, and the survey work which they were able to accomplish. The journey itself was the longest single traverse ever made; that the depots were provided by air, rather than by preliminary sledge journeys, in no way detracts from the fact that they traveled in the field continuously for five months. Rather it emphasizes that the best use of dogs may be obtained when they are supported by air, thereby making a long journey possible in one season where otherwise it would have to be spread over two.

XVI

The Journey Begins

ALTHOUGH we reached South Ice on November 13, weather prevented us from flying to Shackleton until the 15th. This meant that we were already one day late in starting on our transcontinental journey. At base we found that they had been working very hard indeed to prepare for the main journey but at the same time they were concerned at our slow progress to South Ice. Naturally it had been difficult for them to visualize our difficulties from the brief radio reports that were all that the rather poor conditions had allowed. Now that it had been shown possible to take vehicles over the route and we were all working together again, any sense of despondency that there may have been disappeared, and things went ahead at a great pace.

The new date set for our departure was November 24, and we hoped that we should be able to make up lost time during the course of our journey. From our knowledge of the route, we thought that we should be able to reduce the distance by about 70 miles, and although we should still have to probe our way through the crevasses again, our tracks and the marker stakes left behind would speed our movement.

As the remaining days passed, the tempo of work was maintained at the highest level, and the radio room was flooded with last-minute messages and telephone calls from the London office, our relations, other Antarctic stations, the BBC and the press.

It was then that I sent my last message from Shackleton to Hillary, who had begun his journey on the far side of the continent. This gave a short assessment of the situation at our end, and was to prove unduly pessimistic, for we arrived at Scott Base seven days before the date suggested.

HILLARY

734 OWING TO 39 DAYS SPENT FORCING ROUTE TO SOUTHICE OUR START DELAYED TEN DAYS GIVING 200 MILES TO CATCH UP TO MAINTAIN 20 MPD STOP THIS WILL BE ATTEMPTED STOP DISTANCE RUN TO SOUTHICE 400 MILES BUT WILL BE 330 NEXT TIME STOP SEISMIC SNOCAT ONE WEASEL AT SOUTHICE ONE WEASEL ABANDONED ONE RETURNED TO SHACKLETON EARLY ON JOURNEY STOP LEAVING 24TH WITH 3 SNOCATS 2 WEASELS ONE MUSKEG STOP AIR RECCE TO 84S VISIBILITY TO 85S INDICATES SHACKLETON SOUTHICE MOST DIFFICULT SECTION TO POLE STOP NOT CERTAIN 20 MPD CAN BE MAINTAINED TO SOUTHICE BUT EXPECT OVER 20 MPD THEREAFTER STOP WE COULD BE UP TO FORTNIGHT LATE ARRIVING SCOTT BASE BUT WILL ENDEAVOUR REDUCE THIS THOUGH POSSIBILITY REMAINS WE DO NOT ARRIVE TILL 9 MARCH STOP HOPE TO IMPROVE THIS PESSIMISTIC STATE-MENT ON PASSAGE STOP IF YOUR CONDITIONS DIFFICULT WE CAN ACCEPT INTENDED D700 AT 600 MILES BUT WOULD THEN APPRECIATE PROPORTION OF FUEL YOU SAVE IN ADDITION TO TWELVE DRUMS STOP TIME SO GAINED MAY BE USEFUL TO YOU FOR YOUR WORK ON MOUNTAINS STOP AS IT SEEMS UNLIKELY WE CAN MEET AT D700 WOULD APPRECIATE GUIDE FROM PLA-TEAU DEPOT IF POSSIBLE STOP DELIGHTED YOU HAVE VEHICLES ON PLATEAU AND GOING SO WELL CONGRATULATIONS FROM ALL

BUNNY

Meanwhile packing had begun. A complication was the need to separate items under different headings: those for the main journey; others to go on the last flight to Halley Bay; some to be picked up by the American aircraft from Ellsworth (Captain Ronne had kindly offered to ship out some of our more valuable and personal equip-ment); and, lastly, all those things which we were compelled to leave behind. On November 22, we began loading the sledges with 20 tons of food, fuel and material.

That evening it was clear that if the weather held we should get away on the appointed day, so John Lewis prepared a special fare-well meal as our last festivity at Shackleton. All the heavy loading was completed on the following day, but work went on far into the night and many of us did not get to bed until five o'clock in the morning. It was, therefore, hardly surprising that, in spite of our intention to leave at half past two on November 24, we did not get away until 6:40 A.M. Just as we were leaving, a party from the Argentine station twenty miles away arrived, and together with our RAF contingent and Geoffrey Pratt stood waving us good-by. Geoffrey was to fly to South Ice to relieve Hal Lister, the latter joining us in the field.

By the time of our departure the vehicles had all been nicknamed by their drivers, and we left in the order: Sno-cat *Rock n' Roll* — a characteristic enjoyed by all the species; Sno-cat *Able,* named by David Pratt; two Weasels, *Rumble* and *Wrack and Ruin,* belonging to Allan Rogers and George Lowe; next came the Muskeg tractor *Hopalong,* bearing the emblem of a jumping kangaroo and named by our Australian, Jon Stephenson; and the rear was brought up by the Sno-cat *County of Kent,* named by Roy Homard in memory of his Kentish origins.

In spite of the late start, we made 15 miles before camp was pitched. We had also picked up the sledge with twelve barrels of fuel which had been abandoned when Roy's Weasel returned to Shackleton on the second day of the South Ice reconnaissance journey. On November 25, we passed over the filled chasms safely enough, and after 14 miles thought that we were well on the way for a long run. Then, in a twinkling, a snow-bridge fell away beneath *Rock n' Roll,* leaving David Stratton and myself suspended in midair over an impressive chasm. The hole we had made was about 15 feet wide and 60 feet deep, to the first step in the walls of the crevasse below. Peering out of the right-hand side, the situation looked distinctly uncomfortable, for it was impossible to tell how firmly we were wedged against the sides, and in any case there was nothing to step out onto — even the pontoons were inaccessible. Meanwhile, David found that on his side he could reach the rear pontoon, and I followed him out crawling over the ladder-like track as it hung in space.

At first sight recovery seemed almost an impossibility and our immediate reaction was to remove everything from the body of the vehicle. Then David Pratt and Roy moved the two other Sno-cats into position side by side behind *Rock n' Roll* and attached them to the rear towing hook. Next, after careful prospecting along the length of the crevasse, a point was found where George and Allan could take the two Weasels over and bring them round in front of *Rock n' Roll*. There they were joined in tandem, and attached by steel cable to the Sno-cat's front axle. In this way they formed an anchor, preventing the front of the vehicle from falling vertically into the crevasse when an attempt was made to pull it out backward. On a Sno-cat each pontoon is able to swivel freely about its axle, hence it was extremely difficult for us to move the left front pontoon into the correct position to rise over the edge of the crevasse as the vehicle was hauled out.

This was accomplished by lowering David Stratton on a rope into the crevasse where he cut a suitable ledge, then, using the Muskeg as a fifth recovery vehicle, we pulled the recalcitrant pontoon into position and *Rock n' Roll* was drawn slowly backward.

The necessarily simultaneous movement of the five recovery vehicles was a complex maneuver, and it is doubtful if we should have succeeded had we not had the immense power of the other two Sno-cats, using their emergency low gear known to us as "Grandma." On this occasion it showed what it could do when we discovered, at the end of the recovery, that *Rock n' Roll* had been left in forward gear the whole time!

As soon as David and I had stowed all the gear back into our cat, we went off to camp with the rest of the party on the far side of the crevasse. It had taken us about five hours of hard labor to recover *Rock n' Roll* and we were glad to rest.

Pressing on to "Corner Flag Camp," we crossed many more crevasses. From our previous experience we believed them to be quite small, but then we received another warning when a crevasse lid 15 feet wide fell in only a few feet in front of the *County of Kent*, after all the other five vehicles had passed over it. When Roy Homard stopped, his tracks were only three feet from the brink, and he and Ralph Lenton had a great deal of trouble because the two heavily loaded sledges behind him could not be pushed backward, thus preventing him from reversing more than a few feet at a time. After that, we went ahead over the route, probing for crevasses and finding a great many, and this in an area which had caused us no concern on the first journey. Undoubtedly the sun of the previous six weeks had weakened the crevasse bridges and we were now committed to an even more careful examination than we had previously had to make. Several times it seemed that we were leaving the crevasses behind, but as soon as we began to feel happier a new batch of monstrous black caverns would be found beneath the surface.

By the evening of November 29 we had arrived at the 50-mile depot where the temperature was +25°F in contrast to −20°F when we were last there on October 14.

All the time minor mechanical troubles beset us, and David Pratt and Roy were constantly changing radiators, hunting for coolant leaks in the very complicated engine systems, or trying to cure obstinate ignition troubles. We were particularly worried by the appearance of considerable wear on the rollers of *Rock n' Roll's* front left track. This had apparently occurred since it fell into the crevasse but we were unable to discover the cause. It seemed that there was little likelihood of it going for more than a few more miles, and it would therefore be necessary to have a completely new pontoon and rollers sent out by air from Shackleton.

It was now noticeable that some of the party were feeling depressed by our slow rate of progress, but then most of them had not been conditioned by the experience of the previous journey. However, it was only the sixth day out and too soon to be unduly concerned about our schedule, or to prejudice the success of the whole venture by pressing on regardless of the pitfalls.

On leaving the depot everyone was a bit happier, because we not only cleared the remaining 4 miles of crevasses, but covered 27 miles in the day. On December 1, we moved another 41 miles, but that night *County of Kent* drove into camp misfiring badly in spite of all that Roy had done during the previous days. That night we also began to dismantle the damaged pontoon on *Rock n' Roll* and to inspect the bearings. This and other maintenance work held us up until the 3rd, when we traveled for 13 hours and covered 65 miles over the broad undulations of the ice shelf. These undulations seemed to have the form of multiple domes and basins, presumably due to the conflicting forces of the northward-moving ice, from the foot of the "ice wall," and the westward forces of the great Slessor Glacier, entering the ice shelf from the east. The amplitude from crest to hollow appears to be of the order of 30 to 40 feet, with a maximum interval of about 1½ miles, while the general tendency of the surface is to decline from the east to the west.

We were now only seven miles from the eleven-mile-wide crevasse belt lying in front of the "ice wall," and with confidence we set out to find the checkered flag which we had planted in October to mark the first of the crevasses. Presently we saw it ahead, and I was about to say to David Stratton, "I should stop a little way before you get there," when we felt that horrible, prolonged sinking sensation. The bonnet rose up and up in front of us, then there was a jolt and a pause, long enough to make us think it was over, followed by a further lurch as the back sank again and our minds raced over the possible causes and consequences of that second movement. Carefully we crept out and scrambled to the firm snow surface, where we found the front pontoons clawing at the other edge of the chasm while the back of the cat was nearly level with the surface. When the others arrived, they reported that we had been breaking a number of small holes through the surface and that they had been trying unsuccessfully to attract our attention. Here again was an area where the later season was revealing dangers that had not been apparent on our first run.

As we worked to recover the vehicle, it was discovered that the cause of our second lurch was the breaking of four bolts holding the towing hook, for this had torn away from the cat and allowed the back to drop deeper. The recovery took less time than before, but when we had *Rock n' Roll* on the surface once again, we found that the large cast-aluminum steering platform for the rear pontoons had been snapped on both sides. Fortunately David Pratt had brought a spare, and repair work began at once. This went on late that night and during the next day, while the rest of us began the endless business of probing our way through the eleven miles of crevasses. We had the advantage of the old tracks which were almost continually visible along the route, while here and there we had left stakes to mark the worst holes. These aids, together with our greater numbers, enabled us to make slightly better progress than in late October, but it was still slow work.

Owing to lack of time, the engineers had been unable to construct three more of the complicated forward-towing attachments which had been devised for the seismic Sno-cat *Haywire* on the reconnaissance journey. Therefore our three Sno-cats could not be roped together, and remained more vulnerable to crevasses. For this reason, and because the loss of a Weasel was less important than the loss of a Sno-cat, we now sent the two Weasels and the Muskeg ahead, roped together, the leading Weasel to act as a crevasse detector.

On December 9 we were moving forward in this new order over a section of the prodded route when David Stratton, who was skiing ahead to guide my leading Weasel over the prepared track, suddenly pointed back. There behind us we could see two loaded sledges, but no third Sno-cat. At first I feared that David Pratt had dropped right into a crevasse, but then I could just make out a part of the vehicle standing up in front of the sledges. Clearly he was in a bad position and figures could be seen moving about and gesticulating, presumably to recall us. As we skied back, Hal Lister met us to say that all the vehicles would be needed for the recovery, so we unhitched from our various sledges, prodded a turning place for each vehicle, and started back over a course like a switchback, where the numerous smaller crevasse bridges had sunk or broken through. Arriving at the scene, we found *Able* resting in the crevasse with only the very tips of the front pontoons on the surface, the main weight of the vehicle being supported by the back of the body and the rear pontoons hanging free.

Here again was another and different recovery problem. It would be necessary to support the rear pontoons from below when the vehicle was drawn forward, for there was certainly no possibility of hauling it out backward. Happily there was a local closure of the crevasse about 25 feet down, and after some discussion we all set to with shovels to fill in the entire crevasse below the cat until it was possible for men to stand on the snow filling we had made, and to set our crevasse-bridging units in place beneath the pontoons. To secure the bridges, ledges were cut into the walls of the crevasse upon which they could rest at a sloping angle beneath the tracks. They had been specially constructed in 14-foot lengths, each weighing 125 pounds and stressed to carry 4 tons.

It was impossible to put the bridging into position on both sides at the same angle, thus the whole structure looked even more precarious than it really was, and we were particularly concerned about the strength of the ledges at the lower end. On them the whole weight of the body would be bound to fall suddenly as the back dropped free from the side of the crevasse. So as to make the structure more secure, steel rope slings were placed round the ends of the bridging pieces and fastened above to "deadmen" set in the snow above. When all was ready, two Sno-cats began slowly to pull ahead, while two Weasels acting as anchors gradually gave way at the back. As *Able* started to move we held our breath; there was a loud crunch as the ledges under the bridging gave way and the vehicle lurched sideways to sink momentarily deeper but the "deadmen" held; then, like some monster rising from the deep, it appeared to heave and wallow its way to the surface, finally to come safely clear.

When the reloading of *Able* was complete, and all the tools, steel cables, shackles, boards, bridging, ropes and other equipment had been returned to the various vehicles, we all set off for the third time over the broken and sagging crevasse bridges along the trail we had already made. With a few diversions, and great care in driving, everyone reached the sledges, hooked up and continued safely to the end of the probed route.

The day after these events, John Lewis arrived with Fred Morris in the Otter and began to circle the area looking for a place to land. We were scattered over the ice far from the vehicles and by the time some of us had skied back, they were safely down after a remarkable, but necessarily short, landing run of about 100 yards. John had brought us the spare Sno-cat pontoon and four dozen heavy steel track bars and rollers, besides the numerous smaller spares, tools and a few delicacies to vary our sledging rations. An hour later he made a remarkable take-off with the unloaded plane in just over 60 yards, and flew back to Shackleton where the Otter was immediately loaded with the stores waiting to go out to Halley Bay.

At last, on December 10, we cleared the crevassed area and, having confidently increased our speed to a steady 8 mph, arrived safely at the foot of the "ice wall" after a 16½ hours' journey. Expecting to encounter sunken and weakened crevasse bridges on the "ice wall" and over the wide chasms at the top we decided to change to night travel in order to take advantage of the lower temperature which would give a crisper surface, and perhaps add something to the strength of the bridges. We also took this opportunity to change from Local Time to Greenwich Mean Time. This meant that we had to put our clocks forward three hours, sleep through the next day and start our working "day" on the night of December 11–12. We would thus have the added advantage of synchronizing our traveling time with Hillary's party on the far side of the Pole, for on the 26th we were due to open direct communications with him.

Again we prospected on skis to the top of the "ice wall," where the same soft patches of snow existed as before, but we could now see several wide crevasses clearly revealed which had not been apparent before. Here the sun had really been active, for the wide bridges near the top were now deeply depressed, the largest 30 feet wide, having fallen in at one place to leave an immense hole 15 yards to the right of the track. Careful examination showed 20 to 30 feet of snow filling, and this gave us confidence to cross, even with the train of six heavy vehicles. Returning to the vehicles, we started up and again the Weasels were in difficulty in the deep, soft patches, but with some digging clambered their way to the top without further assistance. Crossing the upper crevasses, with a sense of relief we drove straight on to the abandoned Weasel half a mile away.

The idea of flying out a new engine had been carefully considered, but it was not safe to land an aircraft at the top of the "ice wall." As the work would have had to be done before the arrival of the main party and there was no means of transporting the heavy engine from the smooth ice below to the top of the wall, the idea had to be abandoned. Therefore, while many of us were engaged in digging out the sledge that had been left with the Weasel and in stowing properly the items of stores that were with it, the engineers set about stripping the abandoned vehicle of all useful items. Tow hook, SARAH, starter switch, batteries, tracks were taken, even the antifreeze and petrol were pumped out. All this reorganization took several hours. Toward the end of the time, while the newly acquired tracks were being fitted to *Rumble,* I skied a mile ahead to prospect a new route across the great crevasse which had so alarmed us when a part of the bridge fell in beside the Weasel and Sno-cat on the previous run.

The huge hole was still there, made a little larger by subsequent collapse, its margin embellished with a snow cornice formed by the wind. Since this crevasse extended from a heavily fractured area to the south to an icefall on the edge of the "ice wall," there was nothing for it but to find a new way across. After half an hour I was satisfied that I had discovered a reasonable route, and skied back to meet the vehicles. I could see them moving slowly up the slope toward me, with Allan Rogers driving the Weasel *Rumble*. As he approached, I noticed the figure of Hal Lister sitting on the roof, then suddenly there was a lurch, *Rumble* slumped sideways, to be partly engulfed in the snow, and Hal was flung in a heap on the surface. Afterwards I heard that Hal had been acting as lookout for crevasses, but his ignominious disposal by *Rumble,* his torn windproofs and trousers and a nasty scar on the leg, were enough to deter anyone from trying again what was, after all, a dangerous practice. With the assistance of *Rock n' Roll* and *Wrack and Ruin,* we soon had *Rumble* out of trouble, but the appearance of this crevasse, in what we had considered to be a clear area, meant that we should have to start probing again, especially as the crevasse in question ran along the line of our route and at right angles to those we knew to exist ahead.

Work was begun the next day when happily we made good progress, crossing the major crevasse by the route I had found and continuing with the two Weasels and the Muskeg roped together for the next 10 miles. Hoping to travel more quickly we unroped, but after two miles were brought to a halt by four crevasses. Wide and thinly bridged, they were extremely dangerous and we could not understand how we had crossed them without trouble on our previous journey, until we found that on that occasion we had been extremely lucky to strike them 100 yards to the west of our present course, where they were safely bridged. We went steadily on our way in deteriorating visibility, with David Stratton skiing ahead in case of further hazards, and soon we reached the safer area close to the rock of the western end of the Shackleton Range. There, at nine o'clock, we stopped to camp.

Near the camp a glacier flowed down from the east into a wide embayment between the mountains, and although Jon Stephenson had done the general geology of the area during the dog sledging period, I determined to have a look at the rocks which had been denied to me for so long. After pitching camp and pausing briefly for a cup of tea, Jon, Hal, David Stratton and I took the Muskeg and drove up the steep slope of the glacier between the mountains for about three miles, to within a few yards of the screes. Climbing 1500 feet over a series of schists and quartzites, we reached the flat top of the mountain and found it to be entirely covered with rock polygons. From the peak we had a fine view of the surrounding mountains and the endless expanse of ice to the west. We were back in camp by midday and retired after our brief relaxation among the rocks to sleep until it was time to start again that evening.

During the night we traveled 31 miles to reach the first zone of crevassing in the middle of the Recovery Glacier. The following night we started probing the area which had taken us five days to cross at the beginning of November. This time, aided by the markers we had left and the greater number of men, we cleared the route in 14 hours. Only in one place did we feel that there was any real danger. Allan Rogers's and George Lowe's many hours of probing had revealed how broken was the ice below, and when we peered into the dark caverns beneath the surface we could see walls of ice leaning one against the other. Our difficulty was to judge the line along which enough of these reached to the surface to support the weight of our vehicles, but at last a winding route was marked across the surface with a double row of flags. Then, with great caution, I worked *Rumble* gently over, with *Wrack and Ruin* and *Hopalong* keeping the safety ropes tight in case of trouble. Rather to everyone's surprise all went well, none of the vehicles experiencing any trouble, and we were able to camp about half a mile farther on with the whole of the crevassed area behind us. We had crossed the area in one fifth of the time taken on the first journey, and as a result had reached this point in nine days less time than during the October-November journey.

Although we were now ready to go forward, three nights of continuous whiteout, blotting out all surface visibility ahead, made it unwise to approach closer than a mile to the next line of crevasses.

At last, on December 19, the sky cleared and we made an easy passage of the second crevasse belt and the "echelon ridges," but whiteout again made us camp before reaching the "gap" we had found in the crevasses at the foot of the Whichaway Nunataks. Remembering that we had only taken half a day to find our way across this area in November, we had high hopes of reaching South Ice in two more days, but the season had wrought great changes. Probing showed the area to be far worse than we had known and as we worked on we were frequently astounded by our luck on the first occasion. Continually the old tracks led across lids of vast crevasses which could easily have swallowed all our vehicles, and twice in one day we nearly lost Ken Blaiklock.

On the first occasion a bridge gave way beneath his skis. They fell 80 feet to be lost forever, but fortunately the crevasse was narrow and he saved himself. New skis were taken to him, for it would have been foolhardy to walk about on such an area, and a few hours later when he was kneeling on them peering into a hole he had cut in a bridge, Ralph Lenton arrived. As Ralph stood chatting, the bridge beneath Ken fell away leaving him kneeling on his skis in the middle of a four-foot-wide gap! Then, last thing that night, when probing was over and we were walking to our tents beside the vehicles, the snow near my rear sledge gave way beneath Jon Stephenson and left him hanging by one elbow over a deep dark hole from which it is doubtful if anyone could have been recovered, even if he had survived the fall.

After another night of probing we had examined and marked 1½ miles of the route taking us as far as our old friend the "Obelisk." The last mile was the worst, but the tortuous course was gay with colored flags, stakes and ski sticks — 98 of them in one mile, each marking a particularly hazardous point, for minor crevasses we now crossed without concern. In the bright sunlight the scene was suggestive of a course prepared for some nightmare "bending race." David Stratton, David Pratt and I could hardly believe that this was the place through which we had previously found a way in a few hours — this time ten men had spent two days weaving a course among the dark caverns and crevasses we had crossed so blithely. Before going through with the vehicles, I went forward over that part of the complicated course which I should have to drive, for here I would have to pass within a few inches of every marker and it was as well to know what one was up against before making the attempt. Quite by chance, I probed a smooth area toward the far end of the run, to find only two feet of snow forming the center of the proven track! Unluckily, those who had gone before had only found a hard impenetrable windcrust beneath the surface and had missed this narrow soft area in the middle. We spent another hour seeking a way past four overlapping crevasses, each being narrow enough and the intervening walls sufficiently strong to bear the weight of the vehicles.

When at last we began our passage I do not think there were many who thought we should arrive without having had to recover at least one, but our luck was in and when I drew up at the "Obelisk" with all the other vehicles safe behind, we congratulated each other on what we hoped would be the last crossing of a crevasse area between that point and the Pole.

There remained a few crevasses between us and the Whichaway Nunataks, but these were quickly crossed and we soon reached our old camping place not far from the rocks above. Later, four of us, Jon, Ralph, Roy and I, decided to visit the nearby nunatak and perhaps collect a few of the fossils which Jon had already found there on his memorable visit in March. After so much snow and ice, and with the prospect of nothing else but snow until we arrived on the far side of the continent, it was a pleasure and a relief to scramble over the screes, to feel the rock beneath boots specially donned for the occasion, and to find a few fragmentary fossil remains of a bygone vegetation.

After six hours' sleep we were off on the last day's journey to South Ice. Passing various nunataks, we pushed on over the rough sastrugi that still ran across our path reducing the speed to 3 or 4 mph. In places steeper bulges of the ice topography showed heavily crevassed areas, but these were easily avoided, and when breasting the last ridge we found the station lying dead ahead I was able to congratulate David Stratton on his navigation.

At South Ice we were met by Hannes La Grange, who had been maintaining the meteorological observations, while Geoffrey Pratt had busied himself with seismic reflection and refraction and shooting to determine the speed of the shock wave through this higher altitude ice and the depth of ice to the rock beneath. When our vehicles and sledges had been parked, we repaired to the hut for a cup of tea, but it was only built to hold four and, with twelve of us present, all but the two already installed would have to sleep in tents. Here we heard that Major Lassiter intended to fly up to visit us with Captain Finn Ronne, for I had offered the facilities of South Ice if it would assist their flying program. Oddly enough when last I met the major, in Graham Land in 1948, he had been with Captain Ronne. They were also to bring John Lewis on a visit, and had very kindly offered to make up the plane's load with ten drums of petrol from Shackleton, thereby saving us two flights with the Otter.

We were now at well over 4000 feet and temperatures were correspondingly lower, so it was decided to go back to day travel when we left South Ice. As the American plane was due at half past two in the afternoon, when everyone would want to be up and about, it seemed suitable to set this as a deadline for our change from night to day activities, and everyone went off to get as much sleep as he could before that time. When the twin-engined American machine arrived we all turned out to welcome them and to unload the drums of fuel they had brought, before showing the party over the station. An hour later they flew away to Ellsworth leaving us to continue our preparations for departure on Christmas Day. The first loads to be prepared were for the two dog teams, due to leave on the 23rd to reconnoiter the route ahead of the vehicles. The next day they set off carrying 20 days' rations, intending to report progress at eight o'clock that night, and on every date divisible by three thereafter.

On December 22 I sent the following message to Hillary summarizing the situation:

PERSONAL FOR HILLARY STOP WE ARRIVED SOUTH ICE 21 DECEMBER AFTER SEVERE CREVASSE TROUBLE AND THREE MAJOR RECOVERIES OF SNOCATS STOP DISTANCE TRAVELLED IN 29 DAYS 349 MILES BUT CONSIDER THIS WORST STAGE OF JOURNEY AND EXPECT RAPID TRAVEL FROM HERE ON STOP THANKS FOR YOUR INFORMATION AND PROPOSED CREVASSE RECCE HOPE YOU WILL BE ABLE TO MARK ROUTE THROUGH, OR LIMIT OF AREA, WITH SNOW CAIRNS OR STAKES STOP WE LEAVE HERE WITH FOUR SNOCATS THREE WEASELS ONE MUSKEG WILL PROBABLY REACH

YOU WITH FOUR CATS AND ONE WEASEL STOP TWO DOG TEAMS
WILL TRAVEL AHEAD STOP WE EXPECT LEAVE SOUTH ICE 25TH
THEN OTTER AND FOUR RAF FLY THERE TO AWAIT SUITABLE
DAY FOR FLIGHT TO SCOTT STOP HOPE FOR RADIO CONTACT WITH
YOU AS ARRANGED 26TH ONWARDS STOP HAPPY CHRISTMAS TO
YOU ALL

BUNNY

With the dog teams away we turned our attention to unlashing
and reloading the sledges. It was certainly a busy scene, for there
were eight vehicles, counting the two that were already up at South
Ice, together with twelve large sledges and a number of smaller ones.
Everywhere stood piles of material, scores of fuel barrels, dozens of
jerricans, piles of boxes, ropes in profusion, a hundred other items
sorted or to be sorted, stowed and lashed down before we could leave
on the next leg of our journey to the Pole.

Meanwhile, David Pratt and Roy Homard were working hard on
the vehicles, preparing them for the long journey ahead. One major
task which they had expected would be necessary at South Ice was
the replacement of the damaged pontoon on *Rock n' Roll*. We had
been putting this off time after time, on the grounds that the more
mileage we could get from the old one, the further we should be
able to go after fitting the new. This situation still obtained for there
was very little additional wear and we decided to go on carrying the
spares as long as the old parts remained serviceable.

When we went to our sleeping bags on December 24, 320 gallons
of petrol had been used to fill the tanks of all eight vehicles, the
sledges bore another 109 barrels, totaling 5200 gallons and weighing approximately 21 tons. In addition, we were carrying half a ton
of lubricants and 1½ tons of tools and spare parts. The remaining
nine tons of payload included half a ton of explosive for the seismic
work, 1½ tons of food and half a ton of paraffin, major items these,
the rest being made up of scientific equipment, tents, camping gear,
ropes, skis, ice axes and all the other minor needs of a party that is
to be entirely self-contained for three or four months.

XVII

South Ice to the South Pole

AT TWENTY MINUTES TO EIGHT on Christmas Evening we finally left South Ice and set out for the Pole just 555 statute miles distant. There were many last-minute tasks to perform; David Stratton leveled a line of pegs over the snow for 3½ kilometers for Geoffrey Pratt's seismic refraction shots, and then a further line of 50 stakes, extending over a mile, for Hal Lister's glaciological work. While this was going on, Ralph Lenton removed the transmitter from the hut and installed it in the *County of Kent,* replacing it by less powerful equipment which would meet the needs of the RAF party during their brief stage at South Ice, before they flew across to Scott Base. Another major task was undertaken by Hannes, Geoffrey and Ralph: this was to scrub out and tidy the hut itself, so that everything should be in good order for the new occupants. The rest of us were working outside, tidying up the whole area, digging out from the snow the aviation fuel which would be needed for the Otter, and last of all lashing down on top of the sledge loads the tents, skis, crevasse flags, probes and other items required immediately to hand when traveling.

Overriding them all was our determination to listen to the Queen's Christmas Day Broadcast before we left. The radio at South Ice was the only type capable of receiving the particular frequency, and at five minutes to three we were all congregated in the tiny living room. Bulky forms filled every chair, sat on bunks and table, or leaned against the walls, then in silence we listened to that faraway voice speaking across the world. To us, who were, perhaps, the most isolated listeners, there seemed to be special encouragement, not only because we were proud that Her Majesty was the expedition's Pa-

233

tron, but because we were engaged upon a Commonwealth enterprise.

Outside once more, we still found many last-minute things to do and as each vehicle and its sledges was completed, the drivers decorated them in Christmas spirit. Besides Union Jacks and flags of the Commonwealth, a white ensign and the ensign of the RAF appeared, the gay scene being enhanced by the fluttering of dozens of red and black trail pennants, together with the larger red and white checkered crevasse flags. Here and there colored streamers trailed in the wind, while Ralph Lenton's low-slung Muskeg *Hopalong* looked more like a carnival with its motif of tiny Chinese lanterns. As we moved off, the long column was a gay, colorful sight, the vehicles winding their way round the mound that hid the deserted hut, and turning south to follow the trail pioneered by the dog teams.

Blaiklock and Stephenson had already reported that they had found no trouble over the first 32 miles, although the surface consisted of patches of iron-hard sastrugi, with areas of very soft snow lying between. That first evening progress was slow as the vehicles and sledges bumped and banged over the ridges, but we pushed on for three hours to camp at the second of the 6-foot snow cairns built by the dog party. These were constructed of sawed snow blocks placed one on top of the other, and stood up like shining white pillars at a distance of two or three miles.

In the morning, whiteout prevented us from seeing the surface, so that it was impossible to move without the probability of damage to the vehicles. We therefore took the opportunity to make a seismic sounding of the ice and to do some glaciological work. Radio conditions were very bad, and we could hear nothing from either Shackleton, Halley Bay or the Pole Station. This was a pity, as on this day we had planned our first attempt at direct contact with Hillary's field party and Depot 480. Nothing was heard.

By a quarter to six the sky was beginning to clear, and we could see something of the surface, so we moved off over the terribly hard and extensive sastrugi. The course led due south over a series of undulations extending across our path. These appeared to have an amplitude varying from 80 to 280 feet, and a wave length of approximately four miles. We discovered that the worst sastrugi always occurred on the north-facing slopes, while the tops of the ridges were relatively smooth, and the south-facing slopes were only cut to a minor degree. That night we stopped at the dog party's 35-mile cairn, after traveling 25 miles. During the day there had been periodical trouble with coolant leaks on the Weasel driven by Hal Lister, and David Pratt in *Able* was keeping him company. When the time came to camp there was no sign of either of them. When next morning they had still failed to appear, Roy Homard and Allan Rogers went back in the Muskeg, which could travel more quickly and easily over the sastrugi. At half past three I sent Geoffrey Pratt and Hannes La Grange ahead in *Haywire,* telling them to complete the next seismic station 30 miles on, so that we should not be held up by that particular task when we got on the move again.

During this long wait Ralph Lenton made radio contact with Scott Base, and conditions were so good that I was able to speak with John Claydon and to discuss the flying conditions as they would affect John Lewis when he attempted his transpolar flight. This direct voice contact with Scott Base was most gratifying at this long range, but we still could not get in touch with Hillary, who was reported to be 290 miles from the Pole, nor with Depot 480, where a static radio transmitter had been set up.

At last, just before nine o'clock, the breakdown party pulled into camp, having cured the trouble by fitting a new Weasel radiator. Setting off at twenty past ten that night, we were in trouble again when George's *Wrack and Ruin* lost power and was only able to crawl. Roy Homard soon cured this, and we were able to make 15 miles by a quarter to four in the morning, when we stopped at the 55-mile cairn. So developed the picture of travel which was to be our lot throughout almost the entire journey — long hours slowly grinding over hard sastrugi, or through deep soft snow, frequent minor troubles with one or other of the vehicles, time spent every three hours in taking meteorological and gravity observations, and the periodic boring of holes for seismic shooting. Camping, eating, vehicle maintenance and sleeping had all to be fitted into what hours remained. As a result there was generally very little time for sleeping, and at the end of the journey I am sure that we all considered the outstanding hardship to have been lack of rest.

On December 29 we reached the cairn marking 100 miles from South Ice, where we found Ken and Jon with the dog teams, and Geoffrey and Hannes with *Haywire*. The cairn stood in a hollow running east-west to join another deep curious-looking depression which appeared to extend almost north-south. Unfortunately we had no time to investigate, but Geoffrey's gravimeter indicated a sudden shallowing of the ice, and we thought that the surface disturbances were probably due to this. Our position at this time, as observed by David Stratton, was 83°33'S, 29°02'W, and the approximate altitude 5800 feet.

General vehicle maintenance, carried out every 200 miles, was now due, and in addition a number of sledge towbars which had been broken by the heavy going had to be electric-welded. We therefore knew that our stop was bound to be longer than usual, and this had the advantage of allowing the dogs to get well ahead again. Our increasing altitude was making the Sno-cats overheat as they hauled their 6-ton payloads in second and third gears. I therefore took the opportunity of replacing the four-bladed fan on *Rock n' Roll* with another having six blades.

December 31 was a day of beautiful clear weather, but not a good day for us. Troubles came one after another: first the welding of the towbars proved to be a much longer job than we had expected, then there were difficulties with two of the Weasels, and when we were finally about to start, at seven in the evening, Hal's rammsonde became stuck three meters down, and we had to dig a pit to that depth before we could recover it. By half past eight we had moved off, but we did not get very far, for first George Lowe broke a sledge runner, and then Allan's Weasel *Rumble* broke a track and had to be abandoned as no replacement was being carried. Fortunately we had left the Muskeg tractor at the last camp site only six miles back, for it was the first of the vehicles to be dropped, according to plan, when the consumption of fuel had sufficiently lightened our loads. Now, it was possible to go back and pick it up to replace *Rumble*.

As the result of these troubles we camped where we were, but I again sent Hannes and Geoffrey on with *Haywire* to get into position for another seismic shot. At midnight I made the rounds, giving everyone a tot of brandy with which to see in the New Year.

Sno-cat Able before Mount Huggins.

Mount Harmsworth (9300 feet), from Skelton Glacier.
Climbed by the Geological Party from Scott Base.

Sno-cat Haywire on Skelton Glacier; Mount Huggins in the background.

Looking across the open water of McMurdo Sound
to the Western Mountains.

Camp on the Portal, entrance to Skelton Glacier, late February 1958.

Emperor penguins watch the unloading of HMNZS *Endeavour* at Scott Base.

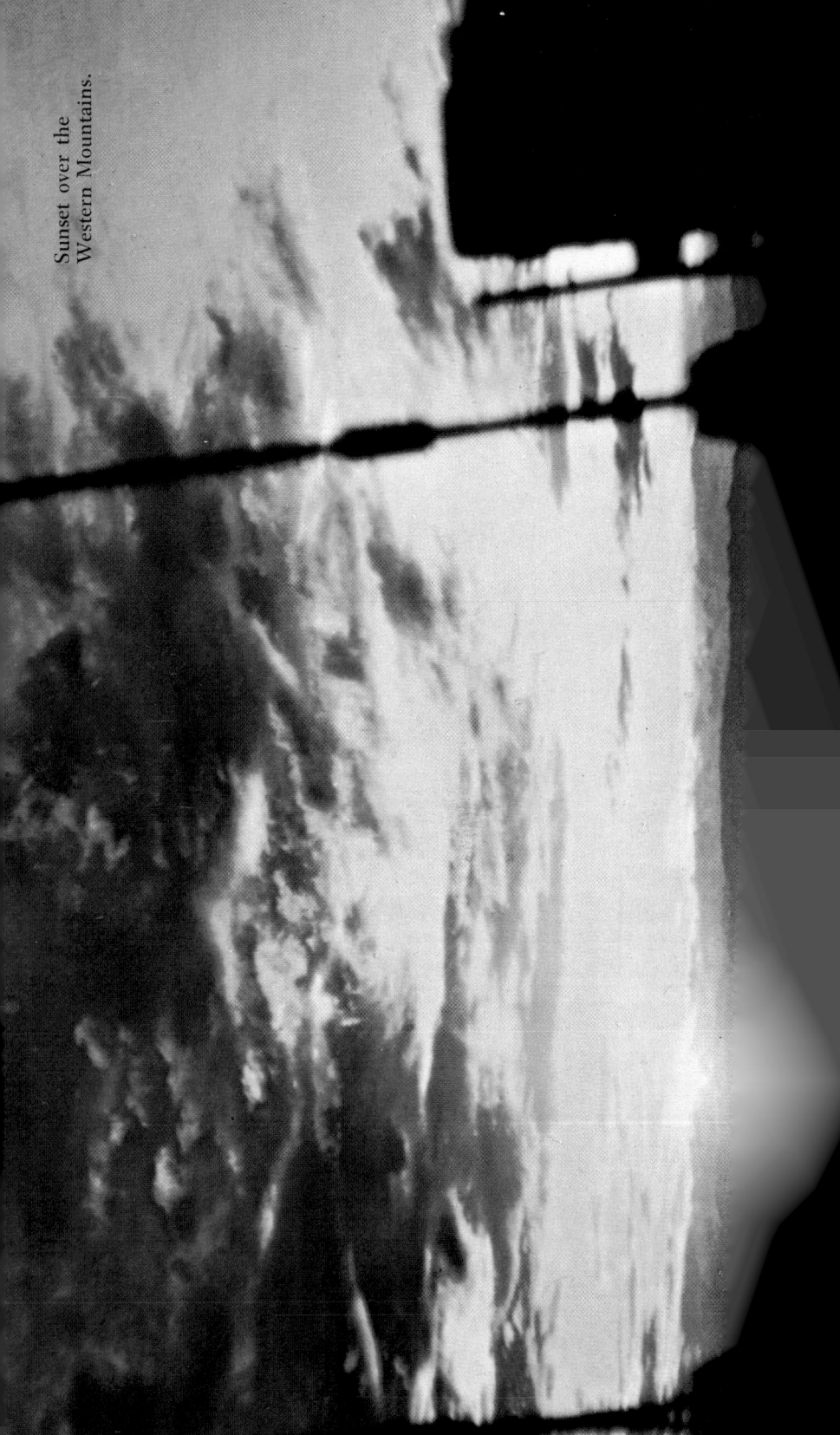

Sunset over the
Western Mountains.

On New Year's Day conditions were so good that we hoped to cover 50 miles, but the surface was too soft for the Muskeg, which was towing two heavy sledges, and it could not travel faster than 2 to 3 mph. Everyone had a soft spot for *Hopalong* because it had gone so far and so well with a heavy load, and had given no trouble. When first we had left it, we had all been sad, then delighted when it had joined us again, but there was no place for sentiment where the efficiency of the party was concerned, and having no Muskeg spares, it must be the next to go. In the circumstances we worked it as hard as possible, saving extra load on the Weasels which would have to travel farther.

To speed our progress the second sledge was taken from *Hopalong* and put as a third behind the *County of Kent,* which seemed to take it easily. *Hopalong* could now keep up 5 mph in third gear, which was reasonable, for it had never been in top gear for the entire 530 miles from Shackleton. In all we covered 39 miles that day, the last nine over increasingly severe sastrugi, which in the end so separated the vehicles that we were forced to camp. This worsening surface was the beginning of our most continuously bad area, and next day, January 2, I wrote:

> Another 30 miles today, but what a labour! All vehicles in first and second gear all the way over the most corrugated fields of continuous sastrugi. The strain on vehicles and sledges is prodigious; particularly I worry about the gear-boxes, for these constant hours of heavy work in low gear is bound to tell on them. Already "Rock 'n Roll's" lay-shaft is very much noisier than it was. One bright spot is that the six-bladed fan now maintains the engines at 160°F even with the radiator doors half shut.

With the dog tracks still extending ahead of us, there was no need for navigation, and Geoffrey and Hannes again went on ahead, followed by the two Weasels and the Muskeg, which were slower than the cats over the murderous sastrugi. It was impossible to go round the high ice-hard ridges, for they formed a great field that extended out of sight in all directions. The best that could be done was for each driver to judge the course for his own particular type of vehicle, and often we found ourselves scattered a mile or two apart, working and weaving our way among the ridges four and five feet high. Sometimes, when there was no easier way, vehicles and sledges had very deliberately to be driven at a speed of half a mile an hour or less over vertical drops. Wending our way, twisting and turning, sometimes at right angles to the course, we tried to keep within reasonable distance of the dog sledge tracks which preserved a fairly steady line and prevented us from making too much extra mileage. When the snow cairns were visible (usually at a distance of about two miles) they were an excellent guide, for we could work steadily toward them. Even the trail of the dog teams wandered considerably and here and there the tracks in the snow revealed the upsetting of a sledge, or where two ski tracks ended abruptly against a ridge we knew that someone had come to grief.

Over this terrain the Sno-cats handled much better than the Weasels, for their articulated tracks conformed more easily to the surface and their great power, and five forward gears, gave easier control. Yet the drivers had their own problems, because the second or third sledges tended to swing more freely and, linked with a wire tow, would catch up and ram the cat or the sledge ahead. The Weasels, on the other hand, did not roll but pitched heavily. Climbing to the top of a sharp-topped ridge, they would tilt up and up, then suddenly dip violently forward, followed by the plunging 2½-ton sledge. Some drivers had the added irritation of towing a dog sledge behind the main load and this, being narrow, would yaw from side to side, often turning over and having to be righted by a fuming passenger. And yet we had good reason for taking these additional dog sledges. Should the vehicles break down, making it necessary for us to walk the remainder of the distance, we had to have sledges that we could manhaul.

Mile after mile this trial of tempers and equipment continued — would it ever stop, we wondered? By now we had expected to be well up on the polar plateau, experiencing relatively easy going instead of these endless sastrugi stretching at right angles to our path. The winds, it seemed, must blow perpetually from the east, scouring and grooving the surface year after year.

As the day progressed, David Stratton and I first found Allan Rogers with a steel towbar that had caught in a snow ridge and been bent right back beneath the sledge. This was unscrewed and replaced with a wire tow. Then, farther on, we found Geoffrey and Hannes together with Hal and George. The seismic spread was ready, but it was essential to wait until the last of the vehicles had ceased to roll, for the extremely delicate instruments would record their vibrations even at a distance of a mile or two. While they were waiting, Hal had decided to drive his rammsonde into the bottom of the pit that had been prepared for the explosive charge. There it had again become jammed in a hard layer of ice several meters down, and a new pit had to be dug before the seismic shot could be fired. When this had been done, we pushed on again to catch up the dog teams, and found them encamped after we covered 30 miles in the day.

That night I was able to speak to Hillary, who said that he was expecting to arrive at the Pole the following day, which for him would be January 4, as he was on the other side of the date line.

All day on the 3rd we traveled over the most vicious sastrugi, the vehicles making very heavy weather and the sledges suffering severely. More and more towbars were getting damaged, so that most of the towing was by steel wire rope which was very hard on the transmissions. We had hoped to make 25 miles in the day, to give us an average of 20 miles per day from South Ice, but all that we could do was 18. By then the blue skies had clouded over, and visibility became too bad to travel over such terrain.

We had taken to traveling by sun compass, for the magnetic compass was already showing some sluggishness. We had therefore mounted a pair of these instruments, one on either side of *Rock n' Roll,* and when the driver's side was obscured by the shadow of the vehicle, the co-driver would call out the heading at frequent intervals.

As the altitude at which we were traveling increased, it was necessary, for the sake of efficiency and economy, to change the carburetor jets on all the vehicles. This we did every 2000 feet above 4000 feet — not, of course, to increase the power of the engines in any way, but only as an economy measure. Indeed, as we gained altitude, our unsupercharged engines were continually losing power, though such was their reserve that no loss was yet apparent, and the Sno-cats continued to haul their maximum loads without trouble. Furthermore, for the last 57 miles we had been running in first and second gears, yet the average for the whole distance that we had traveled was still 1.25 miles per gallon, certainly better than we had expected.

That evening I received a message from Hillary suggesting that, as we were delayed, I should consider stopping at the South Pole and flying the party out with the assistance of the Americans. To this I was unable to agree, and replied explaining the situation. The messages exchanged were as follows:

DEAR BUNNY:

I am very concerned about the serious delay in your plans. It's about 1,250 miles from the Pole to Scott Base, much of the travelling north from D700 being somewhat slow and laborious, with rough hard sastrugi. Leaving the Pole late in January, you will head into increasing bad weather and winter temperatures, plus vehicles that are showing signs of strain. Both of my mechanics regard such a late journey as an unjustifiable risk and are not prepared to wait and travel with your party. I agree with their view and think you should seriously consider splitting your journey over two years. You still probably have a major journey in front of you to reach the Pole. Why not winter your vehicles at the Pole, fly out to Scott Base with American aircraft, return to civilization for the winter, and then fly back into the Pole station next November and complete your journey? This plan would allow you to do a far more satisfactory job of your seismic work, and I feel fairly confident that Admiral Dufek would assist with such a flying programme. Personally I feel the need for a break from the plateau after nearly four months of tractor travel, and there's a lot to do. I prefer not to wait at the Pole station, but will get evacuated to Scott Base as soon as possible. If you decide to continue on from the Pole, I'll join you at D700. Sorry to strike such a sombre note, but it would be unfortunate if the sterling work you've put into making your route through to South Ice and the Pole should all be wasted by the party foundering somewhere on the 1250 miles to Scott Base. I will go ahead with the stocking of D700, and I will leave at the Pole station full details plus maps of the route from Scott to the Pole.

HILLARY

HILLARY POLE STATION:

Appreciate your concern, but there can be no question of abandoning journey at this stage. Innumerable reasons make it impracticable to remount the expedition after wintering outside Antarctica. Our vehicles can be, and have been operated at minus 60 but I do not expect such temperatures by March. Whiteout and drift will be our chief concern. I understand your mechanics' reluctance to undertake further travel, and in view of your opinion that late season travel is an unjustifiable risk I do not feel able to ask you to join us at D700, in spite of your valuable local knowledge. We will therefore have to wend our way, using the traverse you leave at the Pole. The present field of giant sastrugi has extended 57 miles so far, and continues with ridges up to 4 ft. Are we to expect similar fields north of D700, and approx how many miles *in toto*? Main damage is to sledge tow bars, which have to be electrically welded causing delay. Am shortly abandoning second vehicle as planned, leaving us 4 cats 2 weasels. Max interval seismic stations 30 miles, gravity stations 15 miles, rammsonde once or twice daily, meteorology includes fluxplate and radiation measurements. Present position 84°43'S altitude 7,000 ft.

BUNNY

Unfortunately this exchange became known publicly, and although we were quietly getting on with our own work, it gradually became apparent that the press had turned the matter into a *cause célèbre*. It was not until we reached the Pole Station that I began to realize the amount of publicity which the expedition had now acquired. For the next fortnight it was argued and debated in newspapers and journals throughout the world, and much well-meant advice was given to members of the Committee at home, where our small office staff took the brunt of a press onslaught none of us had ever visualized.

Meanwhile I had received encouraging support from the Committee, who told me to take any decisions that might be necessary in the light of the situation in the field. As I, and all my party, had complete confidence in our ability to carry the journey through, and were considerably surprised at the turn of events, there was virtually no decision to make. We continued with our work, and traveled at our normal rate of about 30 miles per day whenever possible, intending to increase that speed by spreading the seismic shots more widely beyond the Pole.

On January 4 Hillary had arrived at the Pole, stayed a few days, and then flown back to Scott Base where he set about building up the supplies of fuel at Depot 700, as I had requested. This seemed a wise precaution, for we had no means of estimating our fuel consumption in the soft snow which, he had reported, lay before us.

At last, on January 5, Blaiklock and Stephenson reported that they were passing out of the bad sastrugi, and it seemed that we should be able to make better progress. This proved to be true and that day we thankfully completed 32 miles. It was with a tremendous sense of relief that we were at last able to drive two or three consecutive miles in top gear. Up to now, the vehicles had ground along in a lower gear nearly the whole distance from Shackleton. We estimated that from Shackleton, 575 miles away, we had traveled, perhaps, 45 miles in "top."

As the time had come to abandon our second vehicle, we again regretfully prepared to leave the Muskeg behind. This also entailed leaving one of the large sledges which could no longer be towed. Together with fourteen empty fuel drums this formed a memorial pile to *Hopalong*, a hard-working and still active friend, whose life ended in latitude 85°15′S.

From January 6 onward the dog teams ran with the vehicles. That day they kept up well, covering a total of 30 miles, and loving the novelty of following a track and the company of the strange-looking tractors.

The days' route took us over almost continuous low, hard sastrugi which, although not so damaging as the really high ridges we had encountered before, was none the less very hard on the vehicles and sledges. The general surface was still undulating, the long rises and falls being steeper toward the north. Here and there during the course of the journey there appeared to be arcuate snow forms, of considerable size, rising perhaps thirty feet or more above the surface. Because of the general nature of the terrain it was difficult to decide whether or not these were a part of the normal, rolling snow ridges, but there were occasions when one gained the impression that we might be seeing "snow dunes" formed in the same way as sand dunes. Having completed another 30 miles on the 8th, we found a broken U bolt on Hal's Weasel, but George Lowe's *Wrack and Ruin* was burning a pint of oil every five miles, with a petrol consumption of 1½ miles per gallon, and soon we should have to decide which of the two should be the next vehicle to be abandoned. The 9th was a maintenance day. Various repairs were carried out and the fan on *Haywire* was changed to a six-bladed type. A seismic shot, fired in a hole 36 feet deep, showed the thickness of the ice to be about 6500 feet. As our altitude at this time was about 7850 feet, the rock below the camp site must have been at 1350 feet above sea level. Although these figures have yet to be worked out in detail, they indicate that where we then were (86°31'S), at 240 miles from the Pole, the rock surface was lower than in the vicinity of South Ice, which was so much nearer to the coast.

When all our work was completed, we made a short run of 20 miles to maintain the daily average which we had at last raised to just above that distance. This brought us up with the dog teams, which had gone on ahead while the maintenance work was in progress. We found the men asleep in their tent, which was pitched not far from the beginning of an extremely bad belt of giant sastrugi. It proved to be 10 miles wide, and was probably "Gordon's Bank," a name given to it because, when flying across the continent, Gordon had reported that around 87°S there was a steep slope with an extremely badly cut up surface which might cause us a lot of trouble. We found that, for a short distance near the bottom of the slope, which was after all only about 200 feet high, there were very high ridges, but after that it was no worse than many other areas. When the day's run of 30 miles was complete we were 192 miles from the Pole, and if the air report was correct we could expect better conditions over the remaining distance. In this we were disappointed, for the next two days provided more and more sastrugi, together with constant whiteout which reduced our movement to 15 and 16 miles. On the 13th the sastrugi continued but it was another misadventure that halted our movement. Both the dog drivers, Ken Blaiklock and Jon Stephenson, had to halt with severe stomach disorders, sickness and temperatures around 101°F. We quickly pitched their tent, and made them as comfortable as possible in their sleeping bags. This was not the first time this curious sickness had hit us, though on this occasion the attack seemed to be much more severe than others had experienced. During the past days Roy Homard, Hal Lister, George Lowe and David Pratt had all suffered the same trouble in varying degrees, and it seemed that some infection was running through the whole party. Our difficulty was to trace the source, for apart from speaking to each other in the open air, there was no other direct association of all the people who were involved. In any event, infections of any kind are rare in the Antarctic, and practically unknown when people have been long isolated from outside communities. Later all the rest of the party, except Ralph Lenton and myself, fell ill with the same complaint.

For the next two days David Stratton and George Lowe drove the two dog teams to give Ken and Jon time to recover from their sickness and subsequent rather weak state. It was here that we abandoned Hal Lister's Weasel in latitude 88°03'S. By now it had four broken U bolts, and for some time had leaked oil in ever-increasing quantities. The leak could not be cured without removing the engine — a three-day task — and we were not altogether surprised when it finally broke down with a "run big-end." Uncertain as to which of the two remaining Weasels would last the longer, we had brought both forward for 100 miles beyond the point where it had been planned that we should drop one on the grounds of fuel economy. Now we were glad that we had done so, and all Hal's glaciological equipment was stripped from his Weasel and transferred to *Rock 'n Roll,* in which he was to travel in the future. We had also to abandon another large sledge, sharing its remaining load among the others. When we moved on, the five surviving vehicles were still transporting 22 tons between them.

By this time we were moving fairly steadily over a surface which was still undulating, with very rough sastrugi on the northern slopes, and were wondering when we should finally reach the smooth level surface which we had expected the polar plateau to present. The maximum day's run was limited to 30 miles, but this was as much on account of the dog teams as it was for the seismic work. On the 13th I had already radioed to Hillary at Scott Base asking him to inquire from the Americans whether there was any possibility that our dogs could be flown out, for they would be too tired to accomplish the increased daily mileage we intended beyond the Pole. Next day I heard from him that Admiral Dufek had most kindly agreed to do so, and this relieved my mind of a considerable weight, because it was certainly impossible to take them with us over the next 1250 miles.

All this time our communications with Scott Base were either direct or through Peter Mulgrew, who had been left by Hillary at the Pole Station. There he was able to use radio equipment in the traveling caboose, which had been left with the three tractors and all the party's sledges and other equipment. This relieved the Pole Station of considerable traffic at a time when they were extremely busy with their own final problems before the supply planes left the Antarctic.

On the morning of January 17 we were camped at 88°45′S when two American planes flew over the camp while we were still in our sleeping bags, but Ralph scrambled outside to speak to them from the *County of Kent*. He heard that they were carrying Admiral Dufek, Ed Hillary, John Lewis and, to our considerable surprise, a posse of nine reporters. It also transpired that it was the evening of their day. Again we traveled 30 miles over sastrugi and undulating country, and it was not until the morning of the 18th, when we began the day's run only 55 miles from the Pole, that the surface at last became smooth and soft. That night our position was 89°37′S, or just over 26 miles from the Pole, and Geoffrey Pratt's seismic shot told us that the rock surface had risen steeply to lie only about 2000 feet below the ice.

When on Sunday, January 19, we began our last run before reaching the South Pole, we found that the surface continued soft and smooth as it had been throughout the previous day, but after a few miles more undulations became apparent.

And then we saw it. At the top of a snow ridge, from which the surface fell away in a long gentle sweep, we had halted to climb on top of our vehicles and scan the horizon for the markers we had been told to expect. Then, suddenly, into the field of vision sprang what seemed to be a small cluster of huts and radio masts. Although it could only just be discerned with the naked eye, it seemed so short a distance from us that our first instinct was to drive straight to the beckoning black spot in the white expanse. But remembering a radio request from Major Mogesson, scientific commander at the station, who had asked us to avoid the snow areas which they were studying and proceed along the 24° meridian, we turned to the southeast and drove along the top of the ridge until we found the line of flags which showed the correct route. At the end of the day I described our arrival in my journal.

Today we have run in to the Pole, the distance being 32 miles instead of only 26 as we expected, because when we sighted the Pole station we were too far west in longitude and they had asked us to come in on meridian 24°W to avoid the snow areas being studied. It took us some time and seven miles to find the barrel and line of flags which marked the route in. When the Pole Station came into view it was about seven miles distant and though apparently on a ridge there was a hollow between us and it.

By the time we had turned south along the line of flags, the dogs were tiring and the convoy moved slowly so that they could keep up and arrive together with the vehicles. The day was a brilliant one, without a cloud and only a light wind from about 80° meridian. As the party moved towards the Pole, I looked back and thought our convoy a brave sight: the orange "cats" and Weasel, together with the loaded sledges, bearing many fluttering flags of different colours. Besides the national Commonwealth flags, there was that of the city of Bristol, a T A E flag embroidered by Ralph, chequered crevasse flags, trail pennants, and a special green one embroidered by Hannes with a springbok on one side, and a protea on the other. Above all this the great exhaust plumes streamed away from the high, open exhausts of the Sno-cats.

Ahead of us we could see two Weasels moving out towards us from the station, but they stopped two miles before meeting us. As we approached nearer we could see quite a crowd, in fact over 30 people all armed with cameras. These included Admiral Dufek, Ed Hillary, Griff Pugh, Peter Mulgrew, the reporters and all the base personnel. Among the latter were Lieutenant Verne Houk, United States Navy Medical Service, in administrative control of the base, and Major Mogesson ("Moggy") in charge of the scientific work.

On jumping out of the "cat," I first shook hands with Ed, then George Dufek and the base leaders. There was such a press of photographers and recorders that it was quite difficult to move about. After the first "milling" had subsided, Houk and Dufek climbed into my "cat" and I drove them on to the base where Houk directed me to the parking site.

The next move was to wash and have a meal, followed by a press conference and a radio recording for the BBC through McMurdo Sound.

Our reception has been a most warm one and we have been invited to sleep and eat in the base instead of our tents. This makes our stay here pleasant, informal and a complete rest.

As we had not crossed the "date line," our day was still the 19th, but we find the Americans are keeping NZ time which makes it 20th January. Their actual time is GMT plus 12 hours. We therefore arrived in our night and their midday. I decided we should change over to their time at once by treating our night as day, and going to bed early if individuals wished. In fact I think most of us have missed a complete night's sleep.

That night Admiral Dufek had to return to McMurdo Sound and flew away in a Neptune aircraft, taking with him Sir Edmund Hillary, John Lewis and all the reporters. We then realized the difficulties with which the Americans had been faced in establishing the station by air, for at that altitude the loaded aircraft, using two jet engines, two piston engines and 16 JATO* bottles, failed to get off in the still air. After several attempts the flight had to be postponed until more JATO bottles could be brought in by another plane. Then, when some of the load had been removed, the pilot got away in great billowing clouds of snow driven by the blast from the soft surface.

Our days at the Pole Station were very crowded, for there was much to do. First of all the loads had to be unlashed and restowed, which relieved us of nineteen empty fuel drums. At the same time our electric welder was set up on *Haywire,* which had been taken into the station workshop. There work went ahead on repairing our broken towbars and battery heating equipment. Outside, Geoffrey Pratt fired a number of seismic shots, but the first of these were unsuccessful, as the records were upset by the high winds and the drift blowing across the station causing static electrical interference.

At a party on the evening of the 22nd each of us was presented with a fine colored testimonial, after the fashion of "Crossing the Line" certificates, stating that we had been around the world on our feet. This was possible because one had only to walk a few yards round the flags marking the site of the Pole itself. These flags were those of the United Nations and the United States, flying side by side on two tall masts surrounded by a great ring of empty fuel drums. At the party, we in our turn presented the station with the expedition pennant in memory of our visit, and were proud to display Her Majesty's signed portrait which we had carried with us all the way from Shackleton. We also unfurled the flag of the Scottish

* Jet Assisted Take Off.

247

National Antarctic Expedition 1901–1903, which had been taken by William Spears Bruce on his voyage in the *Scotia*, when he discovered Coats Land on the east side of the Weddell Sea. This had been handed to me in Edinburgh by the President of the Royal Scottish Geographical Society with the request that we carry it with us to Coats and on across the continent. Another item of interest was Captain Scott's watch which I had worn on a leather thong round my neck since starting the journey. This had been taken from their museum by Smiths of Cricklewood and entrusted to me to take back to the South Pole and on to Scott Base.

We had hoped to leave on the 23rd, but strong winds and high drift still prevented the completion of the seismic work, and this was very necessary. The Americans had flown equipment in and made a sounding at the Pole, and this was the one opportunity of checking the instruments against one another. I therefore decided at six o'clock that we would stay one more night and complete the work in the morning.

XVIII

The Transpolar Flight

While we were still on our way from South Ice to the Pole, the RAF contingent had the task of closing down Shackleton. It was planned that they should then fly across the continent to Scott Base, there joining the Beaver and providing air support in the later stages of our journey.

This would be the first transantarctic flight ever attempted in a small, single-engined aircraft. The following chapter tells the story of their successful achievement.

LATER IN THE SEASON the *Tottan* would again come south to relieve the Royal Society Base, and they had kindly offered to send back to the United Kingdom our Auster aircraft and any equipment, scientific specimens or records we could deliver to Halley Bay. Accordingly, the RAF contingent left behind at Shackleton, while we traveled laboriously to South Ice for the second time, spent long hours in sorting and packing stores.

At the same time, Taffy kept regular radio schedules with us in the field and the Otter was always available to meet our needs. In fact, three supply flights were made with spare parts, and on one occasion they also brought cooked steaks to vary the monotony of our diet. An American plane was due to fly in to Ellsworth from the United States and Captain Ronne had thoughtfully arranged for the pilot to bring personal mail which had been accumulating at the London office. When it reached Shackleton, our pilots at once flew it out to our camp at the foot of the "ice wall." Ironically the office had packed the personal letters for our aviators in a parcel of Weasel spares; by the time this was discovered, the Otter was no longer even a speck in the sky and they had to wait until we had reached South Ice before they could receive their quota.

On December 9 "Operation Pickford" got under way and both the Otter and the Auster were flown to Halley Bay, returning Ivor Beney and Fred Morris who had helped us so much in the last weeks of hectic preparation, and taking Peter Weston to dismantle and prepare the Auster for shipment when the *Tottan* arrived. Taffy Williams remained at base to maintain our radio contacts.

John, Gordon and Peter spent four days at Halley Bay crating the stores which had been flown "loose" to reduce weight, then returned to Shackleton in the Otter to begin the task of closing down the base. Water tanks were drained, windows boarded up, chimneys plugged and the hut swept clean. Apart from their wish to "leave it as they had found it," the thought was in their minds that if things did not go as planned, the ground party might have to make its way back to the base that had been their home for so many months.

Peter Weston was always busy, thoroughly overhauling the plane before its long hop to Scott Base, for a single-engined aircraft cannot afford mechanical breakdowns in the air over the inhospitable Antarctic continent. Then a special auxiliary tank was fitted in the fuselage, doubling the plane's endurance. The total of 356 gallons of fuel gave a flying range, in still air, of 1600 miles, while the distance from South Ice to Scott Base itself was over 1400 miles. This put a premium on accurate navigation.

The party mustered their emergency gear — tents, forty days' food combining the normal sledging ration with the RAF survival rations on which Gordon had already lived during his eleven-day sojourn on the "ice shelf," pots and pans, Primus stoves, sleeping bags, pyrotechnics, shovels, ice axes, ropes: all these had to be checked, packed and stowed.

Now came the problem of weight. The maximum payload of the Otter was one ton, and our pilots had always operated at or just above this limit. Now, with the auxiliary tank fitted, a very large proportion of the load capacity was taken up with fuel, while the four men, fully dressed in bulky cold-weather flying kit and including two heavyweights, John Lewis and Peter Weston, weighed between them 1000 pounds. Ounces counted, and all the rations and equipment were removed from their metal or wooden containers, and repacked in polythene bags which had been "borrowed" from the store where Allan Rogers kept his medical supplies. Every item was weighed before going into the plane.

On Christmas Day we had left South Ice, and now that we were over 50 miles toward the Pole, and no longer needed the plane, they could prepare in earnest to cross to Scott Base. After lunch on the 27th they were ready and, as the plane was loaded exactly as it would be when they made their attempt, the take-off would provide useful experience for their final departure from South Ice. But Shackleton was only 200 feet above sea level and there would still be some anxiety about getting the overladen machine safely off the ground at an altitude of 4430 feet.

The temperature had risen to +15°F, which made the surface tacky, and there was almost no wind as the aircraft started its run. An anxious moment, and then the tail came up — in 500 yards they were airborne. After two or three circuits around the deserted base which would soon become obliterated by the drifting snow, they set course for South Ice.

It was a beautiful sunny day with a gentle breeze — perfect flying weather — and this short trip provided the opportunity for checking the aircraft itself, the navigational equipment, and the radio, under actual flying conditions. As navigation would be of paramount importance, here in John's words is an account of the equipment and methods to be used:

> An astro-compass was mounted on the cockpit combing in front of the second pilot's position and with this the true course could be checked, using the sun. It was made easy at this time of the year because the sun was well above the horizon for the whole twenty-four hours.
>
> A bendix polar-path gyro acted as the master direction indicator, checked for heading precession every twenty minutes with the astro-compass. An ordinary directional gyro calibrated for 80° acted as a standby gyro; a drift sight mounted on the inside of the cockpit door used in conjunction with a radio altimeter gave drift and groundspeed. True course, drift and groundspeed are all that is required to navigate, but obtaining these depends on the weather. Clear skies to see the sun and a visible surface to pick up features

by which to measure the aircraft's drift and groundspeed are essential.

The flight to South Ice was free from incident, and took just under three hours, the Otter landing at five o'clock in the afternoon. While the pilots and Peter Weston at once began to unload the sleeping bags, refuel the plane and prepare a meal, Taffy was keeping radio schedules first with us and then with the American Pole Station. Some time before, the American radio operators had agreed to a daily contact at seven o'clock each evening, when they would pass the weather report from Scott Base together with their own forecasts. From our vehicle party's normal schedule at six o'clock they would hear of intermediate weather conditions, and piecing together the three messages, John would have some idea of conditions over the whole extent of their flight. The only catch was that the weather reports from Scott Base would already be twelve hours old and conditions in the Antarctic can change abruptly in a far shorter time than that.

Taffy was also in daily radio communication with Halley Bay, which was now the link with our London headquarters, and told them that the Otter was standing by ready to fly, awaiting a suitable day. On the evening of the 28th the forecast along the route was bad; in our area it was cloudy with slight snow and the flight was out of the question. On the 29th they spent a long day under cloudless sunny skies, waiting for the evening "sched," but at six o'clock, when Taffy came up on the air, he could get no response from us, owing to bad radio conditions. The four of them sat for another hour round the radio set, waiting impatiently until the Pole Station broadcast — if indeed it was able to get through. Punctually on the hour, contact was made and they learned that some patches of cloud were expected over the Pole and thin, layered cloud in McMurdo Sound. It was not ideal, but it could have been worse. They decided to have a go, and asked the Pole Station to inform Scott Base that they would be leaving.

It had always been planned that they would start from South Ice in the late evening, thus ensuring that throughout the estimated twelve hours of their flight they would have the sun ahead making it unnecessary to circuit the aircraft to take a sight. Now bedding was hastily rolled up, kit packed, the Thermos flasks filled and the aircraft given a last check. Gordon Haslop was to be the pilot, while John navigated, and he opened the throttle, waggling the rudder to free the skis from the tacky snow. This was their great moment: would the heavily laden plane take off at this altitude from a surface made sticky by the blazing sun, and without any helping wind? The aircraft jolted forward, slowly at first, and then, gradually accelerating, the tail came up. The speed crept up to 55 knots, Gordon eased down the flaps to take-off position, the plane bounced twice — and then it was airborne. Four deep sighs of relief were clearly audible. It had taken well over half a mile to get the small plane off the ground. The time was 10:27 P.M. and the sun still shone brightly.

They circled South Ice for what they all thought was a last look, and then set course along the 29°W meridian for the Pole, 550 miles distant and about five hours away in flying time. The Otter climbed slowly at a constant speed, gaining height as the fuel was used up and the plane lightened. The Pole itself lies at an altitude of something under 10,000 feet, and on the far side they would have to cross country known to rise to 11,000 feet. Even if they could coax the aircraft up to 12,000 feet, the margin of clearance was very fine.

For the first hour all went well, and the sight of the vehicle party two miles to port confirmed the accuracy of their navigation. Taffy called up on the radio, but we had had a long day and Ralph Lenton was tucked up in his sleeping bag. They gained a little more height and flew on for another 90 miles when they could see clouds on the far horizon. At 1:52 A.M. on the 30th the Otter was flying above a thin layer of stratus and conditions were deteriorating. Ahead the cloud was thicker and half an hour later they flew into a dense mass which appeared to rise to at least 14,000 feet. The aircraft was now flying at 10,000 feet and the rate of climb was very slow, while the surface below was at 8000 feet and the country ahead invisible and unknown.

One of the objects of this flight was to provide us with a report on the surfaces we could expect between 84°S and the Pole. It was thought that a range of mountains, or at least a disturbance of the surface where they were submerged by the ice, might cross our route, and, if so, some idea of its extent and the difficulties it might present would be invaluable; but at two o'clock, they were still flying in thick cloud at 87°40′S and sticky rime ice began to form along the leading edge of the wings, causing the Otter to lose height dangerously. Cloud still enveloped them and the risk of flying on in the hope that the weather might improve was becoming too much of a gamble. They held a brief consultation and very reluctantly decided that they must return to South Ice.

Their problem was now reversed. If it was too hazardous to fly on to a spot on the map about 1000 miles ahead, it was almost as difficult to turn back 400 miles and pinpoint a small black dot in the middle of miles and miles of nothing after a seven-hour flight. The best hope was that the Whichaway Nunataks and the Shackleton Mountains, lying to the north of South Ice, would act as signposts to the now deserted station. John Lewis took over the aircraft and at 2:45 A.M. the Otter came out of the cloud and flew steadily northwards for nearly two hours. Then four big smiles broke out simultaneously — for dead ahead the vehicle party had come into view! But their anxieties were not yet over.

At five o'clock an ominously dark patch stretched across their path — thick stratus cloud that had moved in from the north. As the aircraft approached the clearly defined edge, they saw that it extended right down to the surface: now what should they do? John lost height but soon realized that he would be flying blind once he entered the murk. They circled round and discussed the next move. Suddenly, immediately below them, the vehicle tracks appeared in the snow. From the outward flight they remembered that these only jinked once, about a quarter of a mile from South Ice. "Flying by Bradshaw," or finding one's bearings by following railway lines, has brought many a plane safely home, and John gratefully accepted the present chance. Without more ado he descended to only ten feet above the ground and skimmed along the "railway lines" for 40 miles until they led him in to South Ice. The visibility was about 100 yards and where the tracks turned sharply right, he closed the throttle, lowered the flaps and touched down, coming to rest not ten yards from the spot where the Otter had taken off over seven hours earlier.

The four men climbed out, frustrated at being back at their starting point; the aircraft was picketed and the sleeping bags moved back into the hut. After a hot drink, they were glad to go to bed, and slept until late in the afternoon of New Year's Eve. Then once again they anxiously awaited the weather reports. On the surface a 20-knot wind was blowing, whipping up thick drift and snow. The day was overcast and bitterly cold; this was not flying weather — indeed in these conditions they could not even refuel the Otter. So with a clear conscience they settled down to welcome the New Year in, with a four-course dinner of soup, fishcakes, stew and fruit, followed by coffee. They drank to the Queen, the vehicle party and themselves — and so to bed to wait for another day and to hope that the storm would blow itself out.

But for the next three days the high winds continued. They chafed at the delay and it was little consolation to hear that conditions at Scott Base were just as bad. On January 4 the wind died down and conditions improved enough for the aircraft to be refueled and for Peter Weston to check it over.

When the complete stock of fuel had been emptied into the tanks the Otter was still short of 25 gallons, or one hour's flying time. The safety margin, narrow enough in the first place, was now nonexistent. Four 40-gallon drums of aviation fuel, all that remained of the original 9000 gallons we had brought down in the *Magga Dan*, had been left behind at Shackleton when the base was evacuated. On the radio Taffy Williams was speaking to Ellsworth, and Major Jim Lassiter, pilot of the aircraft which had carried our mail, hearing of their situation, suggested that he should call at Shackleton, pick up this fuel and bring it to South Ice. This generous offer was gratefully accepted, and early on January 6 the drums were delivered and the Otter topped up.

The weather had cleared and at last it looked as though they might be able to try again. Hoping that the forecast that evening would be favorable, they loaded the plane and again made ready.

During their six o'clock schedule with us we were able to tell them that we were traveling under clear skies with hardly any wind and good visibility. An hour later they were talking to the Pole Station where the forecast was equally good and Taffy passed the message that the Otter would take off at about half past eleven and was expected to take twelve hours to reach Scott Base.

Once more they were feverishly busy. All the emergency gear was rechecked, Thermos flasks filled and skis dug out of the drifted snow. Luckily a light breeze was blowing and the lower air temperature had improved the surface. At 11:48 P.M., and this time with a shorter run, the Otter was again airborne.

Course was set, and speaking to the Pole Station Taffy arranged to call them every thirty minutes until they reached the head of the Beardmore Glacier: after that Scott Base would take over radio control. The Otter climbed slowly but steadily and just over two hours later they sighted our vehicles three miles to port. Taffy again tried to make contact but once more Ralph was asleep as we had not heard from the Pole Station that they would definitely fly that night, and his greetings fell on deaf ears.

A following wind was helping them to eke out their fuel and by four o'clock all eyes were eagerly straining ahead for their first glimpse of the Pole, which they hoped to reach half an hour later. But now the surface became obscured by ice crystals which formed a thick haze, not unlike the smog patch that hangs over industrial towns. At 4:23 A.M. the Otter's loop aerial picked up the transmissions from the M/F beacon at the Pole, and five minutes later the station buildings appeared through the haze, immediately below them. They saw the Stars and Stripes and the United Nations flag marking the Pole itself, and circling round and round — "flying," as John put it, "out of Tuesday, into Wednesday and back again to Tuesday," — they talked to Lieutenant Houk and Major Mogesson. Gordon was delighted to be "in the right quadrant of the globe" once more, and received Maori greetings from his fellow Kiwis at Scott Base before they set course for the Beardmore Glacier.

They had completed the first leg of their journey and their route was now almost identical with that taken by Captain Scott forty-seven years before. All being well, they would cover in a few hours the tragic miles that he and his companions had trudged with such effort over so many weeks.

An hour and forty minutes later a line of mountains came up to starboard and was identified as the Dominion Range. Now the landmarks were coming into focus and ahead on the horizon they could pick out the peaks of the Queen Alexandra Range. At seven o'clock they were over the head of the Beardmore Glacier and marveled at this strange river of ice that wound down 8000 feet, between formidable mountains, to the Ross Barrier nearly 150 miles away.

Our people at home had been anxious about this flight, and remembering that all our office messages were signed "Transpolar," which was their telegraphic address, John now sent an exuberant cable to the Committee giving his position and ending "DOWN HILL ALL THE WAY. VIVA TRANSPOLAR."

In clear skies and brilliant sunshine they lost height and enjoyed the magnificent scenery as they flew down the glacier. To port a mountain called the Cloudmaker lived up to its name, wearing a small cloud like a delicate halo around its summit, and then they could see Mount Hope and the Ross Barrier, which stretched to the horizon like a huge frozen lake.

Now friendly voices were coming over the air, and Scott Base was preparing its reception. Gordon was delighted to be back in New Zealand territory, and helping tail winds caused them to revise their time of arrival to eleven o'clock. Passing the message, Taffy took the opportunity of ordering "four bottles of very cold beer."

The aircraft droned on, every minute bringing it nearer to the end of a unique flight. At half-past nine Mount Discovery jutted out of the slight haze and then the low dark line of Minna Bluff came into view. They were nearly there. Passing the end of the bluff, the plane crossed between Black and White Islands, and then Ross Island loomed up ahead, with its twin volcanic peaks, Mount Erebus and Mount Terror.

Here they were met by an aerial reception committee. Two United States Navy Otters from the base at McMurdo Sound flew out to greet them, both crammed with Americans and New Zealanders, packed, as Gordon described it, "like quills on a porcupine, and everyone of them with a camera trained on us." There was much waving and gesturing, but as the aircraft were controlled on different frequencies by the two bases at McMurdo Sound, the ribald messages they were anxious to exchange had to be relayed through Scott Base and lost some of their originality in the process.

The escorting planes took station on either side of them as they approached Scott Base. Ted Gawn, the radio operator, could not bear to miss the party when they landed and so excitedly shouting, "There you are! You can see the landing strip now — I'm off to be there when you get down," he abruptly went off the air and raced for the runway.

As they circled the base, more American aircraft, Dakotas and Otters, came up to meet them and described exuberant circuits of welcome. The Otter went down, the two American planes flying slightly ahead on either side to guide it in. The Americans came right in with them, almost to ground level and then as our Otter triumphantly touched down, they roared upwards to join their compatriots in the air — much to the chagrin of all the enthusiastic photographers now borne out of range.

After a flight of exactly eleven hours and 1430 statute miles our little aircraft had made it. As the party clambered stiffly out, they were engulfed by a friendly crowd of Americans and New Zealanders, for everyone in McMurdo Sound was there to greet them. Ed Hillary, who had himself only just flown back from the Pole in an American aircraft, led the congratulations and there was a special welcome from John Claydon and Bill Cranfield, the two New Zealand pilots, who could perhaps best appreciate the problems of their flight.

A happy touch was the story of "Taffy's Tankard." During the winter months at Shackleton, our regular radio schedules with the Pole Station had created a firm friendship between Taffy and Ralph, their radio operator. Knowing that the American was due for relief, there was constant chitchat and some betting as to whether he or Taffy would reach McMurdo Sound first. It had been agreed that whichever did would greet the other with a glass of beer. Now, as our four airmen were lined up to be photographed from every angle, a stranger, carefully nursing a tankard, stepped out of the crowd and handed it to Taffy. A promise had been kept.

Finally the Otter was safely picketed down and the party, accompanied by all their American and New Zealand well-wishers, climbed into and onto every available vehicle and moved off to Scott Base, where the "very cold beer" ordered during the flight awaited them.

That evening, through the operators at the Pole Station, we heard the news that the flight had been successful. John Lewis was famous for the comment he invariably made on any kind of good news. "Jolly good," he would say. "Jolly good, bloody good, first class." We were all delighted to know that they had made it and our message of congratulation was simple and direct:

"JOLLY GOOD, BLOODY GOOD, FIRST CLASS!" — and indeed it was.

XIX

The South Pole to Scott Base

On January 24, 1958, precisely two months after our departure from Shackleton, we left the South Pole on our way north to the other side of the world. The distance to Scott Base was 1250 miles, behind us lay Shackleton only a little over 900 miles away. By no means had we reached the halfway point in our journey, but we knew that now every advantage lay with us. We had fewer vehicles to maintain, and when we dropped the last Weasel we should be able to increase our speed; the dogs would no longer hold us to 30 miles per day, for they were to be flown to Scott Base; the seismic soundings would be spaced more widely, and for the last 290 miles from the Plateau Depot to base there would be no need for them. Lastly, and very important, Ed Hillary and his parties had pioneered a route, and provided all we needed in the way of food and fuel. During the last 700 miles we should be within range of both the Beaver and the Otter, which could fly from Scott Base to drop anything that we might need.

So far as weather was concerned, we did not expect temperatures below −40°F until well into March, and we had already operated our vehicles down to −60°. For ourselves, we knew from the winter experience of the Shackleton Advance Party that we could endure temperatures as low as that in the tents, uncomfortable though it might be. Our only real concern, therefore, was the persistence of strong winds and drift, or long periods of whiteout.

These could delay us, and if an early freeze-up in McMurdo Sound forced HMNZS *Endeavour* to leave, we should be committed to another winter in the Antarctic. This we had always known, even before leaving England, and an extra year's supply of food and fuel

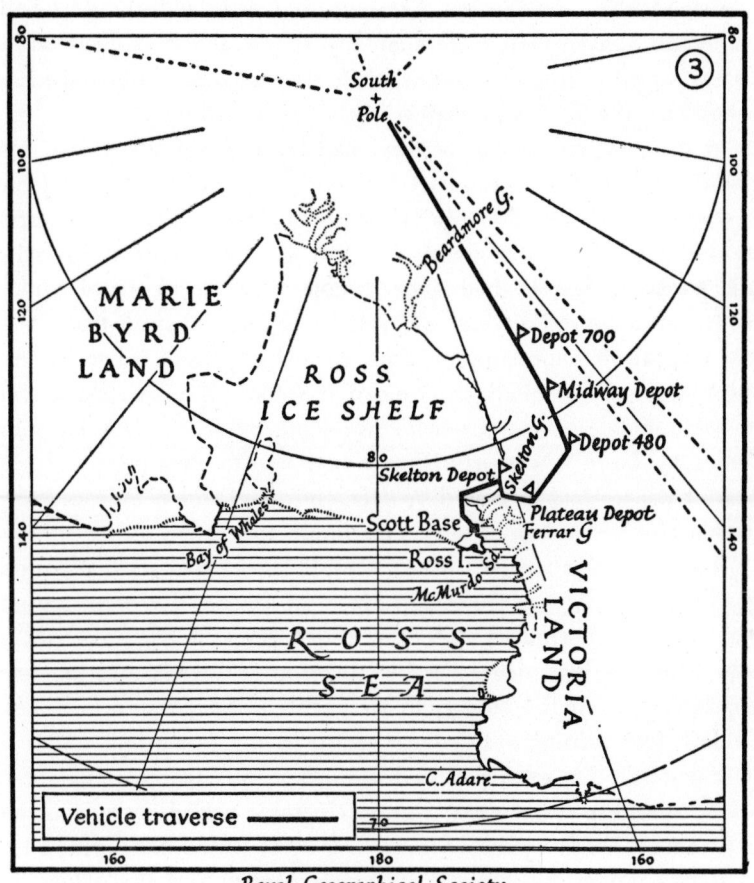

Royal Geographical Society

South Pole to Scott Base.

had been ordered for both Shackleton and Scott Base. None of us wanted to winter again, certainly not those who had already spent two consecutive years in the Antarctic, but, as Blaiklock and I had both found on an earlier occasion, this is one of the chances taken by anyone who visits the continent. If, after all that can be done has been done, the die is cast against you — well, bad luck!

In the morning all the welding had been completed at last, for David Pratt and Roy Homard had worked throughout the night. *Haywire,* which was the only Sno-cat which could drive the electric welder, was released to enable Geoffrey Pratt to complete his seismic work. At first he had some trouble with the electrical equipment, but a second attempt was satisfactory and showed that there was a depth of something less than 8000 feet of ice. When the results have been properly determined it seems likely that there will be a reasonable comparison with the depth found by the American sounding. To us it was surprising to note that in 25 miles the thickness of the ice had increased by over 5000 feet, for it indicated the presence of some form of buried mountain range.

It was five minutes past five in the afternoon when we finally said good-by to Lieutenant Houk and Major Mogesson. The temperature was −14°F, the wind 25 mph as we drove along the 156°E meridian into light but high drift. Passing the ring of barrels and the two flagstaffs marking the Pole itself, we motored slowly round in a close circle before turning onto course again. In the two minutes that it took us to do this we had passed through twenty-four hours of time and returned to the present. During the same period every point on earth except the few yards of snow close by had been due north of us.

It was interesting, and slightly confusing, to find that when we turned north onto our course the magnetic compasses still showed us to be traveling south, so that when driving it was necessary to remember that any diversion to the east was really to the west! In fact, to our surprise, our magnetic compasses were still operating fairly well, but we knew that as we moved north and reduced the distance between ourselves and the Magnetic Pole, still 1250 miles distant, there would come a time when they would be virtually useless.

For the first 18 miles small trail flags had been planted every tenth of a mile by the Americans, so that we could follow the same route they had used and not plough great ruts across the virgin snow areas. At the time these little flags were a great assistance, because the visibility was so restricted that after passing one it was a little while before the next could be seen. At the end of the line, which was marked by a number of fuel drums, we altered course by 15° to bring us over to the 141°E meridian which we intended to follow so as to pick up the tracks of Ed Hillary's vehicles.

When we stopped that night we had covered 25 miles in seven hours, over a very soft, gently rising surface, until we were about 150 feet above the Pole Station. The power of our engines had now been reduced by the altitude to about half the sea level output of 200 hp, and our fuel consumption was rising. In the 25 miles we had covered from the Pole, *Rock 'n Roll* had used 27 gallons and all the others were similarly affected. For all five vehicles this worked out at about 2 tons of petrol for 100 miles, but we were still driving *Wrack and Ruin,* which could be dropped whenever necessary, and I was not unduly worried.

In the morning we fired a seismic shot which told us that the depth of ice was something less than 2000 feet. This showed that we had again reached a high rock area covered by a relatively thin mantle of ice. It seems, therefore, that the Geographical Pole is situated on a great ice-filled basin some 50 miles wide between two rock massifs. These observations were borne out by the gravity readings taken at intervals of approximately 15 miles.

On January 25 and 26 we ran 35 and 40 miles respectively, bringing our total to 100 miles in three days. All the time we had been traveling in consistent whiteout, with fairly strong winds and some drift, but then visibility improved and on the 27th, after 20 miles, we suddenly saw some dark objects a little less than a mile to the left. We knew these must be the sledges, food, paraffin, bottles of gas for welding, tarpaulins, old tents and other unwanted items that Hillary had left behind when the high altitude and soft snow held up his tractors. We picked up four boxes of man-rations, as it seemed a pity to leave them, and continued on our way over an increasingly hard surface, to make 42 miles in the day. By the time we had bored the hole for the seismic shot next morning and Hal had established his thermometers in it, it was nearly four o'clock — but we had long since resigned ourselves to late hours, and endeavored to gain sleeping time when not actually driving.

At ten o'clock we began the shoot but, for the first time, the charge failed to explode. Almost immediately afterwards David Stratton came to tell me that he had found Geoffrey Pratt unconscious on the floor of the Sno-cat *Haywire*. His face was unhealthily pink, his eyes closed and his limbs twitching — altogether an alarming sight. David at once called Allan Rogers who immediately diagnosed carbon monoxide poisoning, and hastily fetching a bottle of oxygen from the gas welding equipment, improvised a crude mask from a handkerchief and administered sufficient to bring him round. Geoffrey was then carried to his tent, where more oxygen was given; but we had at most five hours' supply, which was insufficient to ensure his complete recovery. We were at 10,000 feet, where the rarefied atmosphere was impeding his breathing, and we needed to get him down to sea level quickly.

Discussing what would be our best course of action it was established that Geoffrey and Hannes La Grange had been keeping the windows of their Sno-cat closed, and exhaust gas leaking into the engine compartment had been pumped by a heater fan between the two windscreens to de-ice them, and thence into the cab. Over a period of days Geoffrey's blood had been increasingly affected, until at last his life was threatened by the destruction of so many blood corpuscles. Although we believed that he would recover, there was clearly a danger that unless he was taken to sea level or provided with more oxygen than we had available, he might suffer heart trouble. Another consideration was the difficulty of carrying a sick man for a period of ten days or more in conditions hardly suited to convalescence, for we had to continue traveling. We were at the extreme range of our Otter from Scott Base, and even if the plane came to us it would probably be unable to take off again at our altitude. I therefore signaled Ed Hillary, asking him to approach Admiral Dufek and find out whether one of the United States Neptunes could come out and fly our patient down to sea level.

While Ralph Lenton was trying to break in on one of the schedules, we continued with the firing of the seismic shot. Allan Rogers, who was familiar with electronic equipment from his work in electrophysiology, undertook to work the recording apparatus. To help him, Geoffrey was carried out on a stretcher to Haywire and laid on the floor so that, without moving, he could tell Allan the correct sequence of events. After the firing George Lowe successfully developed the recording. Once Hal Lister had read the gravimeter, all Geoffrey's work had been done, and we continued along the 141°E meridian from our position of 87°59'S — our patient lying in the back of the *County of Kent* where there was more room than in *Haywire*.

By eight o'clock that night two Neptune planes had taken off from McMurdo Sound, carrying Dr. Pugh of the British Medical Research Council who was undertaking a summer physiological program there. As it happened he had specialized in carbon monoxide poisoning and came in one of the planes in case Allan needed any emergency advice when they arrived. They also brought two large oxygen bottles which were parachuted to us, as it was felt that the risk of landing was too great unless Geoffrey's condition was still thought to be dangerous.

When the aircraft reached us we had moved forward ten miles, and the clear blue sky had become completely overcast with cloud lying only 800 feet above the surface. In the circumstances the pilots, Captain Coley and Lieutenant Cook of the U.S. Navy, performed a fine feat of navigation in coming in to us on the first run. While Dr. Pugh and Allan discussed Geoffrey's condition by radio, the planes circled and then made their runs to parachute the oxygen bottles and breathing apparatus. After waiting to see that we had collected them and to make sure that nothing had been damaged, they flew away on their 800-mile return trip to McMurdo Sound.

Soon Geoffrey was receiving a three-hour dose of pure oxygen, followed by many further hours at a strength equivalent to the atmosphere at sea level. Now we had no further worries about him, and felt confident that it would be only a short time before he was back to duty — as was, in fact, the case, for Allan allowed him to resume his work on January 30.

All the next day we traveled over sastrugi, fortunately directed along the line of our course — quite a change after so many hundreds of miles when they lay athwart our track. We totaled 60 miles, the first 40 in a complete whiteout, which made driving difficult. After 55 miles, *Wrack and Ruin's* engine gave trouble and it had to be towed into camp.

We could have repaired the engine, but at this high altitude the Weasel had suffered from frequent vapor locking, and now that we had sufficiently reduced our loads we did not really need it any more. In latitude 87°01′S, longitude 141°00′E, it was abandoned.

January 30 was set aside for maintenance, and additional duties prevented any travel that day. The seismic shot had to be fired twice, the stores carried by *Wrack and Ruin* restowed on other sledges, while George Lowe transferred all his photographic equipment to *Haywire*, where he was to ride in future with Geoffrey Pratt and Hannes La Grange.

The next day we traveled 70 miles, thereby making up the distance lost the previous day. It was a record run for the journey so far, and the first occasion since long before reaching the Pole that it had been possible to drive in top gear. We were certainly finding the surfaces on this side of the Pole very much easier than those we had previously experienced. After the first 5 miles there was a noticeable rise, but then the ground gradually declined to about 9600 feet — this descent, which had begun during the 29th, was to continue steadily for many days to come.

After traveling 51 miles, Roy Homard reported that the outer main bearing of one of his pontoons had broken up, and would have to be replaced. This was the first of the series of different Sno-cat troubles that now began to haunt us. Perhaps this was not altogether surprising since they had all traveled over 1200 miles from Shackleton.

On February 1 we descended a series of long shallow steps, where the surface was hard, and bearing some sastrugi which were oriented along our course. Bowling along at 8 to 10 mph we had covered 45 miles by a quarter past eight, then stopped to take a longitude sight when the sun became visible through the thin overcast at the end of the day.

By the evening of the 4th we had moved forward another 108 miles, but one after the other the Sno-cat tracks had begun to give trouble. These had gradually become looser, until a point was reached when they jumped the lower guide rail and jammed solid with a nasty, jarring noise. To tighten all four tracks, 592 steel links had to be bent by hand with a special tool — a long job, taking an hour for each track and requiring considerable judgment, for it was essential to make, by eye, an equal adjustment all round and yet arrive at the correct degree of tension at the end. The fact that there was no means of bending the links back, if one should go too far, tended to make the operator overcareful, and he would end his task only to find that the track was still too loose. Then the operation would have to be begun all over again.

The 4th being a maintenance day, nearly all the track tensioning was completed, and, in addition, 296 points on the tracks of each cat were greased and the two gearboxes and two differentials topped up. All this, besides other greasing and maintenance work, was an unpleasant task with the temperature at −20°F and the wind blowing at 25 mph. Most of us had long since put on one side old pairs of gloves and windproofs for this work. Filling grease guns was a slimy, slippery process, and the waste grease exuding from the nipples in thin wormlike threads blew about in the wind, to become mixed with snow and finally to adhere to the unfortunate who was humping his way to and fro, like a seal, between the tracks.

The trials of maintenance day were added to on this occasion by the discovery that the main steering attachment for the front pontoons was loose on three of the cats. Metal locking tags had therefore to be made, like one already fitted to *Rock 'n Roll*. As a result of all this work, we did not start until half past eight that night, but I was determined to cover a reasonable distance each day when the weather was suitable, since we should have enough trouble when we had to travel in bad conditions. For 33 miles we ran over hard sastrugi, but fortunately these were fairly low and it was possible to drive round the isolated groups of high ridges and deep hollows. That night bedtime was again at four o'clock in the morning.

During all these days of relatively good going our fuel consumption had been getting better and better, and from the very low figure of 0.9 miles per gallon we had now attained to 1¾ miles per gallon. With only four vehicles, there was now no worry about our fuel supply.

During February 5 both Ken Blaiklock and David Stratton took separate meridian altitudes, and both agreed that we had passed the crevasse belt that Ed Hillary had reported to be in the area. This was good news, and it was quite possible that the crevasses which he had had to cross formed a local patch which did not extend far in any direction. To make sure, we ran on for three more miles before turning onto a course of 053°T toward Depot 700.

We had only traveled three miles on our new course, and were congratulating ourselves on missing at least one patch of trouble, when David Stratton, who was driving *Rock 'n Roll,* stopped suddenly with his front pontoons only just short of a sunken crevasse bridge 12 feet wide. That was at half past eight — it was to be several hours before we pitched our tent and climbed into our sleeping bags.

Skiing on ahead for a quarter of a mile to climb a high ice hummock, I crossed nine more wide crevasses before reaching it. From the top at least two more miles of crevasses were visible, stretching at right angles across our path. To east and west they could be seen extending into the indefinite distance, so that it was apparently unprofitable to move to right or left of our course. Far to the right I could see a crevassed slope, which I thought must be that crossed by Hillary, for leading away from it and toward our position were regular rows of sharp white mounds which clearly marked the lines of numerous crevasses.

On top of the high hummock I was joined by David Stratton, who went on to investigate the area beyond while I returned to tell the others that we would be camping, and that they should be preparing for the seismic shot in the morning. Later I skied for two more miles on a more southerly course in the hope of finding a better way through the area, but without any result. Later, when Stratton and I compared notes, we came to the conclusion that there would be no advantage in diverting our course, and that it would be best to tackle the crevasses and chasms directly ahead.

Next morning a number of us began probing a way across, but after a few hundred yards Roy Homard and I returned to fetch our Sno-cats, leaving the other vehicles to follow along the proved route later on, when the seismic work had been finished.

Sno-cat Able at speed.

covering Sno-cat Able from a crevasse, using light aluminum bridging.

Vehicles halted among high sastrugi.

A Weasel trapped by an invisible crevasse.

Firing a seismic shot to sound the depth of the ice.

One of the many snow cairns built by the dog party
at five-mile intervals to guide the vehicles.

A typical Sno-cat load of five tons. David Pratt is sounding
the depth of fuel in one of the barrels.

The end of the transpolar flight from South Ice to Scott Base.
Left to right: Peter Weston, John Lewis, Taffy Williams,
Ed Hillary, and Gordon Haslop.

the South Pole. Left to right: Sir Edmund Hillary, Dr. Vivian
Fuchs, and Rear Admiral George Dufek, USN

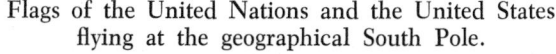

Flags of the United Nations and the United States
flying at the geographical South Pole.

The crossing party
at the South Pole.

Left to right,
back row:
David Pratt
Hal Lister
Ralph Lenton
Ken Blaiklock
George Lowe

Front row:
Dr. Fuchs
Allan Rogers
Geoffrey Pratt
David Stratton
Jon Stephenson
Hannes La Grange
Roy Homard

Sastrugi at seven thousand feet, between
the Pole and Depot 700.

Geoffrey Pratt taking a gravity reading. The bell was rung
to warn people to switch off engines and stand still.

About to break camp after an all-night blizzard on the Skelton Glacier

Sunset over the Skelton Glacier.

No sooner had I begun warming up the engine than the bell was rung and I had to switch off. This was a ship's bell brought by Geoffrey Pratt who used it to warn everyone to stand still and switch off engines before a seismic shot was fired or a gravimeter reading taken. Both instruments were delicate enough to record any movement at a considerable distance. This time 10 pounds of explosive was fired, divided between three shallow pits, for the gravity readings had indicated that the rock beneath was comparatively near the surface, as one might have expected in an area of so many crevasses. When the charge went off, three gigantic but perfect smoke rings shot whirring into the air for several hundreds of feet. Thereafter Hannes, who had dug the pits, amused himself by devising bigger and better pits, purely with the object of obtaining greater and more perfect smoke rings.

No sooner had I restarted the engine to continue warming up than Hannes came over to urge me to inspect the local crevasse lids which, he now declared, had been displaced by the explosion. At each crevasse I found some subsidence of the lids along both sides, which was scarcely encouraging to one who was about to pioneer a route across a whole series of unpleasant-looking chasms.

The party of six, who were now well ahead, were probing the edges of the great chasms that varied in width from 12 to 75 feet. So sunken were the bridges, and so parallel the sides, that they seemed like a great series of parallel canals. At first, as I drove slowly over these lids, there was the familiar uncomfortable expectation that one would feel the whole thing collapse. Soon I was more concerned with the side-swing of the trailing sledges than with the strength of the bridges I was crossing, for many of the wider ones had steep slopes leading down for as much as four or five feet to the sunken level of the bridges.

When at last we arrived at the far side of these obstacles, we had crossed fifty major crevasses in 3½ miles, but found no trouble with any of them. All the time we had been expecting to see the others following us, but there was no sign of them. After a long wait, Jon Stephenson started skiing back to tell them to report by radio what was the matter. In due course, we heard that David Pratt had been in trouble when his hydraulic steering iced up, but now they were on their way to us. We therefore pushed on over a rough surface to a smoother but undulating area beyond. After 25 miles, I suddenly noticed a small crevasse, apparently about two or three feet wide, running across our path. Thinking nothing of it, I drove straight over, intending to stop on the far side and prospect ahead. The front pontoons crossed without trouble, but the rear pair broke through with an ominous crash, then slowly climbed out on the far side, followed by the two heavily laden sledges. Scrambling out to see what had happened, we found a hole eight feet wide, for the crevasse had been larger below than had appeared at the surface.

As *County of Kent* was coming up behind, Stratton and I began to search for a better and narrower crossing point. Believing we had found an excellent place, I beckoned Roy across, but he fared no better, broke through just as we had done, and only just avoided having the rear pontoons caught in the crevasse. Unhappily he was not as lucky as we had been with *Rock 'n Roll,* for inspection showed that the large, cast-aluminum rear steering platform was badly cracked. Roy and Ralph spent the next few hours blocking and strengthening the weak place with timber and rope. Meanwhile David Stratton, Hal Lister and I skied away in various directions to examine the area for the next two or three miles. One after another parallel crevasses crossed our paths, but although none were wider than 15 feet, all were thinly bridged and impossible to cross. About two miles from the vehicles I found a hollow where the crevasses ended, but this was a complex region of hummocks and short irregular-shaped holes with uncertain bridges which it would be wise to avoid.

In the end we decided that it would be better to follow the edge of the crevasse field toward the southeast in the hope of finding Ed Hillary's route, for he had reported crossing a few small crevasses in this area and marking them with snow cairns. By this time the other two vehicles had arrived, but in making a sharp turn *Able* sheared the pin linking the forward steering arm with the steering platform, and a new part had to be fitted. To save time, *Rock 'n Roll* and *County of Kent* went on to reconnoiter the route, leaving *Haywire* to keep company with *Able.*

Carefully we drove along the length of the first crevasse, keeping a sharp lookout for any sign of tracks or cairns. Once or twice up-standing white sastrugi were mistaken for man-made mounds of snow, but by the time we had traveled six miles and found nothing, the seemingly endless crevasse still ran beside us. By half past one in the morning it was certain that we had overshot Hillary's track and we decided to camp, intending to make another attempt to force our way over in the morning. Hal Lister normally tented with George Lowe who had remained behind with the repair party. That night he shared pemmican with David Stratton and me and slept in the back of *Rock 'n Roll.*

As soon as we began route finding in the morning it was discovered that here the bridges were stronger, and by using the thicker places where drift ridges crossed the crevasses it was possible to move over safely. Two pairs went on in front to seek suitable places, while Roy and I followed slowly after with the cats, weaving our way up and down between the crevasses, from crossing point to crossing point. From time to time during the day we spoke to the repair party, and at last heard that they had started after us. Behind us we had left a number of flags at critical places, and there was also the intricate winding track of our vehicles which they could follow. We therefore felt little concern for them and pushed on toward Depot 700 when we found ourselves in the clear after crossing nineteen crevasses.

Gradually the region became more and more undulating, until we began to rise and fall over a series of ridges which surrounded basin-like depressions a few miles across. The north-facing slopes were very hard and rough, bearing large sastrugi, while the southern slopes were relatively soft and smooth. It seemed that here the ice sheet was already crumpled by its movement toward the mountains to the east, and perhaps by the underlying rock topography gradually molding its movement into the channels which carry the glaciers through the mountains.

At twenty minutes to nine in the evening of February 7, I spotted the depot three miles ahead and a few degrees to our right. Thirty-five minutes later we drew up beside the tall mast with its waving flag, surrounded by barrels of fuel and boxes of rations. Now, indeed, there was a sense of accomplishment, for at 82°58'S, 146°02'E, and 8370 feet, we had reached the end of the supply line laid out to meet us from the other side of the continent. From the Pole we had traveled 521 miles in 15 days, giving an average of 34½ miles per day. Over the whole distance of 1427 miles from Shackleton, our average was now up to 19 miles per day.

Shortly before our arrival Ralph Lenton had spoken to Scott Base and told them that we should be reaching the depot in less than an hour. Reporting that we had perfect weather with blue skies, he was told that down at base there was heavy overcast, whiteout and some falling snow, making flying out of the question. It was therefore impossible for Ed Hillary to join us immediately as we had hoped. Later I spoke to Ed, telling him that we were committed to wait at the depot for the other two Sno-cats which had not arrived. But we agreed that if, after we had re-formed our party, the bad weather at Scott Base continued, then we ought to push on, leaving him to join us at some point along the route.

Late that night David Pratt and Allan Rogers arrived to fetch another spare steering pin for *Haywire,* which had suffered exactly the same damage as *Able* only a few miles before. All the next day we waited. The repairs to *Haywire* were still going on and the weather at Scott Base remained too bad for flying. David Pratt had gone back to the damaged vehicles by himself, leaving Allan with us, so he was able to attend to a tooth of mine which had been giving considerable trouble ever since we had left the Pole. Dentistry in a small pyramid tent is necessarily a primitive maneuver, the patient reclining with his head on a box, or between the operator's knees, the latter's legs doubled up beneath him, and instruments inconveniently disposed in precarious positions. At least on this occasion Allan had the advantage of electric light derived from one of the cats, and he did an excellent job which relieved me of much pain, and probably saved the tooth.

During the day 405 gallons of petrol were pumped into our tanks and into the drums which had already been emptied, and extra food supplies were loaded onto the sledges. In fact, though we were still in a strong position so far as food was concerned, the many "extras" that we found in the depot — chocolate, sweets, curry powder, dates and raisins, to mention but a few — were very welcome indeed.

February 9 too we spent at Depot 700, but by the end of the day our position had improved, for at half past ten that night the two Sno-cats, *Able* and *Haywire,* arrived at last, and three quarters of an hour later the Beaver, flown by John Claydon, circled over the depot bearing Ed Hillary and Wright. They had taken off from Scott Base almost six hours before, and had encountered very poor weather which would normally have turned them back; but we reported excellent conditions on our side of the mountains, so John, who was determined to get Ed to us if it was humanly possible, flew on up the glacier leading into Barne Inlet, through the cloud lying over the mountains, and on to the depot. This was the first time that anyone had flown over the Barne Inlet route, and they reported the glacier to be tremendously crevassed.

Before landing, John flew Ed around the crevassed area which lay seven miles to the north of the depot, for he hoped to find a route by which we could avoid this when we started off the next day.

After the first greetings, and when the plane had been unloaded, we began refueling the newly arrived cats and the Beaver. The aircraft had to be picketed, for the weather was too bad to attempt the long flight back that night. Besides mail, they had brought us some eggs and fruit, which rapidly froze solid; the eggs would be none the worse, but it was certainly going to be difficult to thaw the apples and oranges sufficiently to eat them!

Next morning "outside men" were called for eight o'clock after four or five hours' sleep. At twenty to ten Claydon and Wright took off in the Beaver, and we later heard that they had reached Scott Base safely, although Claydon was compelled to land in bad visibility. Precisely at ten o'clock the vehicles moved off, Ed Hillary joining David Stratton, Hal Lister and myself in *Rock 'n Roll.* After an uneventful 10 miles we believed ourselves clear of the crevassed area and altered course to intercept Ed's old track farther to the west, but we had only gone another mile when we broke through a six-foot-wide lid which was invisible on the surface. The sledges passed over the hole quite safely, but it was clearly time to prospect ahead. While David drove, Ed, Hal and I skied forward probing the innumerable crevasses which we now encountered. Many of them were 20 to 30 feet across and we made a number of diversions, but they all seemed reasonably well bridged, and we won clear of the area after 2½ miles without any real difficulty.

Meanwhile *Able* was again in trouble at the back, with a broken rear spring — the only one to break throughout the journey. However, David managed to replace this in under an hour while we were moving slowly forward, and the party was not delayed.

Shortly after clearing the crevasses we found Ed's old tractor trail showing on the surface. This we followed for mile after mile, over undulation after undulation, until we reached a snow cairn left by one of the dog sledge parties at 52 miles from Depot 700.

On February 11, we drove 53 miles to reach Midway Depot at 81°30'S, 146°09'E, where we found the altitude to be 7600 feet. At first visibility was bad, but gradually it improved and the tractor route remained clearly visible, making the driving much easier. After traveling 20 miles, we heard by radio that *Able* had now got a fractured weld of the main steering crossbar. This meant that Roy Homard and Ralph Lenton in *County of Kent* had to go back with the spare that they were carrying. Three hours later, as we grew colder and colder waiting in our vehicles, we heard that the repair was going well and David Pratt urged us to go on.

Continuing over increasingly rough and hard surfaces, in rather hilly country, we reached a wide valley running from east to west. In the bottom, for half a mile or more, there was no crevassing, but for many miles great chasms could be seen on either side. These were up to 15 yards across, and ran parallel to one another, their direction being inward toward the center of the valley, and "upstream" toward the west. One after another we examined these ominous-looking places, but all were very solidly filled and we passed over without trouble. There seemed no doubt that the valley formed the upper reaches of one of the glaciers flowing east through the mountains, almost 100 miles away, perhaps to debouch into Shackleton Inlet.

Near the bottom we came upon the Weasel that Ed had abandoned on his way south. We had brought a spare part for it, and if one of our Sno-cats had broken down irretrievably we would have repaired the Weasel and taken it on with us. As it was, we were satisfied with the condition of the cats and did not want to reduce our rate of travel to that which it had been before we abandoned *Wrack and Ruin*. We therefore left the Weasel where it was and climbed up out of the valley on the north side.

On the further slope were three miles of crevasses, 2 to 5 feet wide, that took us an hour and a half to cross, with David, Hal and Ed working steadily ahead. These were the last that actually delayed us, for from here onward the information acquired by Ed enabled us to avoid all bad areas. Another 15 miles over hard and increasingly hummocky sastrugi brought us to Midway Depot at twenty past four in the morning.

Next day maintenance came round again but the work was held up by the absence of *Able* and the *County of Kent*, for they carried some of the equipment we needed. We heard that when they were five miles beyond the point where they had repaired the steering, *Able's* main transmission box had broken up, and they had had to fit a spare — another long and laborious task with the temperature in the region of −20°F. When we had completed the seismic work and whatever maintenance we could do, there occurred the rare opportunity of catching up some of our lost sleep. Then, during the afternoon of the 13th, the others arrived out of the light snowdrift that obscured the scene.

At last, on February 14, we set off again, but the promise of the previous evening was not fulfilled, and we were unable to see the old tractor trail in the whiteout which prevailed. Later the visibility improved, and after 16 miles we picked out a number of black dots ahead a few hundred yards off course. These proved to be four empty drums left during Ed's outward journey, and they served to give us some confidence, because at the time we were passing an area of crevasses which were known to be parallel to our course and might therefore form a most uncomfortable hazard. It was now noticeable that the surface undulations were trending in a north-south direction and not east to west as had been the case up to now, but we had risen again during the day to 7685 feet.

Next morning we started with high hopes of reaching Depot 480 just 80 miles to the north. The weather was bright, with increasing blue sky, so that we were able to follow the tracks once more. Surprisingly enough, after driving 50 miles the previous day in poor visibility, we found the tracks only 20 yards to the west of our tents. So confident had we been that they lay to the east of us that Ed Hillary had skied a mile or two in that direction and was much chagrined to find he need never have left the camp.

While traveling over the very rough and hummocky surface, I found it increasingly difficult to steer, but put it down to the side-pull of the sledges sliding off the icy swells. Then, when we had covered 13 miles, *Rock 'n Roll* took charge and described an S-bend over which I had no apparent control. Clearly something was wrong, and on climbing out I could see that the front and rear pontoons were obviously pointing in quite different directions. Investigation showed that the same welds had given way as had failed on *Able*. Having no more spares, the only possibility was to re-weld the broken parts. When the others joined us and we settled down to camp and to dismantle the steering, David Pratt and Roy Homard inspected the same welds on the other cats and found that the break had gone almost as far on *Haywire,* although it had not yet affected the driving.

Now our special Terylene traveling tent, for work on the cats, which had so often been useful in the past, really came into its own, for a brisk breeze and a temperature down to −38°F made it essential to have cover for the preheating and prolonged cooling of the heavy metal parts, quite apart from the actual electric welding. This preheating and after-cooling was carried out with blowtorches over a period of some hours, and it was not until half past five in the morning that the two Davids, Roy and Jon climbed into their sleeping bags. Even then the job was not completed, and it took all the next day to finish the welding and reassemble both cats.

At last, on February 17, we got away again, to cover the remaining 63 miles to Depot 480 (79°51′S, 146°00′E, at 7950 feet). Over the hard surfaces of this undulating country we were able to travel at 8 to 10 mph. Some of the slopes were considerably longer and steeper than those we had encountered previously, and we saw the vehicles as small dark shapes at a distance of, perhaps, two miles and seemingly high above us. As we approached the depot, which was clearly visible from a distance of four miles, the white flanking cairns gleamed in the sun for two and a half miles on either side.

There we found fuel, lubricating oil, gear, oil, grease, and food — in fact all that we could possibly require.

Up to this time we had relied on the sun compass for navigation, or, when the sky was overcast, fell back on the magnetic compass. Here at Depot 480, when we set off on the 18th in a complete whiteout, the magnetic compass failed to respond. Apparently, while following the old tracks for the last 80 miles, we had moved into an area where the compasses were so sluggish that their rate of response made it impractical to use them. With no possibility of seeing anything in front in the whiteout, I was driving with eyes firmly fixed on the compass when David Stratton drew my attention ahead. There I saw three Sno-cats coming toward me! I had turned completely round and was heading straight back along our track. Halting the others, we experimented several times, with similar results. Realizing that we should make no progress in this way, we sought other means of keeping course.

The first scheme to be tried was a method by which four of us skied ahead carrying bundles of trail flags. Starting with three sticks carefully oriented by a prismatic compass, which had been allowed to steady for a long time, we could plant one flag after another in line with the first three, at intervals of about 200 yards, and thereby produce the original line into the indefinite distance. The vehicles then followed the flags, a man on the last sledge picking them up for use farther on. After some miles, this was found to be both slow and arduous. We therefore devised a means by which the markers were placed alternately by two men riding on the sledges of the leading vehicle. The problem was then for the driver to maintain a more or less straight course, as it was impossible for him to see behind. This was accomplished by Ed standing on the front seat of *Rock 'n Roll*, with his head and shoulders through the escape hatch, facing backward, and calling "left" or "right" to the driver. In these ways we managed to travel 15 miles in the right direction, but it was not enough.

The whiteout still prevailed on the following day, and flagging had to continue, but the method was modified so that the driver looked backward out of the open door while steering with his right hand behind him. Forward vision and accelerator control were provided by the passenger. This certainly speeded things up, but the strain on the driver's arms and neck was considerable, especially as his left hand had constantly to grip the window frame to ensure that the lurching did not precipitate him through the open door and beneath the rear tracks of the cat. By changing drivers every two hours we managed to move 42 miles in the day, and felt that we had devised a means by which we could travel satisfactorily in whiteout.

So it went on, maintenance on February 20 followed by 25 miles of route flagging, another 39 miles flagged on the 21st; then relief the next day when slight visibility made it possible to see surface irregularities, and for 15 miles we drove "sastrugi hopping" — that is, driving from one selected ridge to the next, thereby maintaining a reasonable course.

When camping the previous evening the first distant rocky mountains had just been visible over the snow horizon to the east — the first rock that we had seen since leaving the Whichaway Nunataks 1450 miles away. Now we made progress in rapidly improving visibility, and more and more snow-clad masses, with a few dark patches of rock, began to show themselves as our course brought us closer and closer to the edge of the plateau. At the end of the day we had traveled 52 miles, and when we stopped, Mount Feather, with a small plume of cloud, was clear against the blue sky. This, Ed told us, formed a good marker for "coming in" on the Plateau Depot, and for the last hour of the day we had been watching for the snow cairn that marked the point where we should alter course. But we did not find it. Fortunately we had obtained a sun sight, and knew that we could not be more than 1½ miles off, so camped where we were — glad to get into our tents out of the sharp wind and a temperature of −28°F.

Continuing on the 23rd over a series of steep snow ridges which mark the margin of the plateau, we gained height for about 29 miles before making a very abrupt descent. There, for the first time, the trailing sledges showed signs of catching up the Sno-cats. Then two more miles, and we saw first the cairns, then the Plateau Depot itself. Twenty minutes later we had arrived, but without the rest of the party, for two hours after starting, the forward steering arm of *Haywire* had dropped and, catching in the snow, had buckled back

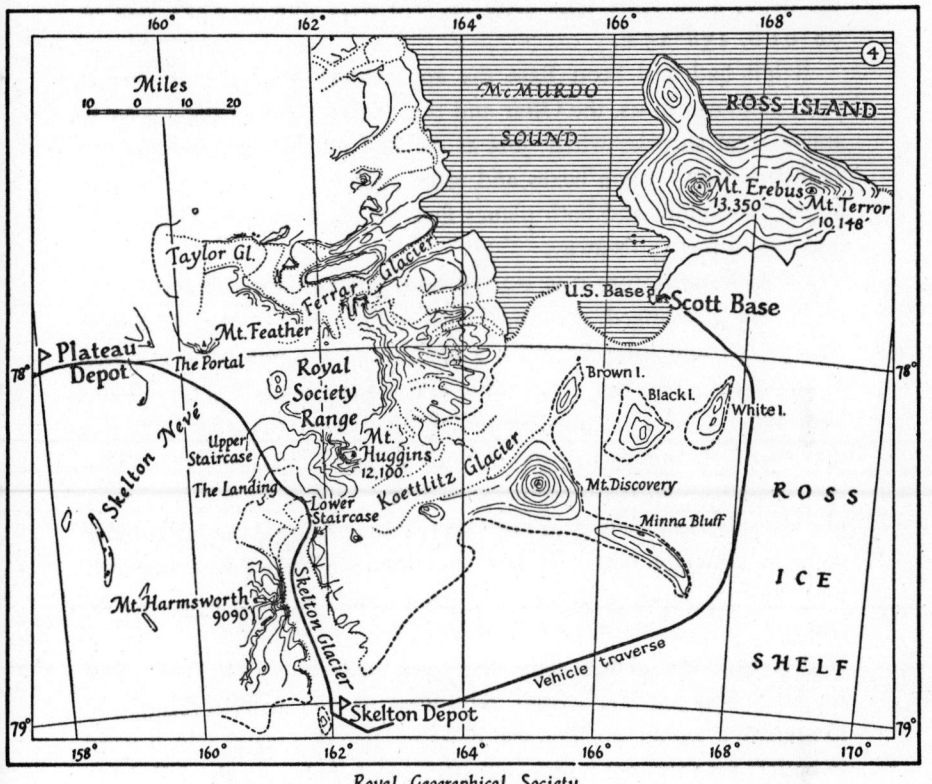

Royal Geographical Society

Plateau Depot to Scott Base.

under the vehicle to be completely destroyed. The fitting of a new spare would take an hour or two, so we did not expect them to reach the depot until some time after us. We were now at 8275 feet in 78°01′S, 158°25′E.

Ralph had told Scott Base the approximate time of our arrival and, unknown to us, the Otter and the Beaver were on their way. It was a great surprise when, just as we had finished digging out the fuel drums and ration boxes and were pitching our tents, there was a roar of engines and both planes flew low over the depot, to circle and land a few yards away.

As the temperature was −30°F both engines were kept running while we exchanged greetings with John Lewis, John Claydon, Wally Tarr and Buzz Burrows, a member of the relief I.G.Y. party at Scott Base, who had flown up to take some magnetic observations. We then loaded a certain amount of superfluous material from the depot into the aircraft, together with a Nansen dog sledge. While this was going on, the other vehicles arrived and a brief "party" took place inside the fuselage of the Otter, where fourteen of us congregated to share the bottles of beer that John Lewis had brought with him, and to shout vociferously at each other over the noise of the engine.

Presently the planes took off again, carrying with them Ken Blaiklock and Jon Stephenson, who were needed at base. They had to prepare a winter stock of seal meat for two dog teams which were to be left for their use on a small venture of their own the following season.

That night we laid out the seismic gear for the last time. As the task was completed, the sun disappeared beneath the southern horizon, a reminder that the season was drawing to a close, and it would soon be time to leave the high plateau where we were still at over 8000 feet. With the clouds lit red by the hidden sun, and the snow mauve in semi-shadow, yet flecked by darker colors in every hollow, we walked to our tents, knowing that the next day we should plunge over the edge and wind our way down through the unfamiliar scene of rocky mountains and towering cliffs.

On the 24th, when the seismic shot had been completed, we entered the wide area which Hillary's parties had called "The Portal," and began the long descent of the Skelton Glacier. Within a few miles the sky clouded over, the guiding rocks were hidden from view by drift, and we began again to flag our route — Ed's tall figure planting the markers one after the other in an invisible surface. Soon the following wind began to fill the cab of *Rock 'n Roll* with snow, and the cold became too great to endure the necessarily cramped and twisted driving position. When we stopped to camp after 15 miles we found the wind speed to be 35 mph and the temperature −38°F.

Knowing that the wind was almost certainly a local katabatic effect we rose next day determined to push on in the hope of finding better conditions a few miles below. Our hope was quickly justified, for soon the wind dropped, the sky cleared, and for 52 miles, as we descended the Upper Staircase, over the Landing and down the Lower Staircase, we had the most brilliant weather. Toward the end of the day the wind rose again, and before we could pitch camp it was gusting to over 60 mph. Using the vehicles as windbreaks, we had little difficulty in erecting the tents, but all night the poles were bending ominously and we listened to constant noisy flapping.

Next day we waited only until Ed could pick out his landmarks through the drift, then broke camp while it was still blowing at 40 mph, and continued down the glacier. Within a mile, as we descended a steep slope, the wind dropped, the drift cleared and we again enjoyed the most perfect weather. Looking back, it seemed that there was a solid wall of impenetrable mountains, dominated by the 13,000 feet of Mount Huggins. There was no sign of the upper reaches of the glacier which were hidden by the rocky spurs.

As we went down the steeper inclines we found them so smooth and hard that the sledges slid from side to side completely out of control. Those linked to a Sno-cat by a solid bar came to no harm, but Roy's sledges were on steel wire tows, which allowed them to follow after the cat, smashing into the rear pontoons, and again damaging the broken steering platform. At the same time a solid wooden beam carried on top of the front sledge pierced the rear door of the *County of Kent,* nearly transfixing those inside. After this escape, and when the repairs were done, Roy continued, using a heavy rope brake under the sledge runners to reach the bottom of the slope.

In its lower reaches the Skelton Glacier was completely bare, the rough blue ice being hard on Sno-cats and sledges. For several miles innumerable crevasses crossed its surface, but it was easy to pick a route where they were too small to cause any trouble. Here again, as all the way down the glacier, Ed's firsthand knowledge saved us many hours of route finding and possible difficulty. After crossing 15 miles of blue ice, we ran again onto a snow surface, which became more and more ridged as we approached Teale Island. These ridges were wind-blown forms like small sand dunes, two to three feet high, and all oriented across our course. Only the next day did we see them clearly, for that night whiteout conditions had again come upon us, and only by the feel of the driving was it possible to know what the surface was like.

Then, away in the distance, some dark specks began to show, and this we knew must be the Skelton Depot (79°03′S, 162°15′E), on the Ross Ice Shelf. This was the last of the depots, and now there remained but 130 miles of level traveling on the ice shelf between us and Scott Base. That night we got into our sleeping bags at quarter past four in the morning, only to rise again at ten o'clock.

Now came the last day of maintenance, which occupied us until late in the afternoon. We were happy to think that it would be some time before we would have to fill a grease gun again, or become covered in a mixture of oil and drift. All the depot stores were dug out, and we selected those which we hoped to fly back to Scott instead of leaving them to be lost in the field. Unfortunately, it was impossible to find a place for the planes to land safely. Until we could do so we were compelled to stack the boxes on top of our already full loads and take them with us until we came to a sufficiently level place for the aircraft to land.

When finally we set out that evening, we drove first on a course of 110°T for 10 miles to avoid the crevasses which were known to flank the Skelton Glacier where it pushed out into the ice shelf, then altered course 35° to the north for another 10 miles, before stopping to camp again, this time on a soft smooth surface.

In the morning both planes flew out to us, bringing Dr. Adams, the British physiologist working at McMurdo Sound, who was to accompany us back to Scott Base doing IMP tests with Allan Rogers for the last three days. When the aircraft left they took with them all the extra stores that we had picked up at the depot, together with some other items. During the day we traveled 65 miles and camped some way to the east of the low rocky tongue of Minna Bluff and the badly crevassed area around it.

Just as we were setting off on the morning of March 1, we saw an American Otter flying toward us, then, as it circled the vehicles and we were climbing into the cabs, we fired a "two-star-red" as a gesture of *joie de vivre* before starting. As a consequence, various things happened which nearly resulted in a serious Antarctic traffic accident. Unknown to us, the Americans took our signal to mean that we needed something, so they made a circuit and came in to land.

Looking back from *Rock 'n Roll* I saw them touch down and told Stratton, who was driving, that we had better stop. In a moment the following cat, whose driver was also looking behind him, began to climb up over the top of our rear sledge. When we went back to look at the damage done by the pontoons, which were resting on top of our load, we found that not only was the sledge wheel badly damaged, but a box containing many hundreds of detonators had been smashed into small splinters, and the metal containers themselves were crushed almost flat revealing detonators in profusion. Had they exploded it would certainly have been the end of the "climbing" Snocat, but fortunately nothing happened, and we were able to tow it slowly backward off the sledge without further damage.

In all the excitement we forgot about the plane, which had taxied across the snow, only to take off again without stopping!

The rest of the day was uneventful except that we made the longest run of the whole journey — traveling 75 miles by the time we camped. This left us 22 miles to go — a comfortable distance to travel by 2 o'clock on March 2, which we had estimated as our time of arrival several days earlier. Before starting we decorated the Snocats for the last time with all the available flags, and then headed off toward Castle Rock, where we had been told we should find a fuel drum marking the start of a line of flags that would lead us to a prepared route through the pressure ridges. This had been done with the assistance of American bulldozers from McMurdo Station, two miles from Scott Base.

As we ran in toward the island, we began to pick out the huts of Scott Base against the dark rock of Pram Point; then Weasels, Ferguson tractors and Bren gun carriers could be seen streaming out along the track to meet us. Soon we joined up, and as the Sno-cats thundered and weaved between the ridges, escorted in front and behind by a variety of vehicles, scores of figures stood, camera in hand, at every vantage point. At precisely 1:57 P.M. on March 2, 1958, our long journey was over. We had traveled 2158 statute miles from Shackleton to Scott Base via the South Pole. We had estimated that the journey would take 100 days and that our average speed would be about 20 miles per day. We now found that we had completed the trip in 99 days (98 if it is remembered that we crossed the date line at the Pole), and had averaged 22 miles per day.

We knew one man would be particularly happy at our arrival — Captain Henry Kirkwood, RN (known to us all as "Harry Plywood"), commanding HMNZS *Endeavour,* and waiting to take us to New Zealand before McMurdo Sound froze over. He told me later that, according to his calculations, we were one day late!

In front of Scott Base the cats assembled on the sea ice, and confusion reigned as scores of photographers had their way with the somewhat astonished new arrivals. Then we all congregated around the flagstaff and listened to speeches of welcome from our own people and the Americans.

An improvised band from "over the hill" did their worst with our national airs, ending up with what we were told was "God Save the Queen." The band had been formed the night before by calling for all who thought they could play an instrument. The edict went forth — "It doesn't matter if you can play — but you gotta be able to play loud" — and they certainly did.

When at last we repaired to the hut, it was to continue talking, to eat, to wash, but not to rest. All sense of tiredness had vanished and it was late that night when the last of us went to bed.

Three days later, on March 5, 1958, we sailed north over the ice-free waters of McMurdo Sound on our way to New Zealand; but although the Antarctic let us go without even a floe in sight, the Southern Ocean took its toll as *Endeavour* pitched and rolled in the heavy seas.

Twelve days later, in brilliant sunshine, we sailed into Wellington harbor. It happened that the *Magga Dan* had arrived a few days before, and we were delighted to see her red painted hull coming out to meet us early in the morning, carrying our families and friends. We were given a vociferous welcome by the many ships lying in the harbor, with a flight of RNZAF Vampires that roared overhead, and an unforgettable reception by the New Zealand people.

This was the end of the expedition as the public saw it, but for us it is the beginning of a new endeavor—for now we must produce the results, which, we believe, will justify the early faith and vision of all those who supported us in the beginning, and sustained us to the end.

Glossary

Bergy bits   Massive pieces of ice generally less than 15 feet above sea level and not more than 30 feet across.

Beset   Situation of a vessel surrounded by ice and unable to move.

Brash ice   Small fragments of broken ice not larger than 6 feet across; the wreckage of other forms of ice.

Fast ice   Unbroken sea ice of greatly varying width remaining attached to the coast.

Floe   A free piece of sea ice, large or small. Ice up to 3 feet thick forms "light floes," thicker floes are called "heavy floes." Floes may be 10 miles or more in diameter.

Frost smoke   Foglike clouds, due to the contact of cold air with relatively warm sea water in leads or pools.

Growler   A piece of ice almost awash, smaller than a bergy bit.

Hummocked ice   Sea ice piled haphazardly one piece over another, which may be weathered or mantled with snow.

Ice edge   The boundary between sea ice and open sea.

Ice front   The cliff forming the seaward face of an ice shelf.

Ice piedmont   Ice covering a coastal strip of low-lying land backed by mountains.

Ice sheet	A continuous mass of ice and snow of considerable thickness and of an area greater than about 20,000 square miles.
Ice shelf	A floating sheet of ice of considerable thickness. Their seaward cliffs range from 6 feet to 200 feet in height.
Ice wall	An ice cliff forming the seaward margin.
Icing	The accumulation of a deposit of ice on (a) the superstructure of ships, caused principally by the freezing of spray; or (b) aircraft, caused by the freezing of water vapor or supercooled water droplets on a cold surface.
Land water	An area of open sea water forming annually along a coast when the sea ice is forced offshore by the wind. Correctly called a "shore lead."
Lead	A navigable passage through pack ice.
Névé	Old snow which has been transformed into a denser material.
Nunatak	A rock mass, often of pyramid form, entirely surrounded by ice and snow. Usually the top of buried mountains.
Pack ice	Any area of sea ice other than fast ice.
Pool	Any enclosed sea water area in pack ice other than a lead, but not large enough to be called open water.
Pressure ice	A general term for sea ice which has been squeezed, and in places forced upwards, when it can be described as "rafted ice," "hummocked ice," or "pressure ridge."
Rafting	The overriding of one floe on another.

287

Rammsonde   An instrument with a conical point driven several meters into the snow surface by successive blows of a known force. Used to determine the density of successive horizons and the annual accumulation during preceding years.

Rotten ice   Sea ice which has become honeycombed in the course of melting, and which is in an advanced state of disintegration.

Sastrugi   Fluted ridges carved by the wind from a snow surface. Sastrugi may be from a few inches to 5 feet high.

Water sky   Dark streaks in the sky due to the reflection of open water on clouds.

Whiteout   A condition of diffuse light when no shadows are cast due to a continuous white cloud layer appearing to merge with the white snow surface. No surface irregularities of the snow are visible, but a dark object may be clearly seen. There is no visible horizon.

Windcrust   A hard snow layer formed on the surface by wind compaction of the crystals. Usually not more than 6 inches thick. A man walking on windcrust will make no footprints.

APPENDIXES

It has been usual to provide technical appendixes to books about polar expeditions. In this case it has been thought better to leave the account of the expedition's scientific work to appear in a more complete form than is possible so soon after our return.

The following appendixes, containing some technical details of the vehicles and aircraft, give a background to the description of the work they had to do. It should also be said that the effectiveness of our machines could never have been attained without the help of the ninety-six engineering firms that gave practical assistance to the expedition.

APPENDIX A: Vehicle Specifications
APPENDIX B: Aircraft Specifications

APPENDIX A
Vehicle Specifications

Antarctic terrain can provide severe problems for mechanical transport. Soft snow requires a vehicle with first-class traction. Hard snow or ice, especially in the form of sastrugi, requires a vehicle with a good suspension system, and a different type of traction. Thus it is hard to combine in any one vehicle all the features necessary for a versatile polar model. After considerable investigation followed by field visits to America, Canada, Greenland and Scandinavia, the decision was taken to use light, tracked vehicles. We also decided to spread the risk and selected four types of light snow tractor for our trans-Antarctic journey. We expected crevasses and realized that the lighter the vehicle the better the chance of crossing the snow-bridges. Our ship, too, was a small one, and it would not be possible to unload heavy vehicles.

Where engines were concerned, the choice was between petrol or diesel. Diesel engines are generally more economical on fuel than petrol engines, but they have a compression ratio of approximately 19 to 1, and petrol, say 7 or 9 to 1. This higher compression makes the starting of a diesel more difficult in low temperatures. Basic engine weight of the diesel is heavier than that of the petrol, generally less maintenance is required, but if injector trouble does arise it proves more difficult to solve than the problems usually associated with a petrol engine.

We decided upon petrol-engined, light-tracked vehicles distributed as follows:

Transpolar Party	4 Sno-cats
	4 Weasels
	1 Muskeg tractor
	2 Ferguson tractors
Ross Sea Party	5 Ferguson tractors
	1 Weasel

291

SNO–CAT, MODEL 743

The Tucker Sno-cat is made in the United States by the Tucker Sno-cat Corporation. We ordered standard models which we subsequently strengthened in the United Kingdom for Antarctic work. The general specification, after modification, is as follows:

GENERAL SPECIFICATION

Make	Chrysler V-8 o.h.v. Industrial
Model	IND 56
Horsepower rating	200 at 4000 rpm
Number of cylinders	8
Bore	3.81
Stroke	3.624 in.
Piston displacement	331 cu. in.
Compression ratio	8.5 to 1
Oil pressure	45 to 55 psi at 2000 rpm
Transmission	Single-plate dry clutch to 5-speed heavy-duty Dodge truck gearbox to two Dodge differentials
Ground pressure	¾ lb./sq. in.
Cooling system capacity	10 gallons
Crankcase capacity	5 quarts
Drive axles (front and rear)	Standard Dodge, 1 ton with short extension axles fitted to carry the pontoon outer bearings
Petrol tank capacity	3 tanks: 25 gallons left, 25 gallons right, 40 gallons auxiliary
Speed range	15 mph maximum: when loaded, 6 mph to 8 mph on even snow
Miles per gallon	0.8 to 2 mpg under load
Turning radius	28 ft.
Overall width	7 ft. 5 in.
Overall length	20 ft.
Overall height	7 ft. 6 in.
Weight (dry)	7000 lbs.
Pontoon and track	24 × 103 in.

TRACTION

The Sno-cat traction system is unique, and provides almost one hundred per cent traction even when turning in soft snow. An open ladder-type track, made up of tubes with grouser plate castings at each end, passes round the pontoon. The round crossbars of this track provide the grip in soft snow, and have the special characteristic that all forces, from tube to snow, are at right angles to the tube. Thus, as the track passes from the snow at the rear of the pontoon on around the pontoon, each track tube will leave the snow without scuffing or slip, and a perfectly clear track indentation can be seen after the vehicle has passed. For grip upon hard ice, the casting at each end of the track tube has two angled grouser plates so that the harder the ice the less there is of the angled grouser plate in contact, and thus the higher the bearing pressure, the greater the penetration of the angle tip of the grouser plate. In soft snow the grouser plates also provide a good grip. The open gap between each track bar allows the snow to pack up against the bottom of the pontoon, thus providing a compressed surface upon which the pontoon can slide. The tracks are driven by two propeller shafts through normal differentials, and each pontoon is free to turn about its axle and is sprung with semi-elliptic leaf springs attached to the steering platform.

STEERING

The front and rear steering platforms are connected to a hydraulic jack through a system of rods and levers. A conventional steering wheel in the cab actuates, through a steering box and another system of levers, the valve which operates the hydraulic jack. A special point is that when turning say to the right, the front pontoons turn in that direction and the rear pontoons turn to the left, so causing all pontoons to be tangents to the arc of the circle around which the vehicle is traveling. This provides better traction on a turn than that of any normal full-tracked vehicle. For example, in soft snow a Weasel may bog down since the skidding track will dig a deep trough and the vehicle will sink into the snow.

PERFORMANCE

We were able to carry up to one-ton payload inside the body of the Sno-cat and, by using runner material having a low coefficient of friction on our sledges (Bakelite and p.t.f.e.), we were able to haul two sledges with two and a half tons loaded on each. This is at least two tons more than has been pulled behind Sno-cats in the past.

Great care had to be taken by drivers, and we found that over hard snow surfaces speed was reduced to as little as 2 mph. Over level firm snow we were able to achieve 10 mph. This was usually of short duration, and a good cruising speed averaged from 6 to 8 mph.

MODIFICATIONS

Examples of a few of the modifications carried out are as follows:

Engine

The compression ratio was raised from 7.5 to 8.5 to provide: (1) higher efficiency and thus economy of fuel, (2) increased horsepower. Increased horsepower would be useful on the polar plateau at 10,000 feet since the brake horsepower available at this altitude could be expected to be about half that obtained at sea level.

The standard hydraulic tappets were changed for a mechanically operated system.

The standard fluid drive was changed to a normal clutch and gearbox.

Instrumentation

Full instrumentation was provided even to the extent of being able to read battery temperature.

An auxiliary fuel tank was fitted to give greater range. This was a flexible bag tank (aircraft type).

Electrical System

The electrical system was changed from 12 to 24 volts because the battery electromotive force is proportional to temperature and the currents required for ancillary equipment are halved by doubling the voltage. The electrical system was fully suppressed to enable radios to be used on the move and this had the added advantage of providing a waterproof system against melted snow.

The batteries were multiplate, low-temperature type to give greater output at low temperatures, and were of 110 ampere hour capacity. All cables were changed to special silicone rubber insulation.

Radio

Ernest Turner T.R.11.H radio transceivers were fitted to the Sno-cats, this equipment being convenient for use with seismic shooting gear. High and low transmitter power was available, giving 40 or 10 watts. The transmission was crystal controlled and we operated on frequencies between 4 and 10 Mc/s. Consumption working on 12 volts D.C. power used (stand by) 3 amps; receiver, 6.25; transmitter low power 7 amps, and transmitter high power 20 amps. We had 12 and 24 bolt sets.

A D/F loop was mounted on the roof of the cab to deal with the possibility of having to search for and find a crashed aircraft, or even perhaps of finding a manned base in bad weather conditions.

Extensible tube compasses were also mounted on the roof to enable the compass to be positioned a good distance from the metal mass of the vehicle.

A SARAH (Search and Rescue and Homing) beacon was fitted to each Sno-cat. The equipment was originally designed for air-sea rescue work, when the beacon would be switched on, and left on, until rescue had been effected. The vehicle SARAH ran from a light-weight low-temperature nickel-cadmium battery, consisting of an alkaline system using a solution of potassium hydroxide as the electrolyte. These could be trickle charged from the vehicle batteries. The beacon is pre-set to 243 Mc/s and requires no further adjustment.

An aircraft flying at 10,000 feet can home onto the beacon from a range of 60 miles.

Transmission

Extensive track rewelding was carried out to low-temperature specifications. Battery and engine pre-heaters were fitted to enable a reliable engine start to be effected down to −60°F. A power take-off was fitted to the gearbox for driving a portable **D.C.** generator which would provide electric arc welding on the trail.

Cab

Double screens and thermal insulation were fitted to the driving cab. A de-mister unit, blowing warm air between the double screens, prevented the formation of ice on the inside of the front driving screen. In the field it was found best not to let the driving cab temperature get too high, or else any snow that came in with the foot-gear would melt and soak through. Damp feet are dangerous and even the best-brushed feet still have a little snow on them! The air temperature at head level was pleasantly warm, and after driving for a few hours was always above freezing point.

The towing arrangement was modified to give a better towing angle and an escape hatch built into the roof of the driving compartment for use in crevasses.

SNOW PROOFING

Drifting snow penetrates even through pinholes, and the sealing of a vehicle body to keep out the snow must be a hundred per cent job or it is better left undone. We found this out from bitter experience, and, being unable to make a good job of the Sno-cat engine, we found it better to let drifting snow blow in and out again. This would occur when camped and it was a fairly quick job to prise snow out from the moving parts and let it drop through beneath the engine to the ground. In the case of the cab doors, by using low-temperature silicone rubber sealing-strip, we were able to keep them drift-proof.

WEASEL

The Weasel cargo carrier was made in the U.S.A. as an army vehicle for World War II.

GENERAL SPECIFICATION

Make	Studebaker
Model	M.29 (Land Weasel)
	M.29 C (Amphibious Weasel)
	(we selected two of each)

Type	L Head (side valve)
Engine	Studebaker straight six
Horsepower (net) at sea level	75 at 3800 rpm
Horsepower (net) at 3000 ft.	55 at 3600 rpm
Number of cylinders	6
Bore	3 in.
Stroke	4 in.
Piston displacement	169.6 cu. in.
Compression ratio	7 to 1
Oil pressure	40 lbs.
Transmission	Single-plate dry clutch to 3-speed gearbox to high and low ratio transfer box to rear differential drive
Ground pressure	Nominal 1.9 lbs./sq. in.
Cooling system capacity	12¾ quarts
Crankcase capacity	5 quarts
Petrol tank capacity	35 gallons
Speed range	On snow, hauling loads, 8 to 10 mph is a good cruising speed
Miles per gallon	0.7 to 3 (depending upon conditions)
Turning radius	12 ft.
Overall width	5 ft. 7¼ in.
Overall length	14 ft. 6 in.
Overall height	6 ft.
Weight (dry)	4800 lbs.

TRACTION

The Weasel has a conventional full-track system which provides a fair grip on medium surfaces. Steering is obtained by braking on the inboard track through a conventional cle-track system. The traction ability of the Weasel was less than half as efficient as the Sno-cat and we found that, when it was necessary to make a turn in soft snow, the Weasel lost most of its traction and was quite capable of bogging itself down.

PERFORMANCE

We aimed at carrying 1200 pounds inside the body, and usually hauled one sledge with two tons payload. We did, on occasions, haul more, but the most efficient method of load hauling is to reduce the sledge payload and increase the number of sledges until the optimum is reached. Each following sledge will then be traversing snow that has been compressed by the runners of the preceding sledge.

MODIFICATIONS

The Weasels were built during the Second World War, and production had ceased. All available Weasels were therefore second-hand. We obtained two from Hudson Bay, Canada, and two from the U.K., which had come from the Middle East. They were in poor condition and had to be reworked. At the same time an extensive program of mechanical strengthening was carried out: heavier springs, stronger driving sprockets, stronger heavy-duty gearboxes, etc. Special batteries were fitted with a pre-heater system for both engine and batteries. This pre-heater was a kerosene-burning heat exchanger, electrically operated, which blew hot air over the parts requiring pre-heating. Full instrumentation was provided, also radio and SARAH beacon.

RADIO

Pye C.12 sets were fitted to the Weasels and the set weighed 66 lbs.

RECEIVER PERFORMANCE

Audio output: 1 watt available at 1000 c/s into 100 ohms, but usually limited to 500 m/W.

Audio response: 10 db down at 200 c/s and 3 Kc/s.

TRANSMITTER PERFORMANCE

R.F. Power Output: RT—5 watts minimum, CW—9 watts minimum.

Measured in 60 pf+ 10 ohms (dummy antenna).

Anode modulation: 95 per cent capability.

Modulator frequency response: −6 db at 200 c/s and −3 db at 3 Kc/s.

Frequency accuracy: Within 1 Kc/s of incoming signal when adjusted to "Zero Best" on Receive.

Frequency selector: Resetting accuracy within 1 Kc/s.

CONSUMPTION

Input Current (12V D.C. input)

Receiver only	4 amps
Receiver and I.C. amplifier + Tx heater	7 amps
Transmit R.T.	13 amps
Transmit C.W.	11 amps

CAB

We had two special cabs built of light alloy. These were onazote lined with double-screen perspex windows. An escape hatch was built into the roof as an emergency exit. We found these cabs extremely warm, and were often forced to drive with the doors open. Steel wire body-ropes were fitted around the vehicle to enable it to be more easily recovered from a lengthwise crevasse. Front nose attachments were constructed to enable the Weasels to be roped together on the same principle as mountaineers, so that if one fell down a crevasse, at least the driver's life would be saved. In the event of the rear of the Weasel breaking through just as the front was safely through the crevasse, the extra pull from the vehicle ahead would haul it out before it dropped.

SNOW PROOFING

The Weasel engine is inside the cab and so, by waterproofing the hull, we were able to keep out snow from engine and cab.

MUSKEG TRACTOR

The Muskeg tractor, built by the Bombardier Company of Canada, is designed for use over snow or in rough country.

GENERAL SPECIFICATION

	Chrysler straight six, side valve
Horsepower rating	115 at 3400 rpm
Number of cylinders	6
Bore	3.437
Stroke	4.5 in.
Compression ratio	7 to 1
Transmission	Single-plate, dry clutch to 4-speed synchromesh gearbox to controlled type front drive differential
Ground pressure	Approx. ¾ lb./sq. in.
Cooling system capacity	14 quarts
Crankcase capacity	5 quarts
Differential	controlled type front drive
Petrol tank capacity	15 gallons
Speed range	25 mph maximum: when loaded and on snow, cruising speed 10 mph
Miles per gallon	1 to 1.8, hauling 2 tons
Overall width	7 ft. 3 in.
Overall length	11 ft. 8 in.
Overall height	5 ft. 8in.
Weight (dry)	4600 lbs.

TRACTION

The track consists of rubber belts with steel crosslinks. The belts are endless, and made from rubber and fabric reinforced internally with steel cables. Each track runs on eight Monopiece-drop center wheels with 4.50 × 16-6 ply nylon tires. The steering consists of braking through a controlled heavy-duty differential.

PERFORMANCE

Up to one ton can be loaded on the vehicle itself and we found the running boards very convenient for carrying our crevasse bridge.

We were able to haul loads similar to that of the Weasel and found the vehicle easy to drive and sturdy. It performed very efficiently on hard surfaces but had poor traction on soft snow. As a base vehicle it was excellent and extremely fast.

MODIFICATIONS

We did not have sufficient time to carry out all the modifications we would have wished, and we only changed the battery to a low-temperature type and drift-proofed the cab and engine compartment.

CAB

The hull and frame was a watertight, all-steel, welded construction with a hinged one-man cab of small dimensions. Without thermal lagging, we found the driving of this vehicle was a very cold operation on the trail.

FERGUSON

The Ferguson tractor is British built by the Massey Ferguson Company and the total of seven tractors came from Coventry, two of which went in *Theron* to Shackleton and five to Scott Base with the New Zealand party. The complete tractor is manufactured for Massey Ferguson by the Standard Company.

GENERAL SPECIFICATION

Model	T.E.20
Horsepower	28.2 at 2000 rpm
Number of cylinders	4
Bore	3.34 in.
Stroke	3.62 in.
Piston displacement	127.4 cu. in.
Compression ratio	6 to 1
Transmission	Single-plate, dry clutch to 4-speed gearbox through rear-drive differential
Ground pressure	1.3 lbs./sq. in.
Cooling system capacity	15 pints
Crankcase capacity	6 quarts
Petrol tank capacity	9 gallons

Speed range	Up to 10 mph on snow, depending on load
Miles per gallon	1.1 to 1.8 (on the polar journey)
Turning radius	20 ft.
Overall width	6 ft. 1 in.
Overall length	10 ft.
Overall height	4 ft. 4 in.
Weight (dry)	3370 lbs. (with full tracks)

TRACTION

We found that this light tractor, when using wheels on snow, was unable to progress, and so we tried half-track equipment. This proved adequate on ice or really hard snow, but for general conditions the traction was inadequate. So we fitted full tracks over the front and rear wheels, using larger front wheels to give the track sufficient clearance over the steering system. The track consisted of rubber belts with steel crosslinks. The belts were endless and made from rubber-covered fabric.

STEERING

With the full tracks fitted, the normal steering system had to be locked and steering was accomplished by using the standard independent brakes, that is, braking the inboard axle.

MODIFICATIONS

(1) A special epicyclic reduction gearbox was fitted, which not only had the advantage of more gears, but lengthened the tractor, thus reducing the ground pressure and improving the traction.

(2) All electrical leads including the ignition system were changed to silicone rubber cables, and low-temperature batteries of 110 ampere hour capacity were fitted.

(3) The starter motor was changed for a slightly stronger one.

(4) Larger front wheels and full track system was fitted, and a special track made in Scandinavia.

(5) Waterproof brakes were fitted to keep out the snow.

While at Scott Base, the Ross Sea Party carried out a number of modifications:

(1) Stiffening the track rods to the front axle by fitting angle iron stiffeners from the frame to the axle.

(2) Construction of windcheater roofless cabs to protect the driver.

(3) The modification of the standard tracks to the pattern of the experimental one sent out to them. This involved welding on cleats to the outside of the steel crossbars.

RADIO

The Ross Sea Party towed a radio caboose which had its own battery supply with an independent small battery charger. Attached to each Ferguson tractor they had a short-range, two-way telephone system so that the drivers were in communication with each other.

PERFORMANCE

The tractors employed at Shackleton were used for base work, that is to say local load hauling, building, the use of the high lift loader, and digging snow. On hard surfaces they were capable of hauling up to two tons.

The three tractors which made the Pole journey from Scott Base were linked together with ropes and on arrival at the Pole were a gross load of three and a half tons. This is very understandable since the power available at 10,000 feet on the plateau would be less than 15 bhp. To operate on the plateau they adjusted the governor, increasing the engine speed to 3000 rpm and drove continuously at full throttle.

These lightweight tractors were not as fully prepared for low temperature as the other vehicles, but they carried out a most noteworthy journey. Their decreased power and traction at altitude explains the somewhat low payload in relation to fuel consumption. The harder the snow surface the better the traction.

Although more suitable and very useful for base work, they could render excellent service for short-range independent polar journeys at reasonable altitudes.

APPENDIX B

Aircraft Specifications

OTTER

The Otter was built by the deHavilland Aircraft Company of Canada, and was used for reconnaissance, support, the establishment of South Ice, and later for the transpolar flight.

CONSTRUCTION

The Otter is an all-metal high wing monoplane. The strut-braced wings have a rectangular plan form of constant thickness and chord. The aircraft can operate from land, water and snow surfaces. In our case it was fitted with skis and took off and landed on snow.

ENGINE

Pratt & Whitney Wasp R 1340
Type   Air-cooled radial
Number of cylinders   9
Power   600 bhp (supercharged)
Rated altitude   3000 ft.

Special design features are the four exhaust augmenter tubes in which the exhaust gases produce enough suction to pull cooling air through the engine compartment, while at the same time providing a measurable amount of thrust in cruising flight.

PROPELLER

Hamilton Standard, three-bladed, constant speed, counterweight propeller.

DIMENSIONS

Wing span	58 ft.
Height	12 ft. 7 in.
Length	41 ft. 10 in.
Cabin length	16 ft. 5 in.
Cabin height	5 ft.
Cabin doors	3 ft. 10½ in. wide × 3 ft. 9 in. high
Cargo capacity	345 cu. ft.
Wind loading	20.3 lbs./sq. ft.
Power loading	12.56 lbs./bhp.

WEIGHT

Basic weight (dry)	4368 lbs.
Gross weight	8000 lbs.

CAPACITIES

Fuel capacity:	Front tank	51 gallons
	Center tank	85 gallons
	Rear tank	42 gallons
		178 gallons
	Auxiliary long-range tank, inside cabin	177 gallons
Oil		9 gallons

PERFORMANCE

Disposable load	3632 lb.
Rate of climb	830 fpm
Cruising speed at 5000 ft. and 1700 rpm	128 mph T.A.S.
Service ceiling	17,400 ft.
Absolute ceiling	19,500 ft.

GENERAL DATA

Main skis, all-metal construction. Runner surface coated with polyethylene. There are two types of skis, a combination wheel and ski, or a full ski without wheel. We used the full ski, which gives a better snow performance.

MODIFICATIONS

A number of modifications were made, some of the more interesting being:

(1) The electrical system was changed from 12 to 24 volts and was fitted with a heavy-duty battery.

(2) SARAH beacon and receiver.

(3) Bendix Polar Path Compass & Gyro System.

(4) Radio compass.

(5) Radio altimeter.

BEAVER

The Beaver was built in Canada by the deHavilland Aircraft Company. The Ross Sea Party used this aircraft for support, reconnaissance and depot laying in the field.

CONSTRUCTION

The Beaver is an all-metal structure, stressed to an ultimate load factor of 5¾ g and for gust conditions up to 66 feet per second. The aircraft can operate from land, water and snow surfaces. In our case, it was fitted with skis and took off and landed on snow.

ENGINE

Pratt & Whitney Wasp Junior
Type	Air-cooled radial
Number of cylinders	9
Power	450 bhp (supercharged)

PROPELLER

Hamilton Standard, two-blade, constant speed, counterweight propeller.

DIMENSIONS

Wing span	48 ft.
Height	10 ft. 7 in.
Length	30 ft. 4 in.
Cabin length	9 ft.
Cabin height	4 ft. 3 in.
Cabin doors	3 ft. 3 in. wide × 3 ft. 4 in. high
Cargo capacity	134 cu. ft.
Wing loading (5100 lb. gross weight)	20.4 lbs./sq. ft.
Power loading (5100 lb. gross weight)	11.3 lbs./bhp

WEIGHT

Basic weight (dry)	2960 lbs.
Gross weight	5100 lbs.

CAPACITIES

Fuel capacity (normal tanks)	79 gallons
Fuel capacity (long-range tip and belly tanks)	151 gallons

PERFORMANCE

Disposable load	2140 lbs.
Rate of climb (sea level)	1020 fpm
Cruising speed (5000 ft. 300 bph)	143 mph T.A.S.
Service ceiling	18,000 ft.
Absolute ceiling	20,000 ft.

GENERAL DATA

Main skis, all-metal construction. Runner surface coated with polyethylene. Tail ski, Fiberglas. There are two types of skis, a combination wheel and ski or a full ski without wheel. We used the full ski without wheel, which gives a better snow performance.

MODIFICATIONS

A number of modifications were made, some of the more interesting being:

(1) The fitting of supply racks under each wing.
(2) Radio and SARAH beacon.
(3) F.24 camera installation.
(4) Bendix Polar Path Compass & Gyro System.
(5) Winter engine nose shutter.

AUSTER

Two Austers were used, one by the main party and the other by the New Zealand party.

Both parties used their aircraft for reconnaissance and support. They were used with floats from the ship for ice reconnaissance, and converted to skis in the Antarctic for use in the field. The Auster is built by the Auster Aircraft Company in England.

CONSTRUCTION

The Auster has a welded steel tube fuselage. The wings have wooden spars, light alloy ribs, and all surfaces have fabric covering. It is stressed to an ultimate load factor of 5½ g.

ENGINE

Gipsy Major 7G
Type	Air-cooled inverted in line
Number of cylinders	4
Power	145 bhp (unsupercharged)

PROPELLER

Two-blade, Fairey Reed type, fixed pitch.

DIMENSIONS

Wing span	36 ft.
Height	8 ft. 8 in.
Length	23 ft. 2½ in.

Cabin length   8 ft. 10 in.
Cabin height   3 ft. 10 in.
Cabin doors   2 ft. 6 in. wide × 3 ft. high
Wing loading (2450 lb. gross   13.25 lbs./sq. ft.
    weight) float plane
Power loading (2450 lb. gross   16.9 lbs./bhp
    weight) float plane

WEIGHT

Tare weight as float plane   1800 lbs.
Tare weight as ski plane   1565 lbs.
Gross weight   2450 lbs.

CAPACITIES

Fuel capacity (three tanks)   16 gallons
                                    16 gallons
                                    13 gallons

PERFORMANCE

Ski plane load available for per-   885 lbs.
    sonnel, radio, etc.
Float plane load available for   650 lbs.
    personnel, radio, etc.

SKI PLANE

Rate of climb (sea level)   525 fpm
Cruising speed (5000 ft.)   102 mph T.A.S.
Service ceiling   10,500 ft.
Absolute ceiling   11,500 ft.

GENERAL DATA

Skis, wooden construction. Runner surface, Bakelite-covered. The
Auster was fitted with five radio sets and there was space available
for one passenger.

APPENDIX B

MODIFICATIONS

1. Oil dilution system was fitted to engine for cold starting and also a Coffman starter.
2. Electrical system changed from 12 to 24 volts.
3. Special radios, SARAH beacon, D/F loop and radio compass.

This Auster aircraft was modified throughout to enable it to carry out reconnaissance work under Antarctic conditions.

INDEX

Index

SOUTH
AMERICA

Weddell
Sea

P
A
C
I
F
I
C

O
C
E
A
N

A N

ANTARCTICA

Shackleton 1908-9 ·······················
Amundsen 1910-12 ————————
Scott 1910-13 — — — — — —